THE SPIRIT OF 74

THE SPIRIT OF 74

How the American Revolution Began

RAY RAPHAEL AND MARIE RAPHAEL

THE NEW PRESS

NEW YORK
LONDON

Requests for permission to reproduce selections from this book
should be mailed to: Permissions Department, The New Press,
120 Wall Street, 31st floor, New York, NY 10005.

Published in the United States by The New Press, New York, 2015
Distributed by Perseus Distribution

LIBRARY OF CONGRESS CATALOGING-IN-PUBLICATION DATA
Raphael, Ray.
    The spirit of 74 : how the American Revolution began / Ray Raphael
and Marie Raphael.
        pages   cm
    Includes bibliographical references and index.
    ISBN 978-1-62097-126-0 (hardcover : alk. paper) — ISBN 978-1-62097-127-7
(e-book)   1. United States—History—Revolution, 1775–1783—Causes.
2. Massachusetts—History—Revolution, 1775–1783.   I. Raphael, Marie.
II. Title.
    E210.R37 2015
    973.3'1—dc23   2015008420

The New Press publishes books that promote and enrich public discussion and
understanding of the issues vital to our democracy and to a more equitable world.
These books are made possible by the enthusiasm of our readers; the support of a
committed group of donors, large and small; the collaboration of our many partners
in the independent media and the not-for-profit sector; booksellers, who often hand-
sell New Press books; librarians; and above all by our authors.

www.thenewpress.com

Composition by dix!
This book was set in Fournier MT

Printed in the United States of America

10   9   8   7   6   5   4   3   2   1

CONTENTS

INTRODUCTION:
THE MISSING
SIXTEEN MONTHS

On December 16, 1773, patriots whose faces were darkened by lampblack and paint dumped 342 chests of tea into Boston Harbor. On the morning of April 19, 1775, sixteen months and three days later, local militiamen confronted British redcoats at Lexington and Concord, where blood was shed and war began.

The Boston Tea Party and the "shot heard 'round the world" are critical markers in the saga of our nation's founding, and chronicles of the American Revolution inevitably feature both events, linking them in some way. Most say that to punish Boston for its wanton destruction of private property, Parliament passed four bills it called the "Coercive Acts" and Americans later dubbed the "Intolerable Acts." The Boston Port Act, which closed its port, was supposedly the "most drastic" of these, as one textbook claims. Another says that by punishing that city, Britain intended to isolate it, but the act had the reverse effect: "Americans in all the colonies reacted by trying to help the people of Boston. Food and other supplies poured into Boston from throughout the colonies." To support the city and oppose Britain's draconian policies, leaders from twelve colonies convened a Continental Congress in September 1774. Congress sent petitions and initiated a new boycott of British goods—techniques that had forced the repeal of earlier acts—but all to no avail. Intransigent British officials refused to change course; instead, they ordered troops to march on Lexington and Concord.[1]

This story line travels quickly from the raid on the tea ships to the outbreak of war. Months pass unnoticed. Yet in this neglected time, nearly lost in telling, lie answers to questions central to the understanding of America's founding. Why did Boston's act of political vandalism lead to a British military expedition against small towns in Massachusetts sixteen months later? How, exactly, did evolving political tensions result in actual warfare?

In the pages that follow, our story slows, pausing at additional markers that are often bypassed or slighted and featuring events that, step-by-step, drove revolution forward. Only in a full telling is war a plausible outcome.

The catalyst here, as in traditional narratives, is the destruction of tea, which triggered Parliament's punitive response. But if closing Boston's harbor was a severe punishment, it was not Parliament's most "drastic act" or "the final insult in a long list of abuses," as textbooks state. That dubious honor goes to "An Act for the Better Regulating the Government of the Province of the Massachusetts Bay," generally called the Massachusetts Government Act, passed seven weeks later. In this measure, Parliament unilaterally gutted the 1691 Charter for Massachusetts. No longer could citizens call town meetings except with permission of the royal governor, and once they met, they could not discuss any items the governor had not approved. No longer could the people's representatives choose the powerful council, the body that functioned as the legislature's upper house, the governor's advisory cabinet, and the administrative arm of provincial government. No longer did the people have any say in choosing jurors and no longer would the council, now filled by Crown appointees, contest the appointment of judges, sheriffs, or justices of the peace—the officials who could instantaneously upend a person's life.[2]

When the Boston Port Act took effect, colonists far and wide sent relief, held meetings, passed resolutions, or declared days of prayer and fasting. But after passage of the Massachusetts Government Act, citizens in Massachusetts, through collective and forceful resistance, made the act inoperable by shutting down the government. In August 1774, when the act took effect, citizens forced all thirty-six Crown-appointed councilors to resign their posts or flee from their homes. They convened town meetings whenever and wherever they wanted, even in Salem, a stone's throw from Governor (and British general) Thomas Gage's office. They besieged the all-important county courts whenever one was slated to convene and prevented these imperial outposts of judicial and executive authority from doing business of any kind. At their hands the Massachusetts Government Act became "a blank piece of paper and not more," in the words of one contemporary.[3]

Without a shot being fired or any loss of life, Massachusetts citizens eradicated every vestige of British authority in the province—except in Boston, the army's command post. In short order, they replaced British rule with an extralegal assemblage of committees of correspondence, county conventions, and a Provincial Congress, buttressed by militia from every township. If "revolution" denotes a forceful overturning of political authority, the Massachusetts Revolution of 1774 certainly qualifies.

Rebels expected that Crown officials, after losing control of Massachusetts, would try to take it back, so to secure the revolution they had just made they readied for war. This was the premeditated work of months, not precipitous or random. The newly formed Massachusetts Provincial Congress raised tax monies to procure a huge arsenal, acquiring, by March 1775, not only armaments but also provisions to support an army of fifteen thousand men. Congress thought of everything, from ten tons of brimstone for the manufacture of gunpowder, to fifteen thousand canteens, to twenty casks of raisins and barrel upon barrel of beef and salted fish.

In London, King George III abandoned all hope of a peaceful settlement. He declared that Massachusetts was in a state of rebellion and that "blows must decide" the outcome. Royal officials ordered Governor Gage to suppress the rebellion with military force but, recognizing that his soldiers were greatly outnumbered and shying away from direct confrontation, Gage opted instead for a surgical strike on rebel arms and provisions. Intelligence sources indicated two major depositories, one in Worcester and another in Concord. While Worcester was distant and its rebel populace numerous and entrenched, Concord could be reached in a matter of hours.

Provincials easily surmised what Gage was likely to do, and with the coming of spring Concord braced for an attack. When British troops departed Boston, they set off a warning system that had been months in the making.

The rest we know: the confrontations on the Lexington Green and Concord's North Bridge, and the redcoats' bloody retreat. A *war* was under way, but the *revolution* had occurred long before. On April 19, 1775, the Crown initiated a counterrevolutionary campaign to recover a lost province. The iconic importance of that date is not diminished in this rendering but contextualized. The shots fired at Lexington and Concord marked a true turning point. Only after the British strike did other colonies embrace the fight and turn the Massachusetts revolution of 1774 into America's Revolutionary War.

Prior to Lexington and Concord, colonists elsewhere took a measure of what was happening in Massachusetts, knowing full well that events there might soon affect them. The previous September, responding to a rumor that British artillery had set Boston ablaze, tens of thousands of militiamen from all four New England colonies set out for Boston to confront the redcoats. Later that fall, the Connecticut Assembly ordered each local militia to train, check the condition of its military wares, and double its supplies of ammunition. The Rhode Island Assembly approved the formation of independent military companies, appointed a major general for all the colony's militia and independent companies, and pledged to mobilize these forces if necessary. Aware of burgeoning militarization, General Gage warned officials in London that "nothing less than the Conquest of almost all the New England Provinces will procure Obedience to the late Acts of Parliament for regulating the Government of Massachusetts Bay."[4]

Meanwhile, several counties in Virginia formed independent volunteer military companies, distinct from the militia that were nominally under control of the royal governor. In December the extralegal Maryland Convention called upon all men between sixteen and fifty to form militia companies, drill, procure arms and ammunition, and "be in readiness to act on any emergency." Pennsylvania, with its concentration of pacifistic Quakers, did not directly advocate military preparedness, but in January 1775 a colonywide convention did recommend that gunpowder mills increase their manufacture "as largely as possible."[5]

Come spring, military mobilization in several colonies reached a fever pitch. At an extralegal Virginia convention, Patrick Henry introduced a resolution declaring that "this colony be immediately put into a posture of defence" and that a committee devise a plan to embody, arm, and discipline "such a number of men as may be sufficient for that purpose." In April, when Charleston, South Carolina, learned that British reinforcements were heading toward Boston, patriots seized sixteen hundred pounds of gunpowder from two magazines and "eight hundred stands of arms, two hundred cutlasses, beside cartouches, flints, and matches" from the State House.[6]

Such events set the stage for a war to come, but they did not *start* that war. Only in Massachusetts did Britain determine to match force with force and thwart an open, pervasive rebellion.

Although the authority of Crown and Parliament was challenged elsewhere, no other colony dismantled every tier of the governing apparatus, amassed arms and supplies to field a full-scale army, and created a complete military infrastructure with the express intent of confronting the British Army.

Proximate to the outbreak of any revolutionary war, unrest surges, spilling over banks that can contain it no longer. Narratives of this initiating period say much about a rebel people's incentives, capabilities, and character, and because they do, historians as a rule pay them close attention.

Strangely, however, most narratives of the American Revolution do not fully explore this revelatory first chapter. They attend, as they should, to "the spirit of '76," when the United States declared its independence, and to the decade of unrest that culminated in war. But it was the popular furor and unprecedented revolutionary gains in 1774 that provoked armed intervention in 1775. "The spirit of '74" galvanized insurgents who cast off imperial rule in that year and who defended their revolution in the critical months that followed. Their story is at this story's hub.

HOW THE AMERICAN REVOLUTION BEGAN: TIMELINE

1773

December 16—Provincials dump 342 chests of East India Company tea into Boston Harbor (later called the Boston Tea Party).

1774

March 31—Parliament passes the Boston Port Act, which closes the port of Boston until the tea is paid for.

May 20—Parliament passes the Massachusetts Government Act, which disenfranchises Massachusetts citizens by revoking key provisions of the Massachusetts Charter.

May 20—Parliament passes the Administration of Justice Act, which allows officials accused of crimes to be tried in England.

June 6—*Boston Gazette* publishes the Massachusetts Government Act and Administration of Justice Act.

June 17—Governor Gage dissolves the Massachusetts Assembly in Salem.

July 4—Worcester's American Political Society arms its members.

July 25—Berkshire County committees of correspondence suggest closing county courts, which administer county government, rather than allow them to convene under the Massachusetts Government Act. Boston committee of correspondence endorses the idea four days later.

August 1—Massachusetts Government Act takes effect. Town meetings are restricted; council members are appointed by the Crown rather than elected; all administrative officials are removed from public accountability.

August and September—Provincial crowds force all thirty-six Crown-appointed members of the new council to either resign or seek protection from British troops in Boston.

August 15—Worcester committee of correspondence calls for a multicounty meeting to provide mutual protection and coordinate resistance to the recent acts of Parliament.

August 16—In Great Barrington, a crowd of fifteen hundred closes the Berkshire County courts.

August 24—Governor Gage fails to prevent an illegal town meeting in Salem, one block from his office.

August 26–27—A multicounty meeting initiated by Worcester calls for a Provincial Congress in early October.

August 30—In Springfield, three thousand people close the Hampshire County courts.

August 31–September 1—British troops seize gunpowder from Quarry Hill in Charlestown.

September 1 and 2—Tens of thousands of provincials mobilize in response to exaggerated reports of the powder seizure ("Powder Alarm").

September 3—Governor Gage starts fortifying the Boston

Neck and decides not to send troops to protect the courts in Worcester.

September 5—Continental Congress convenes in Philadelphia.

September 6—4,622 militiamen from 37 towns close the Worcester County courts.

September 7—Worcester County committees of correspondence assume responsibility for governmental functions.

September 17—Continental Congress voices support for resistance efforts in Massachusetts by endorsing the Suffolk Resolves.

September 20–21—Worcester County committees of correspondence expand the county's militia and tell towns to create companies of minutemen.

October 3—Governor Gage asks London for twenty thousand soldiers to suppress the rebellion, but his request is denied.

October 4—Worcester town meeting calls for a new and independent government.

October 11—Massachusetts Provincial Congress convenes in Concord.

October 17—Provincial Congress moves to Cambridge.

October 19—British Crown prohibits arms importation in America, alienating other commercial nations.

October 20—Continental Congress's "Continental Association" suspends trade with Britain and calls for enforcement committees in every community.

October 26—Massachusetts Provincial Congress authorizes the procurement of armaments.

October 28—Massachusetts Provincial Congress appoints its own receiver-general to collect tax money from towns.

November 2—Provincial Congress's committees of safety and supplies stipulate that large quantities of food for militiamen be stored at Worcester and Concord.

November 18—King George III tells Lord North that New

England is in a "state of rebellion" and that "blows must decide" whether colonial rebels will remain British subjects.

November 30—King George III tells his new Parliament he will enforce the Coercive Acts with effectual measures.

December 14–15—Provincials seize arms and powder from Fort William and Mary in Portsmouth, New Hampshire.

1775

January 25—Committees of safety and supplies order that all provincial artillery be stored at Worcester and Concord.

February 21—Committee of safety orders the committee of supplies to purchase "all kinds of warlike stores, sufficient for an army of fifteen thousand men to take the field."

February 22—Governor Gage dispatches spies to Worcester to investigate the possibility of attacking there.

February 23—Committees of safety and supplies order the formation of artillery companies.

February 26—Governor Gage dispatches troops to Salem to seize cannon supposedly stored there, but the troops come back empty.

March 14—Committees of safety and supplies establish a network of watches to warn of a British attack.

March 20—Governor Gage dispatches spies to Concord to investigate the possibility of attacking there.

March 22—Provincial Congress reconvenes in Concord.

March 30—Paul Revere carries news to Concord that British troops are on the march, but the troops return to Boston within hours.

April 2—News arrives in Boston that Britain is sending more troops, closing Newfoundland fisheries, and prohibiting all foreign trade. Evacuation of Boston begins.

April 7—Revere carries news to Concord that British troops

are preparing to attack Concord the next day, but troops do not leave Boston.

April 8—Provincial Congress invites Connecticut, Rhode Island, and New Hampshire to join Massachusetts in "raising and establishing" a New England army.

April 14—Governor Gage receives instructions from London to arrest the "principal actors and abbettors" of the rebellion.

April 15—Governor Gage begins preparations for an expedition

April 16—Revere travels to Lexington, Cambridge, and Charlestown to coordinate the provincials' warning systems.

April 16—Printing press of Isaiah Thomas, publisher of the *Massachusetts Spy*, is smuggled out of Boston and taken to Worcester.

April 17–18—Anticipating a British attempt to seize provincial arms, committees of safety and supplies order that military wares and other supplies stored in Concord be disbursed among several towns.

April 18—Lieutenant Colonel Francis Smith and eight hundred Regulars leave Boston to seize and destroy the rebels' stores at Concord. Revere rides westward a fourth time bearing the news. The warning network initiated on March 14 and fine-tuned since is activated.

April 19—Militiamen on the Lexington Green face off against the Regulars. A shot is fired, then more. Eight militiamen are killed. Regulars proceed to Concord but find only a few stores there. Militiamen confront a contingent on Concord's North Bridge and drive them back. Militiamen from across eastern Massachusetts swarm to Concord. On their retreat toward Boston, British soldiers suffer serious casualties at the hands of thousands of militiamen.

April 20—Over ten thousand New Englanders lay siege to the British garrison in Boston.

May 16—Massachusetts Provincial Congress asks the Continental Congress to assume responsibility for the New England army that is laying siege to the British Army in Boston.

June 9—Continental Congress assumes responsibility for a "Continental Army" and starts raising money to support it. Thirteen colonies, through their delegates to Congress, officially join the revolution under way in Massachusetts.

A NOTE ON
NOMENCLATURE

The protagonists of this story are British colonials who, in 1774 and 1775, rejected imperial impingements on their right to govern themselves. They called themselves friends of liberty, patriots, or Whigs, and referred to their political opponents as enemies of liberty, government men, or Tories—sometimes prefaced with "damned." This vilified set, however, rejected that nomenclature. They thought of themselves as Loyalists or friends of government, while the others were enemies of government, rebels, damned rebels, or simply rascals.

Centuries later, what should we call each group?

Most American narratives, in default mode, call the first group patriot, Whig, or rebel and the second Tory or Loyalist. Contemporaries on both sides would bristle at these labels.

Supporters of British government policy thought *they* were the patriots who supported their country, and few considered themselves Tories; that label denoted the political party in England unfriendly to the rights of American colonists.

Opponents of this government policy thought *they* were the ones loyal to the British Crown, the British Constitution, and their colonial charters. Although King George III was misled by conniving ministers, the very purpose of the Crown was to protect British subjects, not oppress them. The designation of rebel was even more troubling. Today, Americans use the word with respect and even pride, but in 1774 rebel connoted treason.

Some modern narratives use the Whig/Tory division, which to our ears sounds neutral. But few if any colonists supported the Tory line, and referencing political parties in England seriously misrepresents the local roots of resistance in America.

Others use patriot/Loyalist. This allows each side to self-identify, even if both, historically, would self-identify with both labels. Despite the apparent balance, though, this approach has a distinctly pro-American bias. Patriot is undeniably positive, whereas Loyalist raises a troubling issue: loyal to what? (Curiously, according to the *National Geographic Style Manual*, Loyalist is capitalized only when referencing the American Revolution or Spanish Civil War.)

To be politically correct, we could say "supporters" and "opponents" of official British policies, whether laws of Parliament, edicts of the Crown, proclamations of Crown-appointed governors, or acts of the British Army. This tedious approach, however, would slow the narrative, defuse the drama, and remove all sense of immediacy.

There are no easy answers. Here, we use an amalgam of terms, opting for those best suited to the moment. We shy from rebel, for instance, until provincials are actually rebelling. We use patriot when viewing a scene through the eyes of activists who see themselves that way. We use Tory, too, but only as a term of accusation. We prefer friend of government or government man—meaning, of course, the Crown-controlled government—to Loyalist, which became more common after Lexington and Concord. Always, our intent is to bring us closer to the action, admitting in advance that language in history can never be perfectly neutral.

THE SPIRIT OF 74

PART I

SETTING THE STAGE

I propose, in this Bill, to take the executive power from
the hands of the democratic part of the government. . . .
I therefore move you, Sir, that leave be given to bring in
a Bill for the better regulating of the government of the
province of Massachusetts Bay.

—Prime Minister Lord North
in the House of Commons, March 28, 1774

1

BOSTON: TEA

The Boston Tea Party, the daring episode of a single night, was in reality the work of twenty nights and days or more, accomplished as thousands rallied to the series of meetings beforehand and conferred in caucuses, committees, and subcommittees. Men confronted officials, stood watch in the harbor, drafted petitions, orated from church pulpits, composed arguments for the press, and speechified endlessly in taverns. If they cried out against taxation without representation, other imperial offenses compelled them equally, increasing tension and resolve. In the decade before, protesters had tormented individual government men or submitted petitions or conducted boycotts, but in December 1773, after purposeful deliberation, they subscribed to an especially treacherous action. They defied not only the Crown but also the East India Company, a seemingly invincible global corporation whose fate and Britain's were inextricably tied. All knew the Crown would protect her own, and that vandalism on this scale could be called treason—any man might hang for it. As fierce activity built to a crescendo, colonials found themselves on a precipice. They came to this place of their own free will.

• • •

Before dawn in Boston on November 29, 1773, men and boys whose names went unrecorded posted a handbill "in all Parts of the Town." People saw it on the wall of a warehouse on Long Wharf or on a wooden fence in a street that twisted this way and that up a hill as if, like the town's headstrong inhabitants, it had a mind of its own. It appeared everywhere.

Friends! Brethren! Countrymen!
That worst of Plagues the detested TEA shipped for this Port by the East-India Company, is now arrived in this Harbour; the Hour of Destruction or manly Opposition to the Machinations of Tyranny stares you in the Face; every Friend to his Country, to himself and Posterity, is now called upon to meet at Faneuil-Hall at NINE o'Clock,
THIS DAY,
(at which Time the bells will ring) to make a united and successful Resistance to this last, worst and most destructive Measure of Administration.[1]

Bostonians recognized signal calls to action in words like "Hour of Destruction," "manly Opposition," "Machinations of Tyranny," and "Resistance." Most had risen at first light, as eighteenth-century people did, and, after seeing the posted message, carried the news wherever they went. On very short notice thousands arrived at Faneuil Hall.

Just half as large as it is now, having room for only twelve or thirteen hundred, the building could not hold the crowd. Men marched purposely for a few hundred yards to Old South Meeting House, on the corner of Milk and Marlborough Streets. Constructed forty-four years earlier for its Puritan congregation, Old South was the largest building in Boston. It could contain even the vast numbers that the evangelist George Whitfield drew when he preached there in 1740; the building then was "so exceedingly thronged that I was obliged to get in at one of the windows," Whitfield wrote. On this late November day it was thronged too—as many as "5,000, some say 6,000 men," according to Samuel Adams, who was present. Respected as he was at the age of fifty-one for his seniority and experience, and expert as he was at forging compromises and maintaining alliances, Adams played a prominent role at the vast meeting.[2]

One hundred and more box pews lined the main floor, and as many as thirty men sat shoulder to shoulder in each. Those who stood filled every gap in every aisle. Men made their way upstairs and settled themselves on the balcony's pews. Others trudged higher still, perching on benches in the upper galleries that extended over the balcony. When there was no more sitting room or standing room inside the meetinghouse, men occupied the three church vestibules, and when the vestibules could not contain another body, they lined up outside the open doors, craning their necks to see into the interior.[3]

Stipulations that limited attendance at town meetings to those holding property were not in force. It was the "body of the people" that had turned out, including men of the "lower sort" who would otherwise be disenfranchised; seamen, laborers, apprentices, and the lesser tradesmen, like shoemakers, swelled the numbers in the conclave. They took their places beside those of the "middling sort"—printers, distillers, engravers, craftsmen and master artisans, clergymen, and small shopkeepers. Also in attendance were men of the "better sort"—shipowners, merchants engaged in international trade, lawyers, landed gentry, and gentlemen born to wealth and influence. Men of any class could have a voice in the day's proceedings, responding to speakers and determining the fate of any motion with a yea or nay. Although women did not participate in bodies such as this where votes were taken, they found other ways to make their mark.

Atop Old South rose a towering steeple, one of more than a

dozen on view in the skyline. These steeples testified to Boston's spiritual leanings, tilting toward a Puritan righteousness that animated citizens who continually occupied the moral high ground in altercations with British authorities. But Boston faced the sea, and mercantile interests and dogged ambition compelled opposition, too. Tossed together, stirred and mixed, the ingredients made a potent concoction.

The export of lumber and fish made up fully half of New England's wealth in trade, and ships bound for distant ports sailed out of the harbor with dried or pickled fish in their holds or boards, planks, wooden shingles, hoops, and staves. Ships traveled regularly to other colonies as well, carrying every manner of saleable merchandise, be it nails, barreled beef, or produce. Also on board were the luxurious English imports that had arrived safely in Boston Harbor after challenging weeks at sea only to be immediately dispatched elsewhere. In the province's chief seaport, in its surrounding towns, and in the backcountry, commercial transactions enriched men of influence, while a fraction of the wealth trickled down in relatively dependable fashion to men who cut sails from huge sheets of canvas with their sharp sheeps-foot-blade knives, or to seamen who clambered up a ship's rigging, or to any of the hundreds upon hundreds of others who kept trade alive and ships afloat. Boston, in short, was a trading town. "The Town itself subsists by trade," a contributor to the *Boston Gazette* explained. "Every inhabitant may be considered as connected with it." In the late 1760s, a merchants' organization called the Boston Society for Encouraging Trade and Commerce had opened its membership to artisans and evolved into the Body of the Trade, often called simply "The Body." Everybody in Boston took note when the mother country enacted some law that affected commerce, particularly if that law was billed as the "worst and most destructive Measure of Administration."[4]

The inflammatory broadside called tea "that worst of Plagues," and Abigail Adams called it "that bainfull weed" when she wrote to the literate Mercy Otis Warren, who was to be her decades-long mentor and correspondent. If the times denied Adams a public forum, her letters often testified to an avid interest in the politics of the day, and in these she could take the podium when she chose:

> Great and I hope Effectual opposition has been made to the landing of it. . . . The flame is kindled and like lightening it catches from Soul to Soul. Great will be the devastation if not timely quenched or allayed by some more Lenient Measures.
>
> Altho the mind is shocked at the Thought of Sheding Humane Blood, more Especially the Blood of our Countrymen, and a civil War is of all Wars, the most dreadfull. Such is the present Spirit that prevails, that if once they are made desperate, Many, very Many of our Heroes will Spend their lives in the cause, with the Speech of Cato in their Mouths, "What a pitty it is, that we can dye but once to save our Country."[5]

But why did Abigail Adams imagine that tea might cause such a commotion and lead to heroes dying and civil war?

Tea itself was a character in the drama by 1773, although when it was first introduced into Massachusetts in the seventeenth century, its consumption was negligible and role only minor. It was almost prohibitively expensive and for good reason. In Canton, tea was loaded on East India Company vessels for an arduous six-month passage to England, where the British imposed stiff importation duties. Twice a year it was auctioned off, and the colonial merchants who placed their bids in London then shipped it across the Atlantic's unpredictable waters. Only an elite set drank the beverage, setting out silver sugar tongs and creamers, tea tables, caddies, and the rest of the required paraphernalia.[6]

But by the last quarter of the eighteenth century, improvements in navigation, the cultivation of trade connections, favorable Parliamentary legislation, and expansive sales led to a drop in the price of tea, as did smuggling—ubiquitous on both sides of the

Atlantic. In Massachusetts about half of probated estates during this period included tea wares, such as silver teapots and fanciful porcelain cups. Other households consumed tea from everyday crockery never itemized in a will, but by now almost all drank it, brewed very dark.[7]

In 1767, when Parliament decided to levy duties on five indispensable colonial items, tea was one. The Townshend duties engendered widespread unrest and led to the reestablishment of nonconsumption and nonimportation agreements that had been used to great effect in Stamp Act times. In less than three years, with funds lost from customs duties, colonists agitating, and British merchants and manufacturers complaining mightily as their sales plummeted, Parliament capitulated. When the Crown relinquished the duties on glass, lead, paint, and paper, resistance did subside, as intended. It refused to relinquish its principles, however, and reasserted its right to tax by retaining the duty on tea, the item that garnered most of the Townsend revenues. Because Britain did not yield entirely, tea became *the* symbol of its oppressive policies. Standing on principle in their turn, colonists shunned it. Some imbibed crude substitutes although the vast majority simply consumed smuggled varieties, primarily tea that arrived from Holland.

By choosing not to consume a given item, women as well as men engaged in civic action. "The wise and virtuous Part of the Fair Sex in Boston and other towns," the *Boston Gazette* boasted early in 1770, "being at length sensible that by the Consumption of Tea, they are supporting the [Customs] Commissioners and other famous Tools of Power, have voluntarily agreed, not to give or receive any further Entertainment of that kind, until those Creatures, together with the Boston Standing Army, are removed, and the Revenue Acts are repealed."[8]

The taxing of tea was doubly resented because its proceeds were put to injurious use. Before 1768, the provincial legislature paid the salaries of the most powerful colonial officials. It was the old story of not biting the hand that feeds you, and as long as the hand was an elected body, officials had to pay heed to the people's representatives. A governor who dissolved an obstreperous assembly, for example, could not receive his salary unless he reconvened it. In 1768, however, the Crown decided to remunerate the chief justice of Massachusetts directly, drawing requisite funds from customs duties, including the duty on tea. Starting in 1771, the Crown disbursed the salaries of the lieutenant governor and the governor and, in 1772, the salaries of five superior court justices, taking yet more officials under its wing. Once recompensed by the Crown, officials were "degraded to *hirelings*, and the *body of the people* shall suffer their free constitution to be overturn'd and ruin'd," as Samuel Adams indicated when reacting to the judicial appointments.[9]

Britain's usurpation of the power of the purse escalated the tension around the tea tax. The Crown not only collected monies it had no right to collect but also funneled them to colonial officials who at once became Crown dependents. When Parliament passed the Tea Act in 1773, a new drama unfolded, with the East India Company cast in a starring role. The company had originated in the reign of Queen Elizabeth I as Merchants of England Trading to the East Indies, when, as a reward for advancing the queen's imperial designs, it received a charter, as colonies did, and, additionally, an advantageous monopoly on Far Eastern British trade. For a century and three-quarters it was akin to a nation in its own right, engaging in battles with England's competitors on the seas while maintaining its own armies in distant lands. The East India Company extracted tea, spices, silks, gold, silver, jewels, and other Far East exotica with one hand and did business in a flagrant manner with the other—selling opium to the Chinese people in spite of an emperor's objections or assuming the civil administration of Bengal and extracting taxes there during a drought that killed more than a million. Its functionaries returned to England as wealthy as lords and approximately as powerful, even if they lacked the proper aristocratic credentials.[10]

Although the East India Company seemed too big to fail, by 1772 it was indeed failing. When speculative banking schemes collapsed throughout Europe, it was hard hit, and by then smugglers were cornering the global markets it once controlled. Seven million pounds of Dutch tea entered Britain in the 1760s according to estimates. During those years, the lieutenant governor Thomas Hutchinson guessed that as much as three-quarters of the tea consumed in Massachusetts was unloaded in darkness onto small colonial vessels and spirited away or admitted into the country after bribes exchanged hands. "We have been so long habituated to illicit Trade that people in general see no evil it," he groused. Unsold tea piled up in company warehouses as a result—to the tune of some eighteen million pounds by 1772.[11]

The impending disaster threatened England as well as the East India Company; their fates were intertwined. The company owed creditors a million pounds and was in debt to the Bank of England for three hundred thousand. Default would cause grievous damage. Meanwhile, if the company somehow marketed its enormous tea surplus, the government would profit, not only from customs duties but because the company paid four hundred thousand pounds to the government in any year that its annual dividends surpassed 6 percent. This was the price Parliament charged for doing business as a monopoly. In Parliament, some argued for a government takeover, but in the end that body simply shored up the company. The Tea Act, passed in the spring of 1773, was a rescue operation.[12]

The act waived the duties on East India Company tea if, after its arrival in English ports, the company then shipped it to the colonies. Since the company had anted up two shillings and sixpence, or thirty pence, on every pound of tea it brought into England, this was a substantial gift, especially when compared to the negligible threepence that colonies paid, a duty that the Crown refused to relinquish. To further curtail company costs, the Tea Act permitted the company to assign its own agents, or *consignees*, and bypass

London's public tea auctions and merchant middlemen. Amply recompensed, its mercantile operation streamlined, the company could drop prices, compete with smugglers for market share, and sell the tea that languished in warehouses. For their part, colonists could purchase legal, desirable tea at very reasonable prices, their tax only nominal. British officials expected tempers to quiet. To their consternation, furor rose.

The Tea Act made tea once again a focal point, inevitably arousing the people's distrust and ire. Large sums of money were on the table this time, the cards dealt out in anything but an even-handed manner. The East India Company selected men in Boston's elite conservative circle as consignees, including Thomas Hutchinson's own sons. Ordinary merchants were shut out, and the Crown intended to shut out smugglers too. These men were not cutlass-wielding outlaws but well-regarded shipowners and traders. Since many colonists considered smuggling a form of resistance to unfair taxation, the reputations of these gentlemen had never suffered and the likelihood of arrest had always been slight. Considering the profit margins, any risk they took was worth taking, but under new arrangements they stood to lose vast sums to the East India Company and its consignees.

Tea was already a symbol of imperial taxation, and now it signified monopoly as well. John Dickinson, the lawyer from Delaware and Pennsylvania who had galvanized opposition to the Townshend duties with his *Letters from a Farmer in Pennsylvania*, went on the attack, this time under the pen name Rusticus. The true villain this time, Dickinson said, was the East India Company, which had "levied War, excited rebellions, dethroned lawful Princes, and sacrificed Millions for the Sake of Gain" in Asia and hoped do the same in America. Dickinson, a prosperous plantation owner, hurled invectives with the intensity of a street revolutionary: "Fifteen hundred Thousand, it is said, perished by Famine in one Year, not because the Earth denied its Fruits, but this Company and its Servants engrossed all the Necessaries of

Life, and set them at so high a Rate, that the Poor could not purchase them. . . . They now, it seems, cast their Eyes on *America*, as a new Theatre, whereon to exercise their Talents of Rapine, Oppression and Cruelty." The Tea Act bestowed monopolistic privileges, and the "Monopoly of Tea," he warned, was "but a small Part of the Plan they have formed to strip us of our Property."[13]

Opponents of the Tea Act employed a time-tested tactic used against the Stamp Act by crowds who forced stamp agents to resign their posts. Now they targeted the Tea Act's consignees. In the port cities of Charleston, Philadelphia, and New York, these merchants bent to public pressure, pledging in public statements not to distribute the company's tea. Bostonians would also attempt to force consignees to resign.

At one o'clock in the morning on November 2, 1773, two men knocked violently at the door of consignee Richard Clarke and delivered a letter to his servant:

> Richard Clarke & Son:
> The Freemen of this Province understand, from good authority, that there is a quantity of tea consigned to your house by the East India Company, which is destructive to the happiness of every well-wisher to his country. It is therefore expected that you personally appear at Liberty Tree, on Wednesday next, at twelve o'clock at noon day, to make a public resignation of your commission, agreeable to a notification of this day for that purpose.
> Fail not upon your peril.
> O.C. [For Oliver Cromwell, England's strong-armed revolutionary of the mid-seventeenth century who did not shy from ruthless tactics][14]

The identity of the authors is unknown, but the next day the North End Caucus, one of Boston's several political clubs, issued a command to the East India Company's five consignees. They were to appear on the following day at the corner of Essex and Orange Streets under the "Liberty Tree," a giant elm that had received its baptismal name in 1765 when an indignant body meeting there forced Andrew Oliver to relinquish his duties as Stamp Act agent. In the same indignant spirit, some five hundred men of all ranks gathered now to confront the tea merchants. In such "out-of-doors" assemblies, as people said at the time, men increasingly determined matters of political consequence, often challenging upper-crust gentlemen in their stiff, powdered wigs who ruled "within doors" or "in chambers." Artisans in this company were plainly dressed, their hair tied at the back in a queue, and laborers or seamen might wear hemp breeches that closed with a draw-string, not a button. Yet all had come on serious business, and by sheer numbers they commanded power. The consignees, how-ever, did not even show up.[15]

The matter did not end there. Two days later, on November 5, the Boston town meeting officially demanded that the consignees stand down. Several times over the next three weeks, delegates delivered this order, in person, to those they could find, but these agents refused to cooperate and advanced a specious argument: their commissions had yet to arrive, so how could they resign a post they did not yet have?

On November 17 the *Hayley*, a ship belonging to John Han-cock, arrived in Boston Harbor bringing news. As he had sailed through the English Channel, the captain observed ships that car-ried tea, apparently headed for the American colonies. That eve-ning, inspired by the news, an ad hoc group that was sponsored by no particular organization gathered outside the town house of Thomas Hutchinson to challenge his sons, who were consign-ees. Finding them absent, they moved on to the home of Richard Clarke and his sons. These consignees were arguing their case when someone in the house fired a shot, at which point the retal-iating crowd threw rocks and whatever hard objects they could find through the lower-story windows and the residents retreated upstairs. Even this unruly group, however, refrained from a full-out mobbing of the house.[16]

The Boston committee of correspondence was an official arm of the town meeting, and in the following days it enlisted the support of committees in nearby Roxbury, Dorchester, Brookline, Cambridge, and Charlestown, who pledged opposition to the tea's landing. Expanding the network outward, these five committees of correspondence dispatched a circular letter asking all Massachusetts towns to resist the Tea Act.

On November 27, within Old South Meeting House, the Body—estimated at over two thousand people—selected twenty-five men to guard the harbor and give the alert if they sighted an incoming tea ship. The very next day the *Dartmouth* arrived, bearing a fortune in tea: eighty chests of strong, black Bohea—the drink of the everyman—as well as thirty-four chests of Singla, Hyson, Souchong, or Congou.

The day after that, at dawn, the urgent handbills addressed to *Friends! Brethren! Countrymen!* appeared everywhere in town and multitudes answered the call. On this morning, at the end of November, they had a December date in mind. They would need to act before December 17 because, by law, vessels carrying dutied goods could not linger interminably in a harbor; ship representatives had twenty days to pay what was owed to customs officers and unload their cargo. This meant that in nineteen days, customs officials would seize the *Dartmouth*'s cargo, certainly under a heavily armed, invincible guard. Any action taken to prevent the tea reaching shore must precede that date.

What was to be done? At that meeting, and at similar meetings in the days that followed, the Body deliberated. Some believed they should once again pressure the consignees. Samuel Adams thought the ship itself should be sent back to London, the tea on board and duties never collected, while Thomas Young made a particularly audacious proposal, in keeping with his audacious reputation. Seven years before, at the age of thirty-five, this doctor had left

Albany for Boston, attracted by its radical disposition. He immediately embroiled himself in its political affairs, through committee and caucus meetings or rowdy street demonstrations that influential political figures like Samuel Adams and Joseph Warren did not attend. Though they were compatriots now, the level-headed and widely respected Dr. Warren had regarded Young with a wary eye in former days, when he accused him of "invincible impudence"— along with "bad grammar and nonsense." Invincible and impudent still, Young rose to tell the people at Old South that they should raid the ship and toss the tea overboard.[17]

Destroying the tea was an idea before its time. For now, Samuel Adams's proposal to turn the *Dartmouth* back won favor, but the governor or some port official had to clear this vessel before it sailed off. At this moment, Governor Thomas Hutchinson was anything but a likely ally. Already he had dispatched his injunction to the gathering: "I warn, exhort and require you and each of you thus unlawfully assembled forthwith to disperse and to surcease all further unlawful proceedings at your utmost peril." When read aloud, it was met with "a long and very general hiss."[18]

In the coming days two more tea vessels arrived, the *Eleanor* on December 2 and the *Beaver* on December 7, with a fourth vessel, the *William*, beached on Cape Cod. Patriots placed a twenty-four-hour armed guard at Griffin's Wharf to ensure no one brought tea ashore. A handbill signed "THE PEOPLE" warned that any who did would be treated "as wretches unworthy to live and will be made the first victims of our just resentment." In the midst of this clamor, port officials and the tea's consignees retreated to Castle William, an island garrison protected by British troops and by cannons that were capable of firing thirty-two-pound balls. Warships guarded the shipping channels. Nevertheless, protesters assembled continually. Again and again, they petitioned the governor to release the ships. Repeatedly petitions were denied.[19]

Later, looking back, John Adams, Samuel's younger cousin by

thirteen years, commented on "the malicious pleasure" evidenced by "Hutchinson the Governor, the Consignees of the Tea, and the officers of the Customs" when they "stood and looked upon the distresses of the People, and their Struggles to get the Tea back to London . . . Tis hard to believe Persons so hardened and abandoned." A lawyer, he enunciated the case for the defense— that in safeguarding their rights, a people might commit illegal acts if every lawful course had been exhausted. After three weeks of wrangling with consignees and officials, such terms had been met. Thomas Young's proposal to raid the ships, seize the tea, and throw it overboard no longer seemed preposterous or, for that matter, criminal.[20]

December 16 was cold and a drenching rain fell. From as far as twenty miles away, provincials headed toward Boston, convinced that the tea in the harbor was as much their affair as Boston's. The muddy roads they traveled had been repaired in early summer, the time universally favored by men who were hard-pressed for time during spring planting but who were required by colonial law to repair them. By mid-December improvements made in June had come undone. Trotting horses tripped on the exposed roots of trees or on rock slides in a turning of the road, and wagon wheels slipped in deep ruts and gullies, but men went on.

On this morning the Body demanded that the beleaguered owner of the *Dartmouth*, twenty-three-year-old Francis Rotch, come before them. Not for the first time, he was told that he must ask the governor to clear his ship and allow it to pass out of the harbor. It would be the last request. No days remained. Captain Rotch then traveled to Milton, where Governor Thomas Hutchinson stayed in his country home, a safe seven miles from Boston and its rambunctious citizenry.

Political considerations aside, it was not likely that the governor would heed the demands of what seemed to him a defiant, disgracefully heterogeneous body. The scholar Pauline Maier suggests that Hutchinson depended on the "carefully calibrated scale provided by an established hierarchical system to measure and know himself," and on that scale he ranked high. His own colonial bloodline dated back to 1634. His ancestors had delved into mercantile and political affairs over the generations, steadily advancing and bequeathing him position, wealth, and scholarship. As Hutchinson took his own measure, he measured others. He talked disparagingly of the Body that met on December 16, when the "lower ranks of people" and the "rabble" mixed in such an untoward manner with "divers Gentlemen of Good Fortune."[21]

Rotch had not returned when the afternoon's session convened. Waiting, the Body turned its attention to a newspaper report of a bonfire in Lexington, fueled by tea leaves that were collected in all parts of the town. Defiant residents there decided to burn the tea rather than drink it. Applauding Lexington's conviction, the meeting resolved "that the use of Tea is improper and pernicious." This business accomplished, notable activists took to the floor. Speeches ensued, occupying time, but at four o'clock there was still no sign of Rotch, nor at five. The day darkened. Candles were lit, their flames wavering as if restless, like the gathering. At last the messenger did return, but his announcement was no more than a reiteration of a governor's past replies. Clearance was denied.[22]

Before long, Samuel Adams said, famously, that "he could think of nothing further to be done." Ninety-two years later, his first biographer equated the words to a *signal*, issued by a commander of sorts, as signals are. Narratives since have almost universally concurred. In her rich, Pulitzer Prize–winning account from 1942, Esther Forbes wrote, "Evidently this was a prearranged signal, for there were war-whoops from the dark galleries, yells: 'To Griffin's Wharf!' and 'Boston Harbor a tea-pot tonight!' Shouts and running feet." Accounts of more recent vintage repeat the story. Immediately after Adams spoke, claims one among many, "Instant pandemonium broke out amid cheers, yells, and war whoops. . . . The crowd poured out of the Old South Meeting and headed for Griffin's Wharf."[23]

Contemporaneous reports do not credit the breakneck time frame. They say Adams spoke and then time passed. "About 10 or 15 minutes later," according to one observer, "I heard a hideous yelling in the street . . . as of an hundred people, some imitating the Powaws of Indians and others the whistle of a boatswain, which was answered by some few in the house; on which numbers hastened out as fast as possible." As they did, "Mr. Adams Mr. Hancock Dr. Young with several others called out to the People to stay, for they said they had not quite done." Adams asked Young to make a speech, and "immediately on the subsiding of the tumult within," the doctor discoursed on "the ill effects of tea on the constitution" and on the "virtue of his countrymen in refraining from the use of it, and also in standing by each other in case any should be called to an account for their proceeding." His speech consumed fifteen or twenty minutes and, in all, a half hour or more passed between the alleged "signal" by Adams and the meeting's dissolution. Other firsthand reports corroborate this.[24]

It was truly dark by the time the Body disbanded. The rain had stopped, and a new moon appeared in the clearing sky. Some one to two thousand witnesses lined the shoreline, and one hundred to one hundred and fifty men boarded the tea ships. The consequences for any who were caught could be dire, and they were disguised so that "our most intimate friends among the spectators had not the least knowledge of us," said a young apprentice to a blacksmith, Joshua Wyeth. "We surely resembled devils from the bottomless pit rather than men."[25]

Decades later, when danger had passed, a few from that anonymous assembly claimed credit and revealed their identities, but mysteries remain. Although lists were made in the nineteenth century, these were based in part on circumstantial evidence, accusations by enemies, and mere assumptions. A close study of firsthand testimony suggests that participants came from all walks of life, that only a minority were over thirty years old, and that recognizable leaders, whom the British would at once target, were not in the company. These are all reasonable conjectures.[26]

One who was there that night was George Robert Twelves Hewes, a shoemaker. Practicing a trade that John Adams once called "mean and dimi[nu]tive," married to the daughter of a washerwoman, having served a stint in debtors prison, Hewes exactly fit Governor Hutchinson's conception of "rabble." Chief Justice Peter Oliver called men of this caliber a "mobility" and said they were "perfect Machines wound by any Hand who might first take the Winch." But patriot chieftains did not drive such men, and Hewes was present for sound reasons of his own. During Boston's occupation by British troops, he had witnessed incidents that seem barely worth recording—the simple rudeness of the soldiers or how one robbed a woman of "her bonnet, cardinal, muff and tippet." The continual slights aroused his animosity, and later he was also "on the ground" at the Boston Massacre when soldiers fired into the crowd. It was Hewes who caught in his arms one of the two sailors that they killed. Afterward, in the early morning hours, armed with a cane, he defied eight or nine soldiers, "all with very large clubs or cutlasses." Later he attended the trials of the soldiers who were accused of murder in the aftermath. He was anything but subservient or mindless. Imperial ruthlessness and Britain's wayward policies goaded Hewes on.[27]

Another participant, a caulker named Samuel Howard, tells of meeting on this day with a band of young men and donning camouflage in a cabinetmaker's shop. He eagerly related his story when in his nineties to a traveler who happened upon him, and even showed off garments he had supposedly worn and kept ever since. Howard said that, once disguised, he and his cohorts hesitated. Before committing themselves, they decided to seek the advice of "influential men." Men of influence came, three in all, but not one would "venture an opinion upon the probable result," although one intimated that they would "find friends." These young men were on their own, the outcome uncertain; they might be shot by a redcoat that night or hang for treason soon enough or live to tell the tale. They made their decision ceremoniously, one man asking each of the others in turn if he would "go ahead." When all said they would, a "Round Robin" pledge was drawn up "bearing upon the circumference the reason of their resolution, and their signatures in the centre." Like Howard, many determined to act only after deliberating with others in their guilds, militia companies, or church congregations or simply with their peers. Collectively, they came to decisions and played out the scripts that they had created.[28]

Participants organized themselves into three crews, one to board each ship. Each crew then chose two leaders, a commander and a boatswain. For commanders, they selected experienced leaders of their militia groups, men who knew how to give orders and maintain organized ranks. For boatswains they chose men who could execute orders efficiently. Those who were to board the *Beaver* wanted George Robert Twelves Hewes to fill that role for a very particular reason: his "whistling talent was a matter of public notoriety." On that still night, working in virtual silence, a whistle was the best method of summoning and directing men to perform specific acts. At this one special moment, people called this ordinary shoemaker, who was turned down for military service because he measured only five feet, one inch in height, "Captain Hewes."[29]

Acting as boatswain, Hewes was to "go to the captain and demand of him the keys to the hatches and a dozen candles" so that the boarding party would not need to hatchet their way into the holds or bumble about in the dark. The business was to be businesslike. Hewes reported how all followed orders after the heavy tea chests were lifted from the hold with block and tackle, "first cutting and splitting the chests with our tomahawks, so as thoroughly to expose them to the effects of the water. In about three hours from the time we went on board, we had thus broken and thrown overboard every tea chest to be found in the ship; while those in the other ships were disposing of the tea in the same way, at the same time. We were surrounded by British armed ships, but no attempt was made to resist us."[30]

Hewes did not realize that those warships were rigged out for action, their officers already on board. Deliberately, the admiral of the fleet, John Montagu, kept them in place. "I could easily have prevented the execution of this plan but must have endangered the Lives of many innocent People by firing upon the Town," he later alleged. The Sixty-Fourth Regiment on Castle William, also at the ready, likewise remained immobile. "I had the Regiment ready to take Arms, had they been called upon. I am informed the Council would not agree to the Troops going to Town," Lieutenant Colonel Alexander Leslie attested. Fear of bloodshed and subsequent mayhem tipped the scales in favor of Hewes and the others. Embedded in a history that memorializes action is a turning away from action, the thing not done. It is an alternate, unaccomplished history.[31]

In the story that we do recognize, the British did not fire, the ship was not damaged, the lock on the hold was not broken but opened with a key, the captain and the crew were not injured, and theft was forbidden. It was anything but a night of riotous abandon; contrarily, it was staged and effectively disciplined. When one man among the company slipped tea into his pocket, Hewes reports, "they seized him and, taking his hat and wig from his head, threw them, together with the tea . . . into the water. In consideration of his advanced age, he was permitted to escape, with now and then a slight kick." A sympathetic visitor from New York, in a glowing newspaper account, confirmed the people's discipline as well as their resolve. "We are in a perfect jubilee. . . . The spirit of the people throughout the country is to be described by no terms in my power. Their conduct last night surprised the admiral and English gentlemen, who observed that these were not a mob of disorderly rabble (as they have been reported) but men of sense, coolness and intrepity."[32]

Almost beside himself, John Adams wrote to his close friend James Warren:

> The dye is cast: The people have passed the river and cutt away the bridge: last night three cargoes of tea, were emptied into the harbour. This is the grandest event, which has ever yet happened since the controversy, with Britain, opened. The Sublimity of it charms me.[33]

British officials did not celebrate. On the morning following the assault on the ships, Admiral John Montagu stood on Griffin's Wharf, fuming at evidence of destruction. Possibly he saw the scene that George Hewes described—"a number of small boats were manned by sailors and citizens, who rowed them into those parts of the harbor wherever the tea was visible, and by beating it with oars and paddles so thoroughly drenched it as to render its entire destruction inevitable." Admiral Montagu's fleet had not fired on Bostonians, but now he concluded, "The Devil is in this people." He angrily questioned men who passed by—"Who is to pay the fiddler?"[34]

In a worried tone, privately to his diary, John Adams posited much the same question:

> What Measures will the Ministry take, in Consequence of this?—Will they resent it? will they dare to resent it? will they punish us? How? by quartering Troops upon Us?—by annulling our Charter?—by laying on more duties? By restraining our Trade? By Sacrifice of Individuals, or how?[35]

News of the Tea Party reached England on January 20, 1774, in the first month of a new year. Enraged by what had happened in the last month of the old one, King George III wanted retribution. In Parliament, furious debate ensued. Who indeed would pay the fiddler, and in what currency would he be paid?

2

LONDON: CRACKDOWN

On March 7, 1774, Lord North, the prime minister of Great Britain, carried a message to the House of Commons from King George III. His Majesty had long been disturbed by the insolent temper of the colony of Massachusetts, and he was outraged by the December 16 raid on the East India Company's ships. He spoke of "the unwarrantable practices which have been lately concerted, and carried on in North America, and particularly of the violent and outrageous proceedings at the town of Boston, in the Province of Massachusetts Bay, with a view of obstructing the commerce of this Kingdom and upon grounds and pretences immediately subversive of the constitution thereof." In a celebratory, nationalistic baptism half a century later, Americans would call that incident the Boston Tea Party. At the time no one spoke of a *tea party*, and a vast majority in England agreed instead with King George III's characterization.[1]

His Majesty trusted that Parliament would "not only enable his Majesty effectually to take such measures as may be most likely to put an immediate stop to the present disorders, but will also take into their most serious consideration what further regulations and permanent provisions may be necessary to be established, for better securing the execution of the laws, and the just dependence of the Colonies upon the Crown and Parliament of Great Britain." Previously the Massachusetts governor and other authorities had tried to put "an immediate stop" to any disorder with a show of force. That was nothing new. At moments, however, facing continuing outcry and riotous behavior, Parliament had thought it wise to give ground and had, for example, repealed the Stamp Act and most Townshend duties. Now the king questioned the efficacy of retreat. He determined that leniency undermined his authority and encouraged sedition. This time he'd give no ground, and he wanted Parliament to strengthen his hand by providing necessary weapons—those "further regulations and permanent provisions."[2]

Prime Minister North gave the king's mandate his unrelenting attention. Two decades earlier, at the age of twenty-two, this eldest son of the Earl of Guilford had entered Parliament. By now he was well versed in parliamentary maneuvering and was a persuasive orator with a sharp wit and a commanding voice. He made a ready ally and would serve George III throughout the revolutionary years. Events were propelling revolution forward in 1770 when North's tenure as prime minister began, and it would not end until Britain's calamitous defeat at Yorktown in October 1781 forced him from office five months later.

At this juncture, however, a week after the king sent his message, North introduced the Boston Port Bill in the House of Commons. Other so-called Coercive Acts would follow that spring, and coercive they were, intended to bring Massachusetts to heel with a painful, unrelenting jerk on its collar. The plan was to penalize a troublesome minority while protecting the colony's loyal majority. Other colonies, responding to this display of royal strength, would turn away from the obstreperous province.

The first of the Coercive Acts, the Boston Port Bill would close that port as of June 1, 1774. It would remain closed until "it shall sufficiently appear to his Majesty that full satisfaction hath been made by or on behalf of the inhabitants of the said town of *Boston* to the united company of merchants of *England* trading to the *East Indies*." Anyone caught either entering or leaving the port would suffer "pain of the forfeiture of the said goods, . . . merchandise, and of the said boat, . . . and of the guns, ammunition, tackle, furniture, and stores, in or belonging to the same." Lord North promoted the Port Bill as an efficient, cost-saving retaliation. "The good of this act is that four or five frigates will do the business without any military force," he asserted. Better a handful of frigates than battalion upon battalion of soldiers.[3]

Although the bill would cripple Boston's economy and affect every one of its inhabitants, North insisted that closure of the port was necessary. Since "Boston had been the ringleader in all riots," he told Parliament, "Boston ought to be the principal object of our attention for punishment." Most in Parliament agreed, and certainly Tory MPs did. Though not a political party in the modern sense, the Tory faction generally supported the established political order and the king's authority, while Whigs assailed manifestations of absolutism in the corridors of government. In the House of Commons, Charles Van trumpeted the Tory line at its most venomous: "the town of Boston ought to be knocked about their ears. . . . I am of opinion you will never meet with that proper obedience to the laws of this country, until you have destroyed that nest of locusts." That Bostonians were Englishmen complicated matters, however. They were not dark skinned and did not speak in foreign dialects or practice alien rites—which in this age was excuse enough for brutal punishments—nor were they a vanquished people, like the Irish or the Scottish Highlanders. They were the inheritors of rights granted to all who were English, and from the first they had their Whig defenders. Speaking for what was a decided but principled minority, men like William Pitt the Elder in the House of Lords and Edmund Burke in the House of Commons took to the floor.[4]

William Pitt was long known as the Great Commoner. Possessing no aristocratic lineage, he steadfastly refused the titles offered him as a mark of royal favor until, at the age of fifty-eight, he reversed himself. Only then, to the chagrin of a number of his populist backers, did he become the Earl of Chatham. Throughout his multifaceted political career, Pitt advanced Britain's global dominance. He advocated for military engagements with France or Spain whenever he thought war advantageous, and during his service as secretary of state, he directed the Seven Years' War. After that war, however, he supported the colonial position on taxation and attacked the Stamp Act. When criticized in Parliament for his stance, he replied, "The gentleman tells us, America is obstinate; America is almost in open rebellion. I rejoice that America has resisted. Three million people so dead to all feelings of liberty, as voluntarily to submit to be slaves, would have been fit instruments to make slaves of the rest." Vilified by many in England for holding views like this, he was lionized throughout the colonies and, of course, in Boston. Now, eight years later, he denounced the Port Bill and called Americans "fellow-subjects" while complaining of Parliament's harsh treatment: "By blocking up the harbor of Boston, you have involved the innocent trader in the same punishment with the guilty profligates who destroyed your merchandise . . . and punish the crime of a few lawless depredators and their abettors upon the whole body of the inhabitants."[5]

Edmund Burke, an ally and admirer of America, had come from Ireland to England to study law and had entered the House of Commons some eight years before this, at the age of thirty-six. Burke was a writer, a philosopher, and a masterful public speaker who regularly defended unpopular causes. British leaders never should have levied taxes to begin with, he argued, and now they were attempting to "sneak out of difficulties into which they had proudly strutted." Oratory turned to prophecy. "Reflect how you are to govern a people, who think they ought to be free, and think they are not. Your scheme yields no revenue; it yields nothing but discontent, disorder, disobedience; and such is the state of America, that after wading up to your eyes in blood, you could only end just where you begun; that is, to tax where no revenue is to be found."[6]

Lord North did not relent. He insisted that it was "time to proceed with firmness and without fear. They will never reform until we take a measure of this kind." Parliament expressed its agreement and voted in favor of the Boston Port Bill by a wide majority. On March 31, the king signed the bill into law.[7]

Parliament had fallen into line behind Lord North and a vindictive king, and in the country at large the mood was rancorous. Invectives filled the pages of public newspapers, broadsides, and pamphlets. English manufacturers, whose interests often intersected with those of the colonies, did not plead their case this time but instead condemned Boston's vandalism. Benjamin Franklin, a colonist who had achieved celebrity status in England, realized that America "never had since we were a people so few friends in Britain. The violent destruction of the tea seems to have united all parties here against our province."[8]

The stage was set. A victorious majority in Parliament pressed on, focusing next on the Massachusetts Charter of 1691, which supplanted a charter that Puritans carried with them to the New World in 1629. Citizens believed that the charter was sacred and inviolable. The Crown claimed that it fostered insubordination in America's most defiant colony and that Parliament must therefore redesign it. Britain could maintain global dominion only if it exerted control in all of its far-flung territories, and Massachusetts was no exception. Two bills would impel submission.

One, the Administration of Justice Act, assured British officials in Massachusetts that they need not be "discouraged from the proper discharge of their duty" or suffer under the "apprehension, that in case of their being questioned for any acts done therein, they may be liable to be brought to trial for the same

before persons who do not acknowledge the validity of the laws."
Accused of murder or another capital offense, a Crown officer
did not have to face jurors in Massachusetts—already the scene
of serious and even deadly incidents—for acts committed there.
Instead he could stand before a decidedly more sympathetic jury
in England or a less hostile one in some other colony. In the House
of Commons one member summarized the oppositional thinking
of a minority: "Surely, Sir, the bringing men over to England to
be tried, is not only a direct breach of their constitution, but is a
deprivation of the right of every British subject in America," he
said. On May 20, both houses of Parliament passed the bill, yeas
prevailing over nays by four to one.[9]

On that same date, and by the same majority, an even more
consequential bill became law. King George had asked that Parliament promote the "just dependence of the Colonies upon the
Crown." When Lord North introduced "An Act for the Better
Regulating the Government of the Province of the Massachusetts Bay," commonly known as the Massachusetts Government
Act, he had that request in mind. "I propose, in this Bill, to take
the executive power from the hands of the democratic part of the
government," North said. It was a simple, obvious prescription,
and, as simple prescriptions tend to be, it was radical. It swept
aside signature provisions in the 1691 charter that had long exasperated British authorities, including Governor Thomas
Hutchinson.[10]

The governor of Massachusetts knew from firsthand experience how difficult it was to rule in Massachusetts. While serving
as lieutenant governor during the Stamp Act controversy, what
he called a "hellish crew" invaded his own Boston mansion on
Court Street in the North End. They slit feather beds, took axes
to interior walls, downed his wine, and scattered papers in his
office, where on more peaceable evenings he might work away
on his *History of the Province of Massachusetts Bay*. In that work,

Hutchinson pointed out that "it was not easy to devise a system of subordinate government less controlled by the supreme, than the governments in the colonies. Every colony had been left to frame their own laws, and adapt them to the genius of the people, and the local circumstances of the colony. Massachusetts, in particular, was governed by laws varying greatly from, though not repugnant to, the laws of England. Their penal laws, their forms of administering justice, and the descent of estates varied from the English constitution and were settled to their own minds."[11]

The Massachusetts Government Act corrected alleged flaws in that insubordinate system by suppressing representative influence and increasing the governor's. It granted him "the power to appoint the officers throughout the whole civil authority." Judges, justices of the peace, sheriffs, marshals, and other offices of the courts would serve at his sole discretion when, prior to this, appointments and dismissals required his council's consent. The act also gave the sheriffs, who were appointed by the governor, the authority to choose jurors. Before, they had been selected from a list of nominees drawn up by ordinary citizens, who imagined that their candidates would be objective and fair and make independent judgments in cases coming before them. The act stated, contrarily, that juror selection "by the free-holders and inhabitants of the several towns, affords occasion for many evil practices, and tends to pervert the free and impartial administration of justice."[12]

After applying strong remedies in the judicial arena, Parliament turned its attention to the legislature, which, the act stated, "hath, for some time past, been such as had the most manifest tendency to obstruct, and, in great measure, defeat, the execution of the laws" and sought "to weaken the attachment of his Majesty's well-disposed subjects in the said province to his Majesty's government, and to encourage the ill-disposed among them to proceed even to acts of direct resistance to, and defiance of, his

Majesty's authority." Under the terms of the act, the king would appoint each and every member in the legislature's upper house, the council, which also functioned as an advisory body to the governor and an administrative arm of provincial government.[13]

Prior to this, although enfranchised inhabitants in each town did not directly elect the council's members, they *did* elect the incoming representatives to the legislature's lower house, its assembly. Representatives to that body, along with outgoing council members, chose the incoming council. In this process, voting citizens placed a hand on the lever of a finely calibrated governing mechanism. Citizens had exerted some control over two of the three arms of the "General Court," a term denoting the three nonjudicial arms of provincial government—the assembly, the council, and the governorship. The Massachusetts Government Act altered the balance of power; henceforth the Crown, unfettered, would appoint both the council and the governor.

Only in the New England colonies of Massachusetts, Connecticut, and Rhode Island did the people have an impact on council appointments. Elsewhere, councils were appointed by the Crown, and since they were, royal governors ignored their vexing recommendations whenever they liked. Not so here. Thomas Hutchinson complained of the council's autonomy in 1770 when serving as the acting governor, and his letter was in fact among the papers on a table in the House of Commons in 1774. Summarizing his complaints, a subcommittee noted that Hutchinson could not "remove any of those who were actually in office, some of whom were inflammatory," nor could he get the council's consent for "discountenancing the usurpation of the powers of Government by the town of Boston." Hutchinson was still complaining. The council, aligning itself with those who wanted the East India Company consignees to resign, was "infected" with the "distemper of the people," he asserted. Royal appointment would put an end to the constant adversarial combat and turn the council into a faithful ally of the governor.[14]

The Government Act addressed yet another obstacle, governance in the towns, where meetings were customarily held "when there shall be occasion for them, for any Business of publick concernment to the town there to be done," Hutchinson noted in his history. Of late, in those meetings people had increasingly busied themselves with business of "concernment" to the British Empire, "contrary to the design of their institution," as the act itself noted, and "had been misled to treat upon matters of the most general concern, and to pass many dangerous and unwarrantable resolves." Men rose to their feet to talk about taxation and nonimportation and rights and liberties. If George III desired a "just dependence of the Colonies upon the Crown and Parliament," these constant assemblies were the last thing he wanted, so the Government Act guaranteed only one town meeting per year. Here people could establish bylaws or elect selectmen, but they were to steer clear of imperial matters. To ensure they did, towns were required to submit an agenda to the governor beforehand, and only if he approved it could a meeting go forward.[15]

Even in the upper house of Parliament, the House of Lords, some were wary of the overwhelming reach of this bill. Certain titled members—men such as the Earl of Effingham, the Earl of Abingdon, and the Marquis of Rockingham—laid a strong protest before the House of Lords. They noted that the Government Act entrusted the Massachusetts governor and his council "with powers with which the *British* constitution has not trusted his Majesty and his Privy Council." Throughout, their dissent was marked by strong language. They stated that the act "may best suit the gratification of their [government's] passions and interests." Meanwhile, "The lives, liberties, and properties of the subject are put into their hands without controul; and the invaluable right of trial by Jury, is turned into a snare for the People, who have hitherto looked upon it as their main security against the licentiousness of power." Compelling as the rhetoric was, no words could affect the outcome.[16]

Two more acts followed, the Quartering Act, which was signed into law on June 2, and the Quebec Act, which became law on June 22. Though frequently counted as Coercive Acts, these new rulings took force in all of the colonies, not solely in Massachusetts, and they were administrative in intent, not punitive. The Quartering Act updated an existing act that had led to clamorous resistance in colonial legislatures at the end of the French and Indian War, when Britain determined to keep troops in the colonies to defend the extensive territory it had won. According to the earlier act, when inns or public houses provided quarter, they were reimbursed at established rates. When, on the other hand, soldiers were housed in barracks or in vacant buildings that were rented out as barracks, funds were drawn from provincial accounts for necessities such as vinegar, firewood, bedding, salt, candles, or allotted portions of beer, cider, and rum mixed with water. Colonials had always resented the financial burden, and they begrudged a stipulation in the 1774 Quartering Act that allowed authorities to shelter men wherever they chose when barracks were insufficient for their numbers or when no barracks were nearby. Potentially they could lodge in inhabited buildings, which before was not allowed. In Boston, with redcoats much in evidence and altercations between citizens and solders commonplace, citizens were leery of the law's expansion.[17]

The Quebec Act, which Parliament passed just as it was retiring, shifted land in what would become America's Midwest into Canadian hands. That disturbed the powerful interests that advocated for westward expansion or held land grants on the other side of the Appalachians. In addition, this act protected the rights of French Canadian Catholics, which stimulated antipapist sentiment.[18]

Passage of these two bills perturbed all colonists, as highhanded intrusion by distant authorities commonly does, but they did not strike at the security or liberty of an entire public body as did the three coercive acts directed at Massachusetts. Here, the

Port Act jeopardized the economic livelihood of Boston and of enterprising citizens throughout the province who relied on its seafaring endeavors. But the Port Act at least provided an escape clause—pay for the tea and the port will open. The Massachusetts Government Act and the Administration of Justice Act offered no such reprieve. Provision by provision, with no chance of egress, they dismantled a constitutional framework and its safeguards. It was a particularly authoritarian provocation.[19]

Only a firm hand could enforce measures that closed a colony's foremost port and confined its entire populace to a newly restricted civic space. Whose hand would it be?

Finding a governor to enforce imperial rule in Massachusetts had never been easy. Prior governors had faced hostile reactions from the populace when they attempted to execute laws of Parliament or dictates of the Crown. In 1768 Governor Francis Bernard was held responsible for bringing British troops to Boston, and the following year William Bollan, agent for the Massachusetts Council in London, obtained letters in which Bernard criticized the council and recommended changing the 1691 charter to diminish its powers. The publication of these letters forced Bernard from his post. Upon his departure, Bostonians celebrated by flying the Union flag from the Liberty Tree, ringing bells, firing cannons, and lighting bonfires. The *Boston Gazette* remarked, "Tuesday last embarked on board his Majesty's ship the *Rippon*, sir Francis Bernard of Nettleham, Bart., who for nine Years past, has been a Scourge to this Province, a Curse to North-America, and a Plague to the whole Empire."[20]

The king hoped Bernard's successor, Thomas Hutchinson, would fare better. Unlike prior governors, who had all been dispatched from England, Hutchinson was Boston-born and -bred, yet he had held firmly and consistently to the belief that British subjects must accept Britain's authority over them, whether living in a colony without the benefit of Parliamentary representation or in England itself—it made no difference. But Hutchinson paid the price for such allegiance. His effigy was often set aflame in the streets of Boston, and furor intensified in 1773 after some of his letters, like his predecessor's, went public. Originally they had come into the possession of Benjamin Franklin, who was in England and who sent them to colleagues in Massachusetts. That June, these men released them, against Franklin's explicit instructions, although perhaps not against his actual intentions. Appearing in the Boston papers, the letters included phrases that damned the governor in the eyes of Massachusetts's citizens, such as one that proclaimed, "There must be an abridgement of what we call English liberties."[21]

Weary of colonial abuse and hoping to stabilize his own financial situation, Thomas Hutchinson asked the king for permission to come to England. Permission granted, Hutchinson was about to depart when, on March 3, 1774, Lieutenant Governor Andrew Oliver died. With nobody to assume the governorship in his absence, Hutchinson had to postpone the journey until the Crown appointed a successor to Oliver. The new lieutenant governor, though, would have to serve as temporary governor once Hutchinson departed, a nearly impossible task. "At present I am at a loss where to find a person who would be willing to accept the post, and who has sufficient knowledge of the Constitution, and sufficient firmness of mind to do the duty of his station, if the command of the Province should devolve upon him," Hutchinson confessed to Lord Dartmouth, secretary of state for the colonies.[22]

Unbeknownst to Hutchinson when he penned that letter, King George III was already searching for a man who possessed the firmness of mind to command the province, and he had a candidate in mind. Thomas Gage, commander in chief of the king's forces in North America, oversaw Britain's sprawling military enterprise from Nova Scotia to Florida, and he happened to be in England at the time. As early as 1768, after customs officials seized a ship belonging to John Hancock and an angry crowd drove these public officers from Boston, Gage had suggested to the Earl of Hillsborough, who was then secretary of state for the colonies, "I know of nothing that can so effectively quell the Spirit of Sedition, which has so long and so greatly prevailed here, and bring the People back to a Sense of their Duty, as Speedy, vigorous, and unanimous Measures taken in England to suppress it" and "reduce them to their Constitutional Dependence on the Mother Country." In 1770 he told Lord Barrington, the secretary of war, "I hope Boston will be called to strict account, and I think it must be plain to every Man that no Peace will ever be established in that Province, till the King Nominates his Council, and Appoints the Magistrates, and that all Town-Meetings are absolutely abolished; whilst those Meetings exist, the People will be kept in a perpetual Heat."[23]

After hearing of the destruction of the East India Company tea, King George III had called the commander in chief to his royal closet for consultation. The exchange so gratified His Majesty that he asked Lord North to "hear his ideas as to the mode of compelling Boston to submit to whatever may be thought necessary." Subsequently, the Coercive Acts would reflect some of Gage's thinking. Who could better execute the new measures and restrain protest than this early proponent? As Thomas Hutchinson awaited a successor to the lieutenant governorship so he could travel to England, the king concluded that Gage would become governor, replacing Hutchinson himself.[24]

On April 9, Secretary of State Dartmouth ordered General Thomas Gage to "return immediately to your command in *North America* . . . on board his Majesty's ship *Lively*, now lying at *Plymouth*, ready to sail with the first fair wind." There was to be no delay. Gage received a new commission, "Captain General and Governor-in-Chief of his Majesty's Province of *Massachusetts Bay*." He maintained his military office while assuming the governorship, dual appointments that granted him inordinate power.

Inordinate power would be required, and the letter acknowledged this:

> His Majesty trusts that no opposition will, or can, with any effect, be made to carrying the law into execution, nor any violence or insult offered to those to whom the execution of it is entrusted. Should it happen otherwise, your authority as the first Magistrate, combined with the command over the King's troops, will, it is hoped, enable you to meet every opposition, and fully to preserve the public peace, by employing those troops with effect, should the madness of the people, on the one hand, or the timidity or want of strength of the peace officers on the other hand, make it necessary to have recourse to their assistance.[25]

There was a caveat, however. By law, as of that moment, a governor required his council's assent before deploying military force. Referencing that precondition, Dartmouth added, "I do not mean that any Constitutional power or Authority, vested in them, should be set aside by any part of these instructions." Six weeks later, however, passage of the Massachusetts Government Act would remove this last remaining restraint. The new councilors, appointed by His Majesty, would no longer claim independent "Constitutional power" or resist the governor's will. With their compliance ensured, the governor of Massachusetts and commander of the king's forces in America would surely "meet every opposition," as his commission required.[26]

PART II

THE REVOLUTION OF 1774

The people of each town being drawn into separate
companies marched with staves & musick. The trumpets
sounding, drums beating, fifes playing and Colours
flying, struck the passions of the soul into a proper tone,
and inspired martial courage into each.

—*Joseph Clarke, describing the court closure*
in Springfield on August 30, 1774

3

SALEM: PROVINCIAL ASSEMBLY
AND TOWN MEETINGS

The new governor of Massachusetts had an ample colonial ré-
sumé, dating from 1755 when he arrived in the Ohio Valley
at the start of the French and Indian War, a captain in command
of an advance guard. Thomas Gage had left behind the open-field
carnage of Flanders and Scotland, with bodies and body parts
strewn on fields of battle, and found himself instead in wild, for-
ested terrain where foes did not stand in regimented lines. They
slipped through the trees, spirit-like, a stratagem that unsettled
the British Regulars he led. In spite of the military defeats that
dogged him at the start, Gage progressed as the war did, even-
tually becoming a major general and then, after Britain's victory
in Canada, the military governor of Montreal. At war's end he
bore a consummate title, commander in chief of North America.
In that capacity he witnessed what he termed the "commotions in
North-America" over the Stamp Act and, in years following, to
his consternation, more of the same and far too much.[1]

The continuing complaint and disruption disturbed an aristo-
crat who was bred to authority through generations and who was
by nature disciplined and exacting. In the public sphere Thomas

Gage's comportment was invariably reserved. He left no trace of private sentiment in the interminable letters, reports, and directives he dispatched. The son of a viscount, he sought a career in the military, as male offspring of noble lineage often did if they did not stand to inherit the family estate under the rules of primogenitor. Both a nobleman and a military man, Gage naturally inclined to the view that hierarchies protected society from collapse and dissolution. He despised what he called the "Democratical Despotism" that ran rampant in the New World. In 1772 he issued a warning to the British secretary of war: "Democracy is too prevalent in America, and claims the greatest Attention to prevent its Encrease, and fatal Effects."[2]

Many in Massachusetts feared the appointment of Britain's own commander in chief to the governorship. On the other hand, when he had served as governor in Montreal, Thomas Gage had exercised great restraint in ruling a defeated populace, and during his long service in the colonies, he had avoided conflict when possible. On the surface, he seemed levelheaded and not unsympathetic to colonials, negotiating fairly when negotiation was possible. This won him regard in the eyes of many. Even Joseph Warren, a man who voiced strong Whig opinions, initially considered Gage to be a "man of honest, upright principles" who would attempt "a just and honourable settlement." The historian John Shy points out that "Americans looked to him as their last hope for some reasonable solution of the tea controversy." At the same time, however, Gage's "own government believed that he was the man who could bring Boston to its knees without a civil war," Shy observes. "He could not possibly satisfy both at once, and he was doomed to satisfy neither."[3]

Governor Gage was cognizant of the pitfalls. On the day he first set foot on Long Wharf, resistance flared in one of those mutinous town meetings that soon would be outlawed. "The Act for Shutting up the Port got here before me; and a Town Meeting was holding to consider of it at the time of My Arrival in the Harbour," he wrote in a May 19 communication to Lord Dartmouth. "The late Governor Hutchinson, the Chief Justice, the Commissioners of the Customs, and the Consignees, were either at the Castle, or dispersed in the Country, not daring to reside in Boston." For his first four days in Massachusetts, Gage joined these refugee officials on Castle William Island, protected by the military regiments encamped there and by the waters that separated them from the mainland. It was an inauspicious beginning for the man who embodied British sovereignty in Massachusetts.[4]

Gage's reception in Boston was marked with the customary musket volleys and cheers. "Amid the acclamations of the people," a witness reported, Gage "express'd himself as sensible of the unwelcome errand he came upon, but as a servant of the Crown, he was obliged to see the [Port] Act put in execution: but would do all in his power to serve us." At a reception in Faneuil Hall, Gage offered a toast to "the prosperity of the town of Boston," although in the minds of the citizenry, the recently arrived Port Act signaled ruination. Privately, to Secretary of State Dartmouth, Gage reported that "the Act has staggered the most Presumptuous."[5]

As mandated by the 1691 Massachusetts Charter, the governor's first act was to summon the assembly and the council to Boston for the annual meeting of the General Court on May 25. At that particular moment, nobody in America yet knew that the Massachusetts Government Act would alter the rules under which the General Court operated. On the appointed day, following a long-established protocol, the new assembly and the outgoing council nominated twenty-eight men to serve on the incoming council, but Gage immediately rejected thirteen of these. Although this was his legal prerogative, past governors had turned down only a few nominees from time to time; denying nearly half was a particularly severe intrusion on the assembly's jurisdiction.[6]

Before the assembly and the council had a chance to conduct any further business, Gage issued a shocking pronouncement: "I have the King's particular Commands for holding the General

Court at Salem . . . until His Majesty shall have signified his Royal Will and Pleasure for holding it again at Boston."[7]

When Lord Dartmouth ordered Gage to board His Majesty's ship the *Lively*, which was "ready to sail with the first fair wind," he had warned him not to linger in Boston, dubbing it "the place of anarchy and usurpation." He told Gage that it was "his Majesty's further pleasure, that so soon as the law for discontinuing the port shall have taken place . . . you do make the town of *Salem* the place of your residence; that you do require all officers . . . to attend you there: and that the General Court, and all other courts and offices which are not by law fixed at *Boston*, be appointed and held at *Salem*." That town, nestled in a bay some seventeen miles north of Boston, was deemed safe.[8]

The news shocked and angered the General Court and would shock and anger Bostonians. Already their port was set to close on June 1, less than a week away, and now their town displaced and demoted again. The governor, however, hoped that discontent would recede in time. "Minds so inflamed cannot cool at once," he wrote to Dartmouth, "so it may be better, to give the Shock they have received, time to operate; and I may find the Assembly in a better Temper than usual, and more inclined to comply with the King's Expectations at Salem, to which Place they will be removed after the first of June."[9]

The inhabitants of this new seat of government knew full well what port closure meant to Boston. Originally a Native American trading hub, Salem was by 1774 a center of trade for the colony of Massachusetts in its own right. Numerous wharves reached out to the waters of its wide bay, beckoning ships. Hefty warehouses contained the barrels and crates that awaited export or those that sailors off-loaded from the dozens of vessels that steadily arrived. Nourished by commerce, the town thrived. Traders, sailors, women, merchants, and travelers marched along its crowded streets, past bustling shops and sturdy houses with their steep roofs, brick chimneys, and shuttered windows, and past fish-mongers peddling the recent catch.

On a Sunday the townspeople congregated in Salem's churches—provincial law mandated attendance. The church also served as a meetinghouse, which befitted a people whose civic life and life of worship overlapped continuously, the movement instinctual and rhythmic. Less formally, but regularly, men also gathered in taverns or "public houses," an accurate appellation because it was here, and not in private homes, that they held their unceremonious, animated forums on statecraft. Rum and hard cider drove discussion, but so did native inquisitiveness and concern. Everywhere meetinghouses and public houses hosted an increasingly politicized and restive population. In Salem, political apprehensions even surfaced at the ceremony that marked Gage's arrival. Not afraid to advise the new governor, one speaker urged him to "promote the general happiness of men, which mark the great and good" and "promote the peace, prosperity, and real welfare of this Province." No mention was made of the draconian ruling that closed Boston's port, but the message was clear. Public well-being must be the first concern of any great ruler, not retribution.[10]

When the General Court convened in Salem on June 8, tempers had not cooled as Thomas Gage had anticipated. In fact, the first act of the assembly was to object forcefully to its expulsion from Boston: "*Resolved*, That this House can see no necessity for the removal of the General Assembly from its ancient and only convenient place, the Court House in *Boston*, to the town of *Salem*; and the removal of the said Assembly from the Court House in *Boston* without necessity, is at all times considered to be a very great grievance." The grudge persisted. Two years later, when the Continental Congress detailed its reasons for declaring independence from Great Britain, fourth on its list was this: "He [the king of Great Britain] has called together legislative bodies at places unusual, uncomfortable, and distant from the depository of their public Records, for the sole purpose of fatiguing them into compliance with his measures."[11]

This, as it turned out, was to be the least of their complaints. After thirty-six days at sea, a ship from England had just landed in nearby Marblehead, carrying newspapers from London dated as late as April 26. On June 6, the *Boston Gazette* selected and published items most relevant to British colonials in Massachusetts, as was the custom, and this issue featured the entire texts of two bills being debated in Parliament. One was for "the Impartial Administration of Justice" and the other for "the better regulating the Government of the Province of the Massachusetts Bay." The bills had not yet been subjected to the three readings in Parliament that preceded passage, but all knew this was a mere formality. By the time colonials held copies of the *Gazette* in their hands, perusing the columns of print with increasing apprehension, the bills were in fact the law of the land, to take effect on August 1. They discarded the people's long-held rights, the Crown's pleasure their paramount aim.[12]

Committed activists immediately perceived that Britain had handed them a blueprint for disenfranchisement, and even moderate, undeclared citizens saw that the Coercive Acts dismantled the 1691 charter. Although the label "intolerable" was applied only after the fact in the nineteenth century, it was apt; in point of fact, provincials would *not* tolerate Parliament's dictates. From May 1774 until April 1775 and beyond, resistance would mount, coalesce, and manifest itself in armed, relentless rebellion. A Parliament that had anticipated deference and compliance had miscalculated. That body had been urged on by King George III, Lord North, and the king's prejudicial ministers like Lord George Germain, who considered Americans an inferior breed not fit to govern. If people in the province of Massachusetts "had the least prudence," Germain intoned at the close of hearings on the Administration of Justice Act, they should "not trouble themselves with politicks and government, which they do not understand." Instead, they should "follow their occupations . . . and not consider themselves as ministers of that country." For Germain and many other prominent British officials, Americans were subordinate affiliates in a grand imperial matrix ruled by the Crown. It was a meager portrait, and, like the measures themselves, it was an insult.[13]

The self-portrait that colonials in Massachusetts drew was opposite and prideful. In it, they were the reputable descendants of those who had set out on the harrowing voyage to the New World a century and a half before. Their forebears carried with them all things English—its tools, cloth, leather, wool, seed, gunpowder, fishing hooks, or pins. In a strange land, things English did not always answer, but the immigrants were resourceful. They survived unbearable hardships by turning to what was directly in front of them—the timber of the woods and the water in the streams and the Indian corn, pumpkin, squash, berries, clams, fish, deer, or wild fowl that sustained a native people. They turned to each other. They met in a body to pray. The God they prayed to in their worst trials felt closer to them than a distant king, even if they were his willing subjects. They met in a body to determine strategies and make decisions that would interest a king very little, being too paltry for royal notice. Independence and self-reliance became habit through decades and decades of passing time, and in that time they ministered to their affairs under the terms of their charters. They were able, adept, and, in their own sphere, much practiced at governance. Although, as subjects of the Crown, they recognized royal authority, they resisted untoward and unconstitutional interference.

Alert to intrusions, provincials at once saw just how destructive the new acts were. The refashioning of the judiciary was particularly disquieting. Judgments made in a court could have life-altering consequences, even resulting in imprisonment for debt or the seizure of land, yet in an instant safeguards were discarded. A

man would face judicial officials who were appointed and answerable to a governor only and jurors who were selected by that governor's appointed sheriffs. A citizen entering a courthouse after
August 1 would in effect pass into royally held territory, tilting
the odds against him. Meanwhile, the odds favored a British official accused of capital crimes in Massachusetts, who could now be
tried in England.

If the judicial system seemed rigged, so now did the legislature,
its upper house filled by Crown-appointed "mandamus councilors." The title itself, drawn from the word *mandate*, or decree,
underscored the fact that freeholders would play no part in their
selection. These new councilors could nullify any measure taken
by elected delegates in the lower house, subverting the elective
process.

Additionally, the act dismantled government at the local level
by limiting townships to their annual meetings, at which citizens
could address rudimentary, preapproved business only. To colonial New Englanders, who had called town meetings whenever
they liked and orated on any topic, this interdiction was as abusive
as a prohibition on public worship would have been. Those who attended these animated assemblies were freeholders—not tenants
or transients, but owners of real property. About one-third resided
within town—its clergymen, schoolmasters, tailors, house carpenters, and shopkeepers—while two-thirds were farmers living
on outlying lands who tilled their parcels and pastured their cattle
or horses. Although legislative bodies in London passed imperial
laws and bodies in Boston determined provincial policies, such
men ruled in the local sphere. They might discourse on imperial
policy if they liked, and they determined any and all town policies. Local rule was a matter of fierce pride and of simple common
sense. Who could better decide whether hogs should be yoked or
left free to roam? Who knew better than they did about pasturage
and stock, vagrants, roads, bridges, the education of children, or
disease and the much disputed practice of smallpox vaccination?

These freeholders also appointed officers to oversee the bidding of the town. Surveyors, clerks, and tithing men managed the town's business. Fence viewers ordered property owners to mend their fences, while hog reeves kept hogs off the street at the times determined by the meeting. The more diversified townships might appoint a man who checked the acetic acid content of vinegar or inspected bundles of staves to make sure each contained staves enough for a cooper's barrel. Generally unrecompensed, men who served in such minor posts nevertheless garnered respect by assuming the responsibilities of self-governance. A town meeting also selected a representative to the assembly, but the man they chose was not always free to do as he saw fit once he arrived at the seat of provincial government. A representative generally carried with him a set of agreed-upon instructions, his marching orders. He was to conduct the people's business just as the meeting would have him do it, an overtly democratic practice.[14]

Governor Hutchinson, no great fan of democracy, nevertheless acknowledged its deep roots in the countryside. He noted in his history of Massachusetts that "in very few instances had the interior government of any of the colonies been regulated, or controlled, by acts of parliament." Now Parliament was attempting to correct that oversight by regulating and controlling town meetings, jury selection, and a people's elective influence, while giving the governor unheard-of appointive powers and leaving the appointment of the province's council to the king himself. In bustling coastal ports and in the smallest distant villages, there was a sense of collective, instantaneous outrage. Intent on retribution, Parliament had rattled the cage without ever taking a correct measure of the fierce animal that paced back and forth inside or, for that matter, testing the strength of the bars.[15]

Refusing to be restrained, the elected assembly defied the mandates instantly. At its June 17 meeting in Salem, that body not only contested the new Parliamentary dictums but also asked other colonies to resist as one. If the Crown could dismantle any single colony's charter without its knowledge or consent, they pointed out, the Crown could dismantle another's, and so it was in any colony's interest to join with others in defense. The body resolved "that a meeting of Committees, from the several Colonies on this Continent is highly expedient and necessary, to consult upon the present state of the Colonies, and the miseries, to which they are, and must be reduced, by the operation of certain Acts of Parliament respecting *America*." The idea, the representatives insisted, was to seek "the restoration of union and harmony between *Great Britain* and the Colonies, most ardently desired by all good men," but throughout, their language was assertive, not submissive. "Shutting the harbour by armed force" was "an invasion" and "an attack made upon this whole Province and Continent, which threatens the total destruction of the liberties of *British America*." Further, distant rulers had concocted a "design totally to alter the free Constitution of civil Government in *British America*, and establish arbitrary Governments, and reduce the inhabitants to slavery." Setting an example, the assembly appointed four delegates to the intercolonial meeting. It also suggested a date, "the first day of *September* next," and a place, "the City of Philadelphia." Of one hundred and twenty-nine members present that day, only twelve dissented from this appeal.[16]

News of the assembly's dramatic goings-on reached Governor Gage *as* they were going on, and at once he determined to shut it down. He sent the provincial secretary, Thomas Fluker, to the county courthouse, where the assembly had convened, with a notice proclaiming that the General Court was dissolved, but Fluker found the chamber door locked. When he requested permission to enter, the assembly determined "to keep the door fast." Unable to read the notice directly to the assembly, the envoy could only post it "on the stairs leading to the Representatives Chamber":

Whereas the proceedings of the House of Representatives, in the present session of the General Court, make it necessary for his Majesty's service that the said General Court should be dissolved: I have, therefore, thought fit to dissolve the said General Court, and the same is hereby dissolved accordingly, and the members thereof are discharged from any further attendance.

Given under my hand, at *Salem*, the 17th day of *June*, 1774, in the fourteenth year of his Majesty's reign.

T. GAGE.[17]

Crown-appointed governors had dissolved colonial assemblies before, only to reconvene them later. But the stakes were greater this time. If Gage ever did try to call the assembly back, would anybody come?

At the provincial level, the assembly ignored the royal governor's proclamation and continued to transact business. At the local level, the ban on self-rule was equally unenforceable. All through the summer, intractable citizens continued to hold town meetings, not only despite the prohibition but to some extent because of it. A few town meetings tried to circumvent the Government Act by adjourning each session to some future date, thus eliminating the need to call a "new" meeting; citizens of Marblehead, for example, adjourned the same meeting forty-six times. Others turned their illegally convened meetings into conscious acts of civil disobedience. Boston merchant John Andrews, an inveterate letter writer and astute commenter, took note: "The towns through the country are so far from being intimidated that a day in the week does not pass without one or more having meetings, in direct contempt of the Act; which they regard as a blank piece of paper and not more."[18]

Salem presented a special case. In spite of serving as the current seat of the provincial government, this town too would dare to flout the law. On Saturday, August 20, local leaders called upon "the merchants, free-holders and other inhabitants of this town to meet at the town house chamber next Wednesday, at nine o'clock in the morning" to appoint delegates to a county convention to be held in early September. Two months earlier, when the provincial assembly had appointed delegates to the Continental Congress in Philadelphia, Gage had been taken by surprise; this time he had some advance warning. On Tuesday, the day before the meeting, he held the line, issuing another proclamation:

> Whereas by a late Act of Parliament, all Town-Meetings called without the consent of the Governor (except the annual Meetings, in the Months of March and May) are illegal, I do hereby strictly prohibit all Persons from attending . . . any Meeting not warned by law, as they will be chargeable with all the ill Consequences that may follow thereon, and answer the same at their utmost Peril.[19]

Having learned from his experience with the assembly that a mere proclamation might not be obeyed, Gage took additional measures. First, he summoned the members of the committee of correspondence who had issued the call to appear at his office during the very time the meeting was scheduled to take place. Next, he ordered two companies from the Fifty-Ninth Regiment to stand in formation at the entrance to town on Wednesday morning, armed and ready for battle.[20]

The governor's meeting with resistance leaders did not go well. When he ordered them to walk the few hundred feet to the meetinghouse and disband the people, they told him "that the Inhabitants being met together would do what they thought fit, and that the Committee could not oblige them to disperse." The men then argued that they were acting within "the Laws of the Province," but Gage cut them off: "I am not going to enter into a Conversation on the matter; I came to execute the Laws, not to dispute them." Increasingly agitated, Gage drew the session to an abrupt conclusion. "If the People do not disperse, the Sheriff will go first," he threatened. "If he is disobeyed, and needs Support, I will support him." According to the committee members present, "This he uttered with much Vehemence of Voice and Gesture." True to his word, Gage then sent orders for the Regulars to advance on the meetinghouse. They did as they were told, but by the time they arrived the people of Salem had already ended their meeting, having quickly conducted their business.[21]

Rebuffed and infuriated, Gage instructed Peter Frye, an Essex County judge, to issue warrants for the arrest of the men who had flouted him in his office. Frye was to charge them with "seditiously and unlawfully causing the town to be assembled by those notifications, without leave from the governour, in open contempt of the laws, against the peace, and the late statute." The first two brought into custody posted bail, but the remaining five defiantly told Gage, "If the ninetieth part of a farthing would be taken as bail, they would not give it." Answering Gage's threat with a threat of their own, they also declared that "[i]f he committed them, *he must abide by the consequences.*"[22]

In the end, Judge Frye simply released the men without bail, no doubt influenced by "upwards of three thousand men" who converged on Salem "from the adjacent towns, with full determination to rescue the Committee if they should be sent to prison, even if they were oblig'd to repel force with force, being sufficiently provided for such a purpose; as indeed they are all through the country—every male above the age of 16 possessing a firelock with double the quantity of powder and ball enjoin'd by law." Not daring to risk bloodshed, the governor backed down. "[H]is Excellency has suspended the matter at Salem by dropping the prosecution. Seeing them resolute and the people so determinate, he was willing to give up a point rather than push matters to extremities," John Andrews reported.[23]

With momentum on their side, townsmen continued to press the issue. Although they could not touch the governor, they could exact retribution on those who did his bidding. Judge Frye lived among them and was vulnerable, as anyone would be in the tightly knit societies of Massachusetts. "He and his family were in danger of starving," wrote Andrews, "for the country people would not sell him any provisions, and the [town] inhabitants, however well dispos'd any might be to him, dare not procure him any." When the Essex County Convention formalized measures to isolate Frye, he "resign'd all his posts of *honor* and *profit*." Proffering his "frank and generous" resignation, he promised "not to do any Thing either in my public or private Capacity to execute the Massachusetts Government Act." His hope was "to be restored to that Friendship & Regard with my Fellow-Citizens and Countrymen which I heretofore enjoyed."[24]

A few days after the meeting in Salem, neighboring Danvers called one of its own. Danvers was "right under [Gage's] nose," John Andrews wrote, for it was there that the governor resided. He occupied the Lindens, an estate named for the linden trees that lined the approach to a three-story Georgian mansion with twelve-foot ceilings and interior columns and fine furnishings. The residence had been built as a summer home for a prosperous shipowner from Marblehead who dominated the fishing trade, and it spoke to Gage's status and power—but that power was challenged once again. The populace not only assembled in a town meeting but "continued it two or three howers longer than was necessary, to see if he would interrupt 'em. He was acquainted with it, but reply'd—'Damn 'em! I wont do any thing about it unless his Majesty sends me more troops.' "[25]

4

BERKSHIRE COUNTY: COMMITTEES OF CORRESPONDENCE

Berkshire County lay at the westernmost edge of Massachusetts, a four-day journey from coastal Boston. Toward its
end, a rider passed through dense forests, where he might sight
a wolf or a mountain lion. The hills he crossed extended from
north to south on the county's eastern edge, and in the west the
Taconic Mountains did the same. Like two long arms they held
the region in a protective embrace and shielded it from outsid-
ers. British colonials only arrived in significant numbers during
the first French and Indian War, declared in 1744, and in the one
that ensued a decade later. More settled in the region after war
ended in 1763, arriving primarily from eastern Massachusetts or
Connecticut. Desperate for opportunity in hard times, they populated the narrow alluvial valleys that lay between the two ranges.
When Berkshire separated from Hampshire County to form its
own county in 1761, four thousand resided in this remote region,
only slightly more than 1 percent of the province's population. In
winter months, fierce snowstorms at times cut off contact with the
eastern counties, and spring floods, mud slides, rain, and the common ruts and gullies impeded passage at any time.[1]

Crown officials and soldiers posted along the Atlantic seaboard paid the outpost little heed. Berkshire's citizens were naturally less affected by the Parliamentary rulings that caused heated resistance in Boston and elsewhere, and its representatives to the provincial assembly during this time were among the most conservative in the province. It seemed an unlikely breeding ground for opposition. Yet in 1774, with passage of the Coercive Acts, the inhabitants of Berkshire were as disturbed as any others by the Crown's encroachment. Then, by a quirk of judicial scheduling, Berkshire found itself in the forefront. The Massachusetts Government Act was slated to take effect on August 1, and on August 16, Berkshire County's Court of Common Pleas and Berkshire County's Court of General Sessions were to convene in the town of Great Barrington. There, for the first time anywhere, judges, justices of the peace, sheriffs, and jurors would conduct their business pursuant to the Massachusetts Government Act and the Administration of Justice Act.

The Court of General Pleas was made up of a panel of judges, usually four in number, who reviewed actions of the individual justices of the peace and made decisions that could seriously impact a person's life. Under the new arrangements, provincials had reason to fear their unimpeded authority. The Court of General Sessions was composed of these General Pleas judges and the county's justices of the peace. Acting as the administrative arm of county government, it did such things as grant necessary licenses, determine tax assessments, regulate the configuration of roads, and disperse funds. It had the power to check or permit such a variety of undertakings that in the minds of local people it was more than an administrative arm of the government; it *was* the government.

According to the new acts of Parliament, court officials who wielded such power would no longer be under any obligation to the people. The king, acting through his appointed governor, would be their exclusive source of authority—*if* the acts were implemented, that is. Politically active citizens of Berkshire vowed to prevent this from happening.

Fear of courts ran deep among hardscrabble Berkshire farmers. In 1765, when Deputy Sheriff John Morse tried to arrest Peter Curtis of Lanesborough for unpaid debts, a number of Curtis's friends prevented the sheriff from taking him away. These men and many more—the majority of Lanesborough's farmers, in fact—then formed a compact: if any of them should be arrested for unpaid debts, the others would come to their aid. So when Sheriff Morse returned three weeks later with five deputies to apprehend Curtis and another man, a larger group, armed with clubs, staves, and stones, forced the posse to turn back. Some "very angry, imprudent and profane language was uttered by both parties and they came to blows," a newspaper reported. While Berkshire's officials supported the government in all matters, common farmers showed little deference.[2]

In 1772, when Lord North's ministry determined that Superior Court judges would be paid by the Crown rather than by the provincial assembly, Berkshire citizens realized that they had lost a key check on the court system. This set them on edge once again. As a signal of the shift in the political winds, the people of Lanesborough elected Peter Curtis, the man who had resisted arrest seven years earlier, to represent them in the provincial assembly. There were other signs as well. In Sheffield, the oldest incorporated town in the county, the longtime representative, John Ashley, experienced a sudden change of heart. He had supported the royal governor on all contentious issues through the turbulent 1760s, as men of his standing customarily did. The son of a town founder, he was a colonel in the southern Berkshire militia, a judge for the Berkshire Court of Common Pleas, the town's largest landowner and indisputably its leading citizen, yet he placed himself now at the forefront of resistance. On January 5, 1773, he moderated a Sheffield town meeting that chose a committee "to take into consideration the grievances which Americans in general, and the inhabitants of this province in particular, labour under; and to make a draught of such proceedings as they think are necessary for this town, in these critical circumstances, to enter into." Ashley was chosen to serve on that committee along with a major, three captains, two deacons, a doctor, and Theodore Sedgwick, a young lawyer recently graduated from Yale—leading citizens all.[3]

Gone were the days when respectable men such as these could be counted on to uphold the established order. The document the committee produced, and the town meeting subsequently approved, bemoaned "the design of Great Britain" to deprive colonists of their "invaluable rights and privileges." Foreshadowing the Continental Congress's historic Declaration of Independence, still three and one half years in the future, it declared "*That mankind in a state of nature are equal, free, and independent of each other, and have a right to the undisturbed enjoyment of their lives, their liberty and property.*" Theodore Sedgwick, who likely had a hand in this, did not use the words "equal, free, and independent" lightly. In 1781, he would argue a case for Elizabeth Freeman, commonly called Mumbet or Mum Bett, an enslaved woman who sued for her freedom. Since the first article of the newly approved Massachusetts Constitution proclaimed that "all men are born free and equal," Sedgwick argued that Mumbet could not legally be held as property. Sedgwick and Mumbet won their case, and her master, none other than John Ashley, was compelled to set her free.[4]

Subsequent resolutions argued strongly against the Crown's payment of judicial salaries:

Resolved, That the peaceful enjoyment of any privileges, to the people of this province, in a great measure (under God) depends upon the uprightness and independency of the executive officers in general, and of the Judges of the Superior Court in particular.

Resolved, That if salaries are affixed to the offices of the Judges of the Superior Court, rendering them independent of the people and dependent of the crown for their support; (which we have too much reason to think is the case) it is a precedent that may hereafter, considering the depravity of human nature, . . . [lead to] the most obvious and fatal consequences, to the good people of this province.

The logic was airtight: power of the purse, unchecked, bestows power over the people.[5]

Sheffield was not alone in opposing Crown payment of judicial salaries. Political activists in Boston sensed that country people would respond to this latest "design to enslave us," as Dr. Thomas Young put it. In this they saw an opportunity. "We are brewing something here which will make some people's heads reel," Young wrote from Boston to a fellow radical in New York in the late summer of 1772.[6]

That "something" was a plan to extend the resistance movement into the far reaches of the province. Dr. Young, Samuel Adams, and others of like persuasion first convinced the Boston town meeting to form a committee of correspondence that would communicate "the sense of this Town . . . to the several Towns of the Province and"—in an unabashed addendum—"to the World." This committee drafted an exhaustive list of "the Rights of Colonists" and the "infringements and violations" of those rights— some twenty-nine pages in all, subsequently known as the *Boston Pamphlet*. Once approved by the town meeting, the committee sent this signature document to selectmen in 260 far-flung towns and districts, accompanied by a letter whose tone was simultaneously solicitous and commandeering. Boston was "desirous" to

hear "the collective wisdom of the whole People" and believed the
people would agree "to stand firm as one man . . . to rescue from
impending ruin our happy and glorious constitution."[7]

In those towns and districts, sitting on hard benches within
their meetinghouses, citizens listened to page after page of inflammatory accusations and were told of the dire consequences that
would unfold if imperial abuses were left unchallenged. One example: "Thus our houses and even our bed chambers, are exposed
to be ransacked, our boxes, trunks & chests broke open, ravaged
and plunder by wretches." What would country people, far from
the turmoil that had engulfed Boston, make of all this?

In Boston the returns soon flooded in. At least 119 towns replied to the pamphlet early in 1773 and another 25 by the end of
the summer. More towns participated in this forum than sent representatives to the elected assembly in that year. Most that replied,
like Sheffield, agreed with Boston's radical denunciation of ministerial policies but also relished the opportunity to fashion their
own polemics. Some of the rhetoric was as deeply radical as anything Boston circulated. In language that authorities in London
might consider treasonous, Attleborough's citizens proclaimed,
"We have no natural ascendency and necessary connection with
the Crown in point of government but what springs from our own
choice."[8]

The *Boston Pamphlet* afforded radicals in each town an opportunity to rise to the fore. More often than not, the committee
that drafted a town's response became a committee of correspondence, charged with keeping citizens informed of further threats
to their liberties. Over the previous decade, activists urging resistance to Crown policies had formed ad hoc political groups to
deal with any immediate crisis, but the standing committees of
correspondence piggybacked on a fundamental structure in place
everywhere in Massachusetts—the town meeting. This simple stratagem was well suited to the countryside. Farmers might
live an hour or two away from their meetinghouse, with roads

treacherous in unseasonal weather or in the darkness, and unlike their urban counterparts, they could not attend a steady stream of public forums as issue after issue played out. They did attend town meetings, however, and there, at regular intervals, they would now listen to what their committee of correspondence had to say about events in London or Boston or other towns. Even in the most distant hamlets, imperial business became a town's business. Additionally, radicals who manned the new committees were now legitimate public servants, garnering respect in the community and official accreditation.

Activated instantaneously in any crisis, the committees of correspondence fortified towns by coordinating their resistance efforts. Months later, when the people of Berkshire learned that Bostonians had dumped tea into the harbor rather than abide by Parliament's Tea Act, they used their newly formed committees to let their sentiments be known. The town meeting of Great Barrington, spurred by its committee of correspondence, wrote a letter to the Boston committee of correspondence, which arranged for its newspaper publication. "Imposing Taxes on a free People without their Consent, we consider as an Attempt to enslave us," the town meeting stated, repeating a common refrain. What bothered people most, though, were "the Purposes to which the Money, thus taken from us," was put—including paying judges for "the Administration of Justice." Crown support of judges still topped their list of complaints. "We never heard that Government was not duly supported, or that Civil Officers were not honorably paid, before a Duty on tea was dreamed of," the town stated.[9]

In June 1774, when citizens of Berkshire County learned that the Massachusetts Government Act and the Administration of Justice Act were about to place all court officials and court proceedings totally beyond their control, town committees of correspondence called for a county convention of all the Berkshire committees, the first such meeting of its kind in Massachusetts. On July 6, sixty delegates from nineteen towns and districts convened in Stockbridge to consider what actions, collectively, they might take. All but two of the county's incorporated towns were represented. The convention chose John Ashley as moderator and Theodore Sedgwick as clerk, a position of greater importance then than now since the clerk literally had the final word. Sedgwick, an excellent wordsmith, also served on the five-man committee that drafted the convention's resolutions.[10]

Boston's committee of correspondence, in a circular letter, had asked all Massachusetts townships to join a sweeping boycott of British goods it called a Solemn League and Covenant. "There is but one way we can conceive of" to prevent colonists from becoming "the most abject slaves," the Boston committee wrote, "and that is by affecting the trade and interest of Great Britain, so deeply as shall induce her to withdraw her oppressive hand." Although delegates to the Berkshire convention understood Boston's intent, they found its formulation wanting and offered an alternate plan tailored to rural communities. To make up for the loss of manufactured British textiles, they pledged to plant flax, a fiber crop, and to raise sheep for wool. Berkshire's own covenant also urged people "to avoid all unnecessary lawsuits" so Crown-appointed court officials could not intercede in business that citizens had with each other.[11]

For Berkshire's animated activists, an economic boycott was hardly "the last and only method of preserving our land from slavery," as the Boston committee of correspondence asserted. Even if it worked, it would take time for British manufacturers to feel the pinch and then push Parliament to repeal its oppressive acts. That avenue of resistance was both slow and uncertain. By contrast, there was an immediate and certain way to keep the acts from taking effect: the people could simply close the courts that were slated to convene in August.

On July 25, the Berkshire County committees of correspondence dispatched a missive to the Boston committee of correspondence. The Berkshire County courts were to be "the first in the province after the taking place of those Acts," the letter stated, in case Boston committee members had not yet noted this. But "people this way" would "by no means submit to the New Regulations," and they planned to prevent the courts from sitting "unless we should hear from you." The Berkshire committees asked the Boston committee "for your Advice and Opinion, and desire your speedy sense in this Matter of so great Moment, that we may act in concert with the whole province as much as possible." Despite this obligatory show of deference to Boston's leadership, the Berkshire committees had seized the initiative.[12]

Boston endorsed Berkshire's proposal on July 31: "We acknowledge ourselves deeply indebted to your wisdom. . . . Nothing in our opinion could be better concerted than the measures come into by your County to prevent the Court's sitting on an establishment so repugnant to the Charter and Laws of this Province."[13]

Just days later, on August 4, the Berkshire committees held another county convention in Pittsfield to strategize for the August 16 court closure. The minutes for that meeting are not extant, but we do have a petition adopted by the Pittsfield town meeting on August 15, the day before the court was to convene:

To the Honorable His Majesty's Justices of the Inferior Court of Common Pleas for the County of Berkshire:
. . . We view it of the greatest importance to the well-being of this Province, that the people of it utterly refuse the least submission to the said acts, and on no consideration to yield obedience to them; or directly or indirectly to countenance the taking place of those acts amongst us, but resist them to the last extremity. In order in the safest manner to avoid this threatening calamity, it is, in our opinion, highly necessary that no business be transacted in the law, but that the courts of justice immediately cease, and the people of this Province fall into a state of nature until our grievances

are fully redressed by a final repeal of these injurious, oppressive, and unconstitutional acts. . . . We hope your hon-
ors will not be of a different opinion from the good people in
this county. . . . We ought to bear the most early testimony
against those acts, and set a good example for the other part
of the Province to copy after.[14]

To nobody's surprise, the judges and magistrates of the court
did not heed Pittsfield's petition. On the morning of August 16,
a Tuesday, officials powdered their wigs in preparation for their
court appearance, but simultaneously, some fifteen hundred un-
armed men prepared as well. They gathered at the Berkshire
County courthouse, a one-and-a-half-story wooden structure,
"plain and unpainted, . . . destitute of architectural pretention or
adornment, save a semi-circular window in its eastern gable and
some little carved wood work about the front door." A symbol
of civil authority, the courthouse protruded "so far out into Main
Street as to admit a pass way for wagons, on either side," in the
words of a history of Great Barrington written a century later. "It
occupied a prominent position becoming the uses for which it was
intended, and was a conspicuous object in the ill-kept and untidy
village."[15]

When the judges and magistrates arrived for work, they discovered that the protesters had "filled the Court-House and Avenues
to the Seat of Justice, so full, that no Passage could be found for
the Justices to take their Places. The Sheriff commanded them to
make way for the court; but they gave him to understand that they
knew no court on any other establishment than the ancient laws
and usages of their country, & to none other would they submit
or give way on any terms." Court officials, vastly outnumbered,
offered no meaningful resistance. Judge John Ashley, having
already switched allegiances, submitted willingly to the crowd,
and the other two judges, although reticent, saw no alternative
options. Perry Marsh, son-in-law to Israel Williams, the leading

Tory in neighboring Hampshire County, must have grumbled, but he could hardly force his way through the crowd and into the courthouse. At age sixty-four, Chief Justice William Williams, who had earlier complained to Governor Gage of being threatened with a tarring and feathering, had sense enough to give in quietly. Justices of the peace yielded as well.[16]

Despite his legal obligation to serve on the Court of General Sessions, David Ingersoll Jr., a justice of the peace, never showed up. Following the court closure, some of the crowd decided to pay him a personal visit. Previously respected, Ingersoll had been elected militia captain and representative to the provincial assembly, but recently he had antagonized his neighbors with a full-throated expression of Tory views. Two weeks earlier, before sunrise on August 2, "a vast concourse of people" armed with clubs had surrounded his house. They demanded he arise from his bed. At first, according to Ingersoll's testimony to Governor Gage, he "utterly refused to comply with their insolent requisition," but after the men broke into his house and threatened his family, he obeyed. This did not satisfy the "ruffians," who placed him and his servant on horses and took them to the town of Canaan, just over the Connecticut border and fourteen miles from Great Barrington, where they had erected a "pompous Liberty pole." They accused him of many "crimes," including his support for the Massachusetts Government Act and his opposition to the Berkshire covenant. Finally, after signing a statement he composed himself but not the covenant, the prisoner was set free.[17]

This time Ingersoll fled his house ahead of those who would torment him. Here was a graduate of Yale accustomed to deference, but on the night of August 16 he was nothing but a hunted man who "repaired to the Wilderness." There he spent the night in the muggy August heat, hiding from his pursuers, some of whom "attacked his house and office, broke and Entered both of them, destroyed his Yard fences, his Garden, and greatly damaged his House, papers, &c." Realizing he would never find peace in Berkshire County, Ingersoll made his way eastward, escaping. When he arrived at Chesterfield, some thirty-five miles away, about two hundred men confronted him. This time his captors would not release him until he signed the Berkshire covenant, and at last he did. Again at Hatfield he was "surrounded by about 200 men who ordered him to decamp within a few minutes." Finally, through woods and along back roads, David Ingersoll continued on to Boston, the only place where intransigent apologists of the government could feel safe.[18]

The Berkshire courts never again opened for business under British rule. Although other county conventions of the committees of correspondence would stage similar events, some larger and better organized, Berkshire was the first to close its courts. In the wake of Berkshire's dramatic resistance, Governor Gage informed Lord Dartmouth that "popular Rage has appeared at the Extremity of the Province, abetted by Connecticut, . . . and makes its way rapidly to the rest." Although worried enough, Gage had not yet taken full measure of the people's wrath. It was not progressing from place to place in linear order but was erupting everywhere simultaneously. By referencing the *spread* of unrest, he implicitly denied the legitimacy and the power of local protest. Even in the face of mounting evidence, Gage continued to profess that the real culprit was Boston. "It is agreed that popular Fury was never greater in this Province than at present, and it has taken its Rise from the old Source at Boston, tho' it has appeared first at a Distance," he reported.[19]

Boston's John Andrews described the mood of the times more accurately when he wrote, "The inhabitants of the country towns . . . are prodigiously vex'd." Faced with disenfranchisement, people throughout Massachusetts were responding with a strong and nearly unanimous voice. They had even created an oppositional infrastructure—the committees of correspondence—that could turn "popular Rage" into concerted and effective political action.[20]

5

HAMPSHIRE COUNTY: "RIVER GODS"

In the eighteenth-century world, the social order was highly structured, and one's standing depended to a great extent on family pedigree. At Harvard in 1772, for example, a young gentleman by the name of William Chandler graduated at the very top of his class, but academic merit did not determine his ranking; social standing did, and by that measure William Chandler deserved the honor. His father, John Chandler IV, was politically prominent and vastly wealthy, possessing nine working farms, an elegant mansion, three carriages, multiple shops and mills, five pews at the meetinghouse, and two slaves.[1]

It was Massachusetts gentlemen like this who sat in the forward pews of the church, their ample donations securing first-rate seating. Their sons were received everywhere and married well, as did their daughters. Such marriages established interconnecting dynasties that increased the influence of all members, and political dominance inevitably followed. Members of each county's elite gentry served on the provincial council, and townships elected gentlemen to the lower house of the legislature, the assembly. If commoners had sporadic reservations about the firmly tiered social structure and the authority of those who governed within it, for the most part they did not object. Where, at that point in time, was there any other societal arrangement? Who were they to question long-established cultural norms? Besides, as likely as not, they themselves read haltingly. Perhaps they wrote in a scrawl. It made sense that educated gentlemen would compose legal documents for them or dash off needed petitions, flourishing a quill pen. They were the ones to argue the fine points of law inside chambers in the State House. Drinking and dining with influential patrons, they might procure contracts or intervene on behalf of their constituents in times of need, a thing no ordinary man could manage.

On the other hand, farmers and farm wives, coopers, farriers, milliners, saddlers, doctors, barbers, and others did not feel themselves to be dispossessed or abject. They too had standing in this world. More often than not, they lived in the townships their relatives had lived in for generations, where farms or shops or trades passed from fathers to sons. Women married local men, strengthening connections between families. The people gathered in taverns or churches or in town meetings, and they knew their neighbors well. Undoubtedly that knowledge encompassed gossip and quarreling, but even the gossip and quarrels nurtured the sense of place and of belonging. They inhabited a known world; its climate, rocks, animals, hills, streams, footpaths, history, and family lineages were as familiar to them as lines on their palms.

In their own domain, people might gain respect by dint of their labor or knowledge of restorative herbs or a reputation for simple kindnesses. A woman might act the part of midwife or nurse a neighbor's dying child. Men helped each other at harvest time and took on respected town duties, arranging care for the town's poor or inspecting the quality of firewood being sold. Men could and did speak out at town meetings, exhibiting rhetorical talent. They voted, exercising political control. Although ordinary town and country folk did not occupy the top rungs of the hierarchical ladder, they could, with effort and some good fortune, keep a steady foothold on the middle ones.

In Hampshire County, most citizens farmed land that they owned, which classed them "yeomen," one rung below "gentlemen" in the traditional English hierarchy. As freeholders, most yeomen were enfranchised citizens who participated actively in town meetings. In the small community of Chesterfield, with only thirty families, twenty-one men were elected to at least one town office in 1762. [2]

All higher offices, however, went to a coterie of gentlemen, dubbed "river gods," who possessed fertile land along the Connecticut River Valley in the central part of the county, where they raised fine horses for markets in the West Indies and fattened herds of cattle. Their prosperity stemmed from the area's rich soil and the broad, flat terrain, rare in the heart of New England. Wealthy as they were, they leveraged political control. During the second quarter of the eighteenth century, they occupied all key governmental posts. John Stoddard of Northampton, son of the influential minister Solomon Stoddard, served as justice of the peace, chief justice of the Court of Common Pleas, colonel of the Hampshire militia, commander in chief of the western forces, representative to the House, and member of the provincial council. Many of these positions he held concurrently. A successful land speculator, he used his political and military appointments to garner even greater riches, prestige, and power. No county road could be laid without the approval of Colonel Stoddard, and no contract awarded. Food for the militia would probably be purchased from someone he knew, and when a gentleman's son was ready to embark on a career, undoubtedly John Stoddard would be asked to procure an appointment.

Men such as this bequeathed to their heirs not only fortunes but a dynastic legacy decades in the making. Upon Stoddard's death in 1748, his nephew Israel Williams, of Hatfield, inherited the title of kingmaker. Like his uncle John, Williams was a Harvard

College graduate and, like him, was related to practically every government official in the county, as well as to several of its most important ministers. His cousin Elijah Williams was patriarch of Deerfield, while his nephew William Williams had established his own domain in Pittsfield. He was related by marriage to other members of the county's elite—John Worthington of Springfield and Joseph Hawley and the Dwights of Northampton—and, over several decades, was related to every justice of the Hampshire Court of Common Pleas and every officer of its Probate Court. Williams used his multifarious positions, the same once held by Stoddard, to wield power and influence. Like his uncle, he dispensed his favors carefully, expecting as he did some return on that investment.

Downriver at Springfield, John Worthington, a graduate of Yale, held sway. He was a gentleman farmer, a land speculator, moneylender, justice of the peace, representative to the assembly, member of the council in 1767 and 1768, and the king's attorney in all local cases. While representing the Crown before the Court of General Sessions, he sometimes collected both his attorney's fees and payment for service as one of the court's justices.[3]

"River gods" indeed, for gods they seemed. Set apart and above, they lorded over Hampshire County in ways that perpetuated their dominion. For decades, they went unchallenged.

A fault line crossed through Hampshire County, separating one class of people from another, but before the mid-eighteenth century the fault was dormant and barely acknowledged. Not until midcentury did the initial tremors appear. The epicenter was in the countryside, with its scattered farms, where land had been steadily subdivided. In New England, double-digit offspring were not uncommon and all males stood to inherit family holdings; few fathers bequeathed land to an eldest male heir, as in England. Divided over and over, estates were reduced to a meager size, the smaller holdings by necessity overworked. Inventories of estates in probate began to list "worn land." If their farms could not support them, men and women, called the "strolling poor," moved on, hoping to start anew elsewhere. Each town, in order to avoid the obligation of supporting vagrants, "warned out" transients when they first showed up—and warnings were on the rise. In Hampshire County, the official count increased by 248 percent between 1750 and 1764.[4]

Increasingly, farmers accrued debt and creditors took them to court. If a debtor lost his case, he had to pay court costs as well as his original liability; owing initially very little, a man might lose livestock or acreage. From 1761 to 1765, the annual number of suits in five rural counties in Massachusetts amounted to 22 percent of the adult male population. Typically, the court record listed a creditor as a "gentleman" and a debtor a "yeoman." Threatened by moneylenders and lawyers and dependent on the integrity of men in wigs and robes, a yeoman's hold was tenuous. If a decree went against him, a freeholder might become a mere tenant or even become one of the "strolling poor."[5]

The growing threat to economic security coincided with changes in British imperial policies. The Stamp Act in 1765, which aroused hostility everywhere, created a challenge for Hampshire's river gods. Previously, when they supported the governor and the Crown, their constituencies had not objected so long as local interests were not compromised, but now local citizens vehemently opposed a tax on all court documents, contracts, licenses, newspapers, almanacs, and even playing cards. River gods were in the untenable position of serving two masters who clashed, locking horns. If they supported the new tax, they would enrage their constituents, but if they publicly opposed it, they would alienate provincial officials who bestowed favors. Caught in the crossfire, they had little wish to declare themselves, and whenever possible, they prevaricated or searched for escape routes. Israel Williams, chief justice of the Hampshire County Court of Common Pleas, did not close the court but simply adjourned it until the Stamp Act was repealed. In Berkshire County, the probate judge William

Williams, Israel's nephew, claimed illness and did not show up for work. The crisis was short-lived, and for the most part approaches such as these paid off; the people of Hatfield retained Israel Williams as their representative to the assembly, and Springfield retained John Worthington.[6]

One of their number broke ranks during the Stamp Act crisis. Joseph Hawley, a celebrated war hero, minister, and attorney, agreed to defend Seth Warren, a Berkshire man accused of rioting. Warren had been among the Lanesborough crowd that beat back a sheriff and posse who were trying to apprehend a debtor, Peter Curtis. (See chapter 4.) Ten men were later arrested, and though nine pleaded guilty, Warren chose to have his day in court. Men of Hawley's standing did not normally take on a case like this, but he saw in it an opportunity to elucidate a radical view of governmental authority. At the time of Warren's arrest, a stamp was required on all legal documents, yet no stamps had been issued in the colonies, so Hawley claimed that all legal proceedings against Warren were null and void. Technically, this was correct. For months, lacking stamps, courts everywhere had closed. Juries could not even be called since writs summoning them required a stamp. Hawley could have rested his case on these technicalities but did not. The controversy around the Stamp Act, he argued, had created "almost a total blank in the course of law, a chasm and gap in the administration of justice, when the King's writs did not run in the province. What then was the state and condition of the inhabitants of this province on the 26th of November 1765? Indeed little other than a state of absolute outlawry." Under such conditions, the normal rules of law did not apply. Warren and the others "shewed themselves to be a sensible, discerning, judicious and courageous people" by resisting the incursions of the sheriff and his posse, who were backed by no legal sanction. Conservative judges summarily rejected this profoundly revolutionary argument. Warren was fined three pounds and charged four pounds, six shillings in court costs, and Hawley was suspended from the bar.[7]

Joseph Hawley sided with the insurgents and paid the price. Other river gods were careful to take no side at all, which was sound policy when only a few months separated the enactment of the Stamp Act and its repeal. It was not a realistic stratagem after passage of the Massachusetts Government Act nine years later, when the Crown was intransigent, repeal inconceivable, and the people more infuriated than ever before in the colony's history.

In Springfield, the town meeting of July 12, 1774, raged against the Government Act. Citizens refused to be "dissiez'd of our Property, or any way Punish'd, without the judgment of our Peers." Three times they referred to their "Sacred" charter, which had been gutted by Parliament. They declared that "the propos'd new System of Government, Virtually Annihilating our most Essential Charter Rights, added to the Boston Port Act, gives us such apprehensions of the designs of Administration against our Liberties, as we have never before allowed ourselves to entertain." John Worthington and his fellow river gods could do nothing to quiet the discontent. In a rearguard action, they did persuade the meeting to express "great deference and respect" to "the wisdom of the British Parliament" and oppose any "Insult upon that respectable body," but this perfunctory gesture could not mask an underlying truth: citizens no longer deferred to the river gods and their views. Their position at the top of a long-prevailing hierarchy was no longer secure, and they knew it. When John Worthington and Israel Williams learned of their appointments as mandamus councilors, they concluded, correctly, that they could not possibly accept their posts and retain favor with the people. Immediately they informed Governor Gage that they would not serve, but the people would soon demand much more from them.[8]

The quarterly session for the Court of Common Pleas and the Court of General Sessions for Hampshire County was scheduled

to meet on August 30. This would be the second county to convene its courts under the new acts, and Hampshire's committees
of correspondence called an ad hoc convention to deliberate. In
Hadley, home of a 130-foot Liberty Pole thought to be the tallest
in the province, representatives from twenty-five towns and districts gathered on August 26. Delegates considered various options: they could petition the judges to adjourn, they could disrupt
the court physically, or they could ask the judges to recognize the
authority of the Charter of 1691 rather than the Massachusetts
Government Act. "After mature deliberation and passing of sun-
dry votes," they decided to ask the judges under what authority
they held their offices.[9]

The Reverend Stephen Williams of Longmeadow, uncle of Israel Williams, was unnerved. He wrote in his diary, "I am in fear
& concern, what things will come to. . . . Clouds & thick darkness are round about us—great tumults & uproars among people,
complainings in our Streets." A reverend, he understandably
turned toward God for solace: "I humbly request of him to pity
this people; reform them, pardon them, and in thy great mercy, be
pleasd to help us." His nephew Israel, meanwhile, prepared for an
encounter in Springfield, where the court was slated to sit.[10]

Come Tuesday, August 30, an estimated three to four thousand
people assembled in Springfield, at least twice the turnout for the
court closure in Great Barrington. One eyewitness, Joseph Clarke
of Northampton, Joseph Hawley's adopted son, sent a friend a
vivid account. "The people of each town being drawn into separate companies marched with staves & musick," he wrote. "The
trumpets sounding, drums beating, fifes playing and Colours flying, struck the passions of the soul into a proper tone, and inspired
martial courage into each." The judges and justices of the peace
offered no resistance to "the body of the county," as Clarke called
the men who marched with their towns' militia companies. When
a committee asked them "whether they meant to hold their commissions and exercise their authority according to the new act of

parliament for altering the constitution of the province," they all said they would not.[11]

But the officers of the court were not done. "Amidst the Crowd in a sandy, sultry place, exposed to the sun," John Worthington, Israel Williams, and sixteen other judges, justices of the peace, and lawyers were forced to submit in writing:

> We, the Subscribers, do severally promise and solemnly engage to all People now assembled, in the County of Hampshire, on the 30th Day of August 1774, that we will never take, hold, execute, or exercise any Commission, Office, or Employment whatsoever, under, or in Virtue of or in any Manner derived from any Authority, pretended or attempted to be given by a late Act of Parliament, entitled, "An Act for better regulating the Government of the Province of Massachusetts-Bay, in New England."[12]

Thousands of exhilarated patriots seemed to not want the day to end. Victory in hand yet demanding more, they summoned renowned government men to appear. One by one, they came before the body as if before jury and judge, and Clarke carefully noted how each was treated. Worthington and Williams had not publicized their resignations from the council, and their ostensible appointments made them "very obnoxious" to the crowd. When Worthington was ushered forth, "the sight of him flashed lightening from their eyes. Their spirits were already raised and the sight of this object gave them additional force." Worthington put up a defense, but to no avail. "He attempted to harangue them in mittigation of his conduct," Clarke reported, "but he was soon obliged to desist. The people were not to be dallied with." Despite the rancor, "the people kept their tempers." Worthington was released after resigning from the council a second time.[13]

After witnessing Worthington's ordeal, Israel Williams was prepared to bow to the will of this multitude. Clarke wrote:

He declared in my hearing that "altho' he had heretofore differed from the people in opinion with regard to the mode
of obtaining redress, he would, hereafter, heartily acqui-
esce in any measures, that they should take for that purpose,
and join with them in the common cause. He considered his
interest as embarked in the same bottom with theirs, and
hoped to leave it in peace to his Children."[14]

The social order had turned upside down. The river gods were
out; the body ruled. A disgruntled shopkeeper, Jonathan Judd
Jr., commented on the happenings in Springfield: "[A]ll opposition was in vain every Body submitted to our Sovereign Lord the
Mob—Now we are reduced to a State of Anarchy. have neither
Law nor any other Rule except the Law of Nature which much
vitiated and Darkened to go by."[15]

From Joseph Clarke's perspective, there was no "Sovereign
Lord the Mob," but instead a mindful crowd, their reactions nuanced. "I kept all the time amongst the people, and observed their
temper and dispositions," he wrote. He detailed five additional
interrogations, each decided on the merits of the case. One man
was "brought into the ring" but quickly released because "the
accusation against him was not well supported." Another was
"charged with saying some imprudent things, but none of them
were proved, & he departed." Those who submitted readily were
simply asked to disavow "the new act of parliament" and then
"dismissed, unhurt, and in peace." Jonathan Bliss, a Springfield
lawyer, was "very humble" when his turn came, so the people
were "very credulous." Bliss "asked their pardon for all he had
said or done which was contrary to their opinions; and as he depended for his support upon the people, he beged to stand well in
their favor." That was all the people needed to hear.

Captain James Merrick, from nearby Monson, received much
harsher treatment "for uttering imprudent expressions." Because
he was "very stubborn," the crowd "carted him." Being placed in

a cart and dragged around was seen as the last step before tarring and feathering, and Clarke, for a moment, feared it might come to that. In this case, though, the carting sufficed and Merrick finally "made some concessions." Here was the only application of physical force that Clarke reported. "No man received the least injury, but the strictest order of justice were observed," he declared. "The people to their honor behaved with the greatest order & regularity, a few individuals excepted, and avoided, as much as possible, confusion."[16]

The three to four thousand men who gathered in Springfield to close the Hampshire County courts acted as the "body of the county." Jonathan Bliss ceded as much when he vowed to go along with "the people," whom he depended on for support. So too did the river god Israel Williams when he claimed, disingenuously, that "he considered his interest as embarked in the same bottom with theirs." Jonathan Judd, clearly displeased, summed it up best: "Government has now devolved upon the people," he wrote in his diary on September 7, "and they seem to be for using it."[17]

On the other hand, even the sympathetic Joseph Clarke recognized that there could be problems once the people took matters into their own hands. The daytime proceedings had gone well enough, but what might happen that night, now that traditional constraints had been shattered? He concluded his letter: "I wait till morning, hope nothing will be transacted rashly tonight, for it is given out by the fearful that there is a number looking."[18]

6

MASSACHUSETTS TOWNS AND COUNTRYSIDE: "MOBS"

Shortly before the Massachusetts Government Act was to go into effect, Governor Gage predicted, in a letter to Lord Dartmouth, that unruly colonials were likely to "intimidate the new Counsellors from accepting their Commissions." This proved true, but Gage did not foresee that intimidation would derail the incoming council and render the new law inoperable.[1]

When the act itself arrived in Gage's hands on August 6, six days after it was to take force, the governor assembled eleven councilors who happened to reside in or around the eastern port towns and swore them into office. Via couriers, he summoned the remaining twenty-five. On August 16 only thirteen of these took their oaths, bringing the total to twenty-four, when it was supposed to be thirty-six. Writing to Lord Dartmouth, Gage admitted that a few, including Israel Williams and John Worthington, had declined their appointments, while the remainder were either "wavering, absent, or dead." Even so, despite intimidations, two-thirds had showed up for duty. The new council, an integral component of the governmental apparatus, was up and running, he boasted.[2]

Was it really?

Although he had expected some trouble, Governor Gage underestimated the ease with which New Englanders could bring pressure to bear on individuals who violated group norms. Those who had been appointed by the Crown to serve on the governor's council, gentlemen of wealth and standing, were very much in the public eye. Particularly visible, they were particularly vulnerable, and now, as symbols of the hated act, they attracted their neighbors' ire. Everywhere, they were forced to submit to the popular will—or flee.

On history's pages, those who impelled compliance have been labeled "mobs," suggesting a wrathful horde overpowering individual victims in a mindless instant. Although friends of government used the term consistently, mindless attacks were rare. Crowds deliberated before an event and during it, holding what were in effect mobile town meetings. They elected ad hoc delegates who conducted negotiations with adversaries and returned to the body of the whole, which put the determination to a vote before proceeding further. In Braintree, Abigail Adams witnessed an out-of-doors council such as this from her window. Having successfully seized some gunpowder from the local powder house, a troop of about two hundred men forced the sheriff to burn two warrants he was attempting to deliver. Afterward, some wanted to loudly "huzzah," but it was Sunday. Should they or should they not disturb the Sabbath? "They call'd a vote," Abigail reported to her husband, John, and "it being Sunday evening it passed in the negative."[3]

The simple presence of a multitude ordinarily resulted in a subject's assent, and as soon as he yielded, the crowd was done with him. "No man received the least injury," Joseph Clarke reported at the Springfield court closure. If a man did not submit, numbers might swell, threats ensue, humiliating theatrics unfold, and destruction of property follow. Methods varied. Violence against a man's person was not common, however, and severe forms such as tarring and feathering—which amounted to torture—were extremely rare. Still, the people focused relentlessly on men who flouted the collective will, and in assuming office any mandamus councilor did. The lives of these officials were upended, and their families bore the burden as well, worsening the predicament of any man sworn to serve the Crown. Their situation was precarious. It was not a good time to resist the popular rage.[4]

Even the simple act of going to church could prove troublesome for a mandamus councilor. Consider Daniel Leonard of Taunton, "as respectable a person as any in the Province" and known for his fancy attire. "He wore a broad gold lace round the rim of his hat; he made his cloak glitter with laces still broader," in the words of John Adams, who battled with Leonard through letters in the newspapers. After ceremoniously taking his oath for the council in Salem on August 16, Leonard returned quietly to his home. The following morning, he made the simple mistake of attending divine worship, inadvertently notifying his neighbors that he was back in town. Immediately, a notice appeared on the meetinghouse door, calling citizens to the town green the next day "to deal with me," as Leonard later reported.[5]

When a crowd estimated variously as "five hundred persons" and "upwards of two thousand men" showed up, Leonard's father "promis'd to use his influence" to convince his son to resign; otherwise, the angry fellows "would have pulled his house down." But Daniel had fled. On Sunday after church, with the writing on the wall, or in this case on the meetinghouse door, he journeyed fifteen miles to Staughton. He spent the night there and on the next day journeyed another fifteen to Boston. By the time Monday morning's conclave advanced from the town green to his house, Leonard was out of harm's way, but he heard the reports:

> About five hundred persons assembled, many of them Freeholders and some of them Officers in the Militia, and formed

themselves into a Battalion before my house; they had then no Fire-arms, but generally had clubs. Some of the principal persons came to my house with a message that the People were much incensed at my accepting a Seat at the Board, and begged I would resign it. Upon being informed that I was not at home, they returned to the main Body, who dispersed before night, after having been treated with rum by their Principals.

Such was the face of a country crowd from a conservative perspective: a paramilitary group, its leaders using rum as a lure.[6]

That night, a much smaller group returned to the Leonard house. Under cover of darkness, deeper than our own, different rules applied. Men fired "four bullets and some Swan-shot" into the upstairs chamber inhabited by Job Williams, who had pulled down the notice on the meetinghouse door. This frightened Daniel's pregnant wife. "My family were exposed by it, and I have received repeated advices from my friends at Taunton, since I arrived at Boston, that my life will be in danger if I return," Leonard complained to Gage. Once the troubles passed, he hoped to go back home—but troubles never did pass. Leonard stayed put, serving on the council and busily penning polemical letters to the Boston papers under the name of "Novanglus."[7]

Josiah Edson, another councilor, returned home after taking an oath of office. He too attended church, but "his townsmen at Bridgewater, after some exhortation, thought proper to *send him to Coventry*, nor would they even deign to sing ye psalm after his reading it, being deacon of the parish." Their refusing to sing with him was ultimatum enough, and he too became one of "the new fangled, refugee councellors," in the words of merchant John Andrews. Boston was a haven for those who no longer dared to live among their own.[8]

Returning home to Plymouth after taking his oath with Leonard and Edson, George Watson also went to church. The *Boston Evening-Post* reported what happened:

When he came into the House of publick Worship, a great number of the principal Inhabitants of that Town left the Meeting-House immediately upon his entering it; "being determined not to worship in fellowship with one, who has sworn to support that change of our constitution, which professedly establishes despotism among us."[9]

Unlike Leonard and Edson, however, Watson chose to resign and presented his reasons in a letter to Governor Gage:

By my accepting of this Appointment, I find that I have rendered myself very obnoxious, not only to the inhabitants of this place, but also to those of the neighboring towns. On my business as a Merchant I depend, for the support of myself and Family, and of this I must be intirely deprived, in short, I am reduced to the alternative of resigning my Seat at the Council Board, or quitting this, the place of my Nativity, which will be attended with the most fatal Consequences to myself, and family. Necessity therefore obliges me to ask Permission of your Excellencey to resign my Seat at the Board, and I trust, that when your Excellency considers my Situation, I shall not be censured.[10]

For a Plymouth merchant, Boston held little promise. It was teeming with merchants who had few goods to sell now that the port was closed, and although Watson might find safety there, he could not make a living. Better to submit humbly, however humiliating that might be.

After taking his oath, Abijah Willard, a "large and portly" man from Lancaster in northeastern Worcester County, journeyed to Union, Connecticut, to escape his neighbors' wrath. Yet Union's patriots seized him, tossed him in jail for a night, and then returned him to Brimfield, Massachusetts, just over the border. He was placed in the hands of four hundred local citizens who "called a Council of themselves, and Condemned Colonel Willard to Newgate Prison, in Symsbury; and a number set off and carried him six miles on the way thither. Colonel Willard then submitted to take the oath . . . on which they dismissed him." Willard's resignation was published in the Boston papers:

> Whereas I, Abijah Willard of Lancaster, have been appointed by Mandamus a Counsellor for this Province, and having without due Consideration taken the Oath, [I] do now freely and solemnly declare that I am sorry that I have taken the said oath, and do hereby solemnly and in good faith promise and engage that I will not sit or act in said Council, . . . and do hereby ask forgiveness of all honest, worthy gentlemen that I have offended.[11]

At times, citizens could bend a councilor to their will simply by not singing with him. In other instances, they might write threats, carry clubs, or put a man in prison. Even so, they generally refrained from inflicting bodily harm. During Abijah Willard's ordeal, however, "One Captain Davis of Brimfield was present, who, showing resentment, and treating the people with bad language, was stripped, and honored with the new fashion dress of tar and feathers; a proof this, *that the act for tarring and feathering is not repealed*." We can imagine a ferocious interchange, seeded by "resentment" and "bad language" and escalating terribly until perpetrators decided to do their very worst. Few confrontations were as brutal. Even in extreme cases, the mere sight of a bucket of tar sufficed to ensure compliance.[12]

The inevitable showdown between mandamus councilors and citizens was never amicable, but in the right circumstances it could be civil. Mild-mannered Timothy Paine, who lived in Worcester, ranked fifth in his class at Harvard, when a family's station and wealth dictated ranking, and he reinforced his standing by marrying a sister of John Chandler IV, current head of the elite clan that had held sway in town for three generations. "Madame Paine," Timothy's wife, was reputed to be an exceptionally outspoken friend of government, even for a Paine or a Chandler. Yet, in the face of all this, the town trusted Paine to chair turbulent town meetings in which government men and liberty men went after one other tooth and nail. The tide turned against Paine, however, when he took an oath to serve as a mandamus councilor on August 16.[13]

Even though he knew people were preparing to confront him, Paine did not decamp as most did but stayed in place, apparently unrattled. "I had some private notice of it," he wrote, "but upon the whole I thought it not best to go out of the way, and determined to stay and see how far they intended to carry matters." Although Paine expected a crowd, he might not have anticipated its size. The town of Worcester contained fewer than 350 adult males, inclusive of outlying farmers within the township, but on the morning of August 27 a crowd estimated variously at fifteen hundred, two thousand, and three thousand gathered on the Worcester Common. Three detailed accounts—two newspaper reports and a letter by Paine to Governor Gage—basically agree on what occurred, but Paine's is the most intimate and revealing:

> The people began to assemble so early as Seven o'Clock in the morning, and by Nine, by the best computation, more than *Two Thousand men* were paraded on our Common. They were led into town by particular persons chosen for that purpose, many were Officers of the Militia, and marched in at the head of their companies. Being so assembled they chose a large Committee from the whole body, which Committee chose a Sub Committee to wait upon me. . . .
>
> I received them first at my Chamber Window, but upon assurance from them they had no design to treat me ill,

I admitted them into my house. They then informed me of their business, that they were a Committee chosen by a large body of People assembled on the Common to wait upon me to resign my Seat at the Council Board. I endeavored to convince them of the ill consequences that would ensue upon the measures they were taking, . . . but all to no purpose, they insisting that the measures were peaceable, and that nothing would satisfy the Assembly unless I resigned, and that they would not answer for the consequences if I did not.[14]

Paine submitted immediately, hoping to be done with it all: "Thus surrounded on every side, without any protection, I found myself under a necessity of complying, and prepared and signed a resignation." But a simple resignation was deemed insufficient. Paine needed to issue a full apology and adopt a deferential tone toward the people, most of whom were his social inferiors:

"To Messrs Joshua Bigelow, Thomas Denny, Joseph Gilbert, Edward Rawson and John Goulding,

"GENTLEMEN, As you have waited upon me as a Committee chosen by a large body of People now assembled on the Common in Worcester, desiring that I now resign my Seat at the Council Board; my Appointment was without sollicitation, and am very sorry I accepted, and thereby given any uneasiness to the People of the County, from whom I have received many favors, and take this opportunity to thank them: and I do hereby assure you that I will not take a Seat at the Board unless it is agreeable to the Charter of this Province."[15]

Paine undoubtedly thought this submissive recantation would terminate the unseemly affair, but people wanted to *witness* his capitulation, so the committee ushered him from his house to the Common, where a committee member, with Paine beside him, read the written statement. Again, that was not enough. "Numbers were dissatisfied, requiring that Mr. Paine should read it himself, and that with his hat off," one witness reported. Since only a small number heard him, the crowd "drawed up in two bodies, making a lane between them, through which the committee and he passed and read divers times as they passed along, the said acknowledgment." Timothy Paine, who liked to drive to the court for the quarterly sessions in his "handsome green coach, trimmed with gilding and lined with satin," was duly humbled.[16]

When Governor Gage informed Lord Dartmouth of Paine's resignation, he said that Paine "was seized and roughly treated." But according to firsthand sources, the crowd was orderly and even respectful, as Paine himself admitted. "I met with no insult excepting they obliged me to walk with my Hat off when I passed through them," he told Gage.[17]

At noon that same day, five hundred of the men who engineered Timothy Paine's submission set their sights on other mandamus councilors: John Murray of Rutland and Timothy Ruggles of Hardwick. Both were connected by marriage to elite Chandlers: Murray, like Paine, wedded one of John Chandler IV's seven sisters, while Ruggles's daughter married one of Chandler's sons.

Rutland, home to Scottish-born John Murray, lay some fifteen miles northwest of the town of Worcester. After the administration of oaths on August 16, John and his son Daniel, who was studying to be a doctor, lingered in Boston for a week. When they left for home, they were anticipating trouble and were "well armed and resolute," the Boston merchant John Andrews noted. "I imagine they are determin'd to stand a brush, if opposed," he added, "being both very stout men, near or quite as large as a Forrest." John Murray was in fact reputed to be six foot three, extraordinarily tall for that time, but in spite of his formidable size he was wary. The next day Andrews wrote, "Col. Murray halted yesterday at Cambridge, least too great precipitancy in so bold an enterprise should prove fatal. He has behav'd like an experienc'd commander, and sent to reconnoitre before he advances, with a view to better inform himself of the hostile disposition of his townsmen." Murray had reason to think some might be hostile. He had amassed a fortune by lending money to local farmers at interest over decades, undoubtedly accumulating resentment as well as profit.[18]

On Thursday, August 25, the Murrays did arrive home, but John Murray had no intention of staying when the risk of confrontation was so high. That night, after packing up his belongings, he set out for Boston, leaving Daniel to secure their property. When fifteen hundred aroused citizens of Worcester County arrived at the Murray household two days later, Daniel told them his father was not there. Refusing to accept him at his word, the men "insisted upon searching the house, which was thoroughly done, as also the barns, out houses and stables," a newspaper reported. Faced with a recalcitrant yet elusive adversary, this crowd was far more aggressive than the one in Worcester that morning. They came "armed with sticks in general heavy enough to have levelled a man at a stroke," Daniel Murray reported. In the mid-nineteenth century, Lorenzo Sabine reported that a John Singleton Copley portrait of John Murray, by then in possession of Murray's grandson, had a hole punched through the wig. Family tradition, wrote Sabine, held that "a party who sought the Colonel at his house after his flight, vexed because he had eluded them, vowed they would leave their mark behind them, and accordingly pierced the canvas with a bayonet." Though not hard history, it does seem plausible.[19]

With Murray nowhere to be found, the crowd decided to post a letter in the Boston newspapers, which they composed on the spot and published soon thereafter:

To John Murray, Esq: Sir,

As you have proved yourself to be an open Enemy to this Province, by your Conduct in general, and in particular in accepting of the late Appointment as an unconstitutional Counsellor, in Consequence whereof, a large Number of Men from several Towns are assembled, who are fully determined to prevent your holding said Office as Counsellor, at the Risque of our Lives and Fortunes; and not finding you at Home, think proper to propose to your serious consideration: the following viz:

That you make an immediate Resignation of your Office, as a Counsellor.

Your compliance as above, published in each of the Boston News Prints by the Tenth Day of September next, will save the People of this County the Trouble of waiting on you immediately afterwards.

In the Name and Behalf of the whole Assembly now present, Willard Moore

Despite the threat, Murray did not capitulate. Along with fourteen other councilors who held firm, he continued to serve at the governor's pleasure, but he never did return to his home in Rutland. The following year, when Daniel requested permission from the revolutionary government to visit his father in Boston, his request was denied.[20]

After the crowd left the Murrays', some continued to Hardwick, another fifteen miles to the west, in search of Timothy Ruggles, but Ruggles was not at home, nor had he been for some time. Among the most vilified Tories in the province and a prime object of patriot rage, he was already on the run.

It had not always been this way. When Timothy Ruggles (Harvard, class of 1732) moved to Hardwick in 1754, residents immediately asked him to represent them in the Massachusetts Assembly, where his political skills and connections would be of benefit. He

was also elected to the provincial council, a position he continued to hold longer than any other man of his times. John Adams,
while learning to practice law under Worcester's James Putnam in
the late 1750s, came into frequent contact with Ruggles, who was
judge on the Worcester Court of Common Pleas, among his many
offices. With keen insight, Adams assessed the man's character:

> Ruggles's Grandeur consists in the quickness of his ap-
> prehension, Steadiness of his attention, the boldness and
> Strength of his Thoughts and Expressions, his strict Hon-
> our, conscious Superiority, Contempt of Meanness [low
> social standing], &c. People approach him with Dread and
> Terror.

Noted for his daring in the French and Indian War, Ruggles was
rewarded with a large land grant and the position of brigadier
general.[21]

"The Brigadier," as people called him, was perhaps the best-
known man in the interior of the province, so much so that he was
selected to serve as one of three representatives from Massachusetts to the intercolonial Stamp Act Congress in 1765 and even
presided over that gathering. As president, however, Ruggles refused to sign the congress's "Declaration of Rights and Grievances" and departed in a huff, a sin for which the Massachusetts
Assembly censored him. Having once been highly honored, his
fall from grace was all the more pronounced.

In 1774, local citizens no longer approached the Brigadier "with
Dread and Terror." Even before taking the oath, Ruggles encountered difficulty. Departing Hardwick on his way to Boston, he
had to travel "on the Road near Worcester," where "a Number of
People collected . . . to stop him, but he made his Way through
them." He arrived safely in Salem on August 16, in time to accept
his position. Three days later a friend from Hardwick informed
him that "there are those here, who I am satisfied thirst for your

blood, and they have influence enough over the others to put them upon spilling it." Ruggles took heed and went to the home of a friend in Dartmouth, one hundred miles from Hardwick, but patriots would not tolerate his presence *anywhere*. The following week the *Boston Evening Post* published a letter from Taunton dated August 25:

> We hear that Brigadier Ruggles, one of the new made Counsellors, being at Col. Toby's at Dartmouth, the People assembled there one Day this Week, and ordered him to depart forthwith; upon which the Colonel promised them he would go the next Morning by Sun an Hour high; but before that time the Brigadier's Horse had his Mane and Tail cut off, and his Body painted all over.

A crowd of two to three thousand was expected to assemble the next day to force "Brigadier Ruggles to depart the County immediately." The letter concluded, "Such is the Spirit of this County—they seem to be quite awake, and to have awoke in a Passion. It is more dangerous being a Tory here than in Boston, even if no Troops were there." In the past, local jurisdictions in Massachusetts had "warned out" the transient poor; now, they were warning out mandamus councilors. "Messrs. Ruggles, Edson, Leonard, and Murray," Governor Gage reported to Lord Dartmouth, "have fled from their houses, and been obliged to seek protection among the troops at Boston."[22]

William Pepperell was not a war hero but was descended from one, and this, ironically, only fueled discontent. His grandfather of the same name was widely heralded as the conqueror of the French fortress at Louisbourg in 1745, a military victory of iconic proportion in the mid-eighteenth century. To reward him for this great deed, the Crown had granted Pepperell vast land tracts and bestowed on him the title of baronet, an unprecedented honor for a man born and raised in the colonies. Upon his death, with no surviving son, Sir William Pepperell had bequeathed his sword, his gold watch, and a good portion of his immense estate in York County to his daughter's son—provided, that is, that his designated heir petition the Massachusetts General Court to change his name from Sparhawk to Pepperell. When William Sparhawk complied, he too became a Pepperell, but by accepting a seat on the council, he proved himself in the eyes of many unworthy of his grandfather's illustrious name. Worse yet, he seemed to be currying favor with the Crown to gain his grandfather's title. Sacrificing the good of the people for such an ignoble purpose was a supreme insult. "The time will come, Sir," wrote "a Yorkshireman" in the *Boston Gazette*, "when the character of your father shall cease to protect you, your estate be plundered, your purse . . . be exhausted; your country detest and despise you.—Then, Sir, enjoy the title of a Baronet, like a King without Subjects." Pepperell could retain his seat on the council only by retreating to Boston as Ruggles, Murray, and others had done.[23]

Joshua Loring of Roxbury, known as "the Commodore" for his service on the Great Lakes during the French and Indian War, also accepted an appointment to the new council and, again, that was seen as a betrayal. A victim of intimidation, he elucidated the techniques employed.

> At 12 o'Clock in the night of the 29th Instant I was awaked by a very hard knocking at my door; immediately I jumped out of bed and threw up the window, when I saw five men disguised, their faces black'd, hatts flap'd, and with cutlasses in their hands. I ask'd them who they were, they answered they came from a Mob. I then asked them what they wanted; they told me they came to know if I would resign my Seat at the Board. I answer'd I would not, and went into some discourse with them, asking what right they had to make

such a demand on me or any other man. They told me they did not come to talk, they came to act, and that they wanted my answer: I replied that they had got it already. They then told me they would give me till tomorrow night to consider of it, and then the speaker gave orders to a large party who were in the road, to discharge their pieces, which they accordingly did, and which I took to be pistols. They then told me my house should be safe till tomorrow night, and went off in number about sixty.[24]

Reluctantly but prudently, Loring left home, but afterward his family told him what happened when the crowd returned the following evening:

About 9 o'Clock [Loring's son] heard their noise, and in a few minutes they were up to the house, and immediately knocked at the door; he went to it and found five men disguised, their faces black'd and cutlasses in their hands: they order'd the candle to be put out, and then asked for the Commodore, and said they came for his answer. He told them he was gone to Boston, and then endeavored to reason with them against their demand, but to no purpose; they said this was the second time they had come, and to beware of the third, that if he would publish in the Thursdays News Paper a Recantation, it would be well, if not, he must abide by the consequences, which would be very severe, that his house would be levelled to the ground, and many other of the like threats; and then these Five who seemed to have the direction, I can't say command, of the Mob who were at the gate, retired to them, and during all this time they kept laying on the board fence with clubs, and crying out Don't fire, for God's sake don't fire, keep back, keep back: but the People did not seem to mind them, and continued their hallowing and knocking on the fence with their clubs: all of which was designed to intimidate.

They soon went off, and, as he was informed, to the house of Mr. Pepperell, who not being home, they returned again within the space of half an hour, and in the same tumultuous manner halted in the road opposite the house, and all at once were very silent, occasioned, as he was informed, by some friends speaking to them; a few minutes after they set up their hallowing &c again, and went off. And as it was a very dark night he could not judge of their numbers, but was told they were about two hundred.[25]

During that brief period of silence, the nighttime crowd most likely was considering its next move. Had they pushed the issue enough, or should they do some real damage to drive the point home? A fine line separated destruction born of anger from constructive engagement intended to dismantle the abusive acts of Parliament. This was a common problem. When faced with noncompliance, those who tormented Abijah Willard "called a Council of themselves," and only then dispatched their prisoner to Newgate. When Berkshire County's David Ingersoll was first confronted on August 2, the crowd took "Several votes one way or another" before releasing him.[26]

In this instance, the agitated men outside Loring's home gave the Commodore one last chance to recant. Loring refused. "I have always eaten the King's bread, and I always intend to," he stated brashly. In Boston, at a safe distance, he could speak his mind.[27]

The confrontation with Loring ended with a settlement, but the terms were far from even. Loring would serve on the governor's council, but he and his fellow councilors could wield power only in Boston. Outside that enclave "not a Tory but hides his head," Abigail Adams told John Adams. The incisive John Andrews agreed:

The present temper of the People throughout the Province is such, that they wont suffer a *tory* to remain any where among 'em without making an ample recantation of his principles; and those who presume to be so obstinate as not to comply, are oblig'd to take up their residence in this city of refuge.[28]

At the end of August, when Governor Gage summoned his remaining councilors to Salem, they all refused. They would not venture there, fearing "that they should be watched, stopped, and insulted on the road." Although anointed by the king, they found themselves trapped on a tiny peninsula that was connected to the province they were supposed to govern by a stretch of land no more than a few hundred yards wide, the Boston Neck. The personal skirmishes between angry crowds and mandamus councilors effectively partitioned Massachusetts into two zones: Boston, where redcoated soldiers buttressed the vestiges of an unpopular regime, and nearly everywhere else. Battle lines were drawn, not just figuratively but geographically. Only the towns rimming Boston, which were in rebel hands but subject to the occasional foray by British troops, were contested ground.[29]

7

CHARLESTOWN AND CAMBRIDGE: POWDER ALARM

By the end of August, Governor Gage realized that Boston was not his biggest problem. Massachusetts was. Mobs formed wherever a mandamus councilor dared show his head. Courts had been closed in Berkshire and Hampshire Counties, and Worcester was threatening "resistance by arms" at the convening of the courts in early September. During the confrontation over the town meeting in Salem, the ever alert John Andrews commented that provincials were ready "to repel force with force, being sufficiently provided for such a purpose"; unlike earlier protesters, they seemed to be preparing for actual combat. Unable to derail the growing resistance movement, Gage's best hope was to minimize its destructive potential by limiting access to guns and powder.[1]

Provincials did possess guns. Most were holdovers from the French and Indian War, which had been kept as trophies and passed from father to son, but gunsmiths still made guns that a man could purchase. In common forges blacksmiths fashioned the metal balls used for shot, but the volatile black powder that sent these projectiles through the air was not so easily come by.

Existing supplies were secured in sturdy powder houses made of stone or brick, where much had lain since the Seven Years' War, a goodly quantity deteriorating in the interval. Powder mills were decrepit and the art of making powder largely forgotten, which meant that colonists relied almost exclusively on powder imported from England. If war came, England would supply her own soldiers but not, obviously, colonial rebels. Anticipating the shortage, towns began to take powder they considered rightfully theirs from local powder houses.

On August 27, William Brattle, a government-leaning general of the Middlesex militia, notified Gage of just such an occurrence: "This morning the Select Men of Medford, came and received their Town Stock of Powder, which was in the Arsenal on Quarry-Hill, so that there is now therein, the King's Powder only, which shall remain there as a sacred Deposition till ordered out by the Capt. General." The Quarry Hill arsenal was a thirty-foot-high cylindrical tower with thick walls that were made of stone quarried from nearby ground. Before its sale to the Massachusetts province a little more than three decades earlier, it had served as a windmill on a farm, but it was well suited for military use and currently held the largest supply of powder in the colony. For good reason, one of Ben Franklin's lightning rods sat atop its roof. Though Brattle had declared the king's gunpowder to be "a sacred Deposition" and supposedly secure, Gage decided to move it to Castle William in Boston Harbor, out of the reach of adversaries who were capable, he knew very well, of any audacious move.[2]

Located in a part of Charlestown that is now Somerville, the Quarry Hill powder house was easily accessible to British troops. On the first day of September, well before dawn, some 260 redcoated soldiers (one report said 280) boarded thirteen boats at Boston's Long Wharf. It did not take long for the oarsmen to cross the Charles River and make their way up the Mystic River to a landing at Robert Temple's farm, and after a one-mile march in darkness they arrived at Quarry Hill. Unwilling to carry lanterns with their flaming wicks inside a powder house, they waited for the first light of day, but once day broke they acted quickly. By noon they had carried off the entire store of powder—212 barrels by the *Boston Evening-Post*'s estimate, or 250 barrels, as the *Boston Gazette* surmised. As these troops completed their mission, others seized two field pieces from nearby Cambridge.[3]

Laden with captured munitions, wagons rumbled off on a thoroughfare that took them through bustling Cambridge, Roxbury, and finally Dorchester, where their prize was loaded on boats and carried to the island fortress at Castle William. People noticed and people talked. General Brattle had called it "the King's powder," but they deemed it provincial powder, subject to their own control. Its seizure by the king's troops was, in their minds, sheer theft and another manifestation of high-handed overreach by imperial authorities.

People milled about angrily on Quarry Hill or wherever they happened to be when they heard the news. Come evening, many returned to their homes, but others, dissatisfied, gathered in nearby Cambridge. Intent on action of some kind, this restless, truculent band decided to pay a visit to General Brattle, a convenient target. They had just learned that Brattle was the one to inform Gage about the powder, and his mansion was nearby, on land that descended in stately fashion to the Charles River. The general, however, had already taken himself off to Castle William, "the only place of safety for him in the province," as John Andrews caustically remarked. Not to be put off, the men immediately sought out another well-known Tory, Attorney General Jonathan Sewall, who also lived on "Tory Row." Predictably, he too was absent. While Sewall's wife pleaded for peace, one of his friends fired a shot from a second-story window. In response, the crowd broke some windows before disbanding, and thus ended what the *Boston Gazette* called the "mischief" of the evening.[4]

News of the Quarry Hill seizure spread across the countryside that night and during the early hours of September 2. By eight o'clock in the morning, some three thousand men had congregated on the Cambridge common, drawn to a place where militia traditionally drilled and where the body of the people—the de facto out-of-doors civic body—conducted its affairs. In this assemblage were militia companies from Waltham, Watertown, Concord, Charlestown, and Framingham. Marlborough men, "with a troop of horse and another of foot," appeared after a nighttime march of thirty miles. Although many in these companies had carried muskets on the way, they arrived at the Cambridge common "armed only with sticks, as they had left their fire arms, &c. at some distance behind then," the newspapers asserted. The protest was to remain peaceful if possible, but if British Regulars should attack arms would be close at hand.[5]

Meanwhile, in these hours, facts mutated into fierce rumors that alarmed all who heard them. A traveler from Connecticut named McNeil reported that when boarding at an inn in Shrewsbury, some forty miles inland from Boston, he was awakened shortly after midnight by "somebody violently rapping up the Landlord, telling the doleful Story that the Powder was taken, six men killed, & all the people between there & Boston arming & marching down to the Relief of their Brethren at Boston." In less than half an hour "fifty men were collected at the Tavern tho' now deep in Night, equipping themselves & sending off Posts every Way to the neighboring Towns." The next day, he said, the road toward Boston was in a constant convulsion. "All along were armed Men rushing forward some on foot some on horseback . . . at every house Women & Children making Cartridges, running Bullets, making Wallets, baking Biscuit, crying & bemoaning & at the same time animating their Husbands & Sons to fight for their Liberties. They scarcely left half a dozen Men in a Town, unless old and decrepid, and in one town the Landlord told him that himself was the only Man left."[6]

In Longmeadow, over ninety miles west of Boston, the

Reverend Stephen Williams recorded in his diary the so-called news a rider delivered: "The Ships in ye Harbour of Boston, & ye Army on ye Land Side were allso fireing upon ye Town so that it was like ye Town was Demolished." Understandably, commotion gripped the town. "Ye blacksmith shop was opened—guns carrid to him to be mendd—horses to be Shod—& many Employd making Bullets—& a man Sent to Enfd to get powdr." Well equipped, men then "repaird to ye meeting house—& a number Gave in their names or listd," ready for the long march eastward.[7]

In Boston, news of the people's advance unleashed comparable panic, according to John Andrews:

> Four or five expresses have come down to Charlestown and here, to acquaint us, that between Sudbury and this, above ten thousand men are in arms and are continually coming down from the country back: that their determination is to collect about forty or fifty thousand by night (which they are sure of accomplishing) when they intend to bring in about fifteen thousand by way of the Neck, and as many more over the ferry: when once got possession, to come in like locusts and rid the town of every soldier.

"Such a scheme," Andrews continued, was "so big with mischief and calamity" that "every prudent man set out to oppose 'em." This gave an unexpected twist to the carryings-on. Whig leaders, whom British officials imagined to be the source of unrest, mobilized to contain the mobilization of the people.[8]

The committees of correspondence from Cambridge and Charlestown worried too that General Gage, reacting to the sudden mobilization of militiamen, would send out troops and that the men who had stashed their arms would retrieve them. The escalation of fear on both sides, fueled by misinformation, could easily become a bloodbath. They sent a dispatch to Boston's Joseph Warren, who had emerged as the hub of communications within the committee of correspondence there. Warren reported that "[A] billet was brought, requesting me to take some step in order to prevent the people from coming to immediate acts of violence, as incredible numbers were in arms, and lined the roads from Sudbury to Cambridge." Quickly he summoned other members.[9]

Cambridge committee members also sought out Lieutenant Governor Thomas Oliver, Gage's second in command, who lived near William Brattle and Jonathan Sewall. "I was desired to go and intercede with his Excellency to prevent their coming," Oliver later commented. (Gage was then in Boston, having left Salem four days earlier to attend the province's Superior Court, which could meet only under protection of the army.) "From principles of humanity to the country, from a general love of mankind, and from persuasions that they were orderly people, I readily undertook it," Oliver said, adding, "As I passed the people I told them, of my own accord, I would return."[10]

Later that morning a delegation of six prominent Whigs from Boston, who were heading toward Cambridge to pacify the protesters, met up with Thomas Oliver, who was heading to Boston to pacify Governor Gage. They exchanged encouraging words.[11]

When Boston's committee of correspondence arrived at Cambridge common, Thomas Young, seemingly incredulous, observed that "Judge Danforth was addressing perhaps four thousand people in the open air; and such was the order of that great assembly that not a whisper interrupted the low voice of the feeble old man from being heard by the whole Body." The people were asking Samuel Danforth and Joseph Lee, mandamus councilors who resided nearby, to tender their resignations. The day before, seeing how events were transpiring, each had written a letter of resignation to Gage, but that was done privately, and, as usual, the crowd required public declarations. Danforth and Lee readily submitted.[12]

Next, David Phips, the Middlesex County sheriff who had

unlocked the Quarry Hill arsenal for the British troops, pledged that he would "not execute any Precept that shall be sent me under the new Acts." After each recantation, the crowd voted on whether that would suffice, and each time, without dissent, the vote was yes. The day's proceedings were advancing in an orderly and peaceful fashion, skillfully directed by the representative committee elected earlier from the towns. The Boston men were much impressed by the decorum. "We there saw a fine body of respectable freemen, with whom we spent the day, and were witnesses of their patience, temperance, and fortitude," Joseph Warren told Samuel Adams. Another eyewitness described those freemen to John Adams: "They were dress'd just as they are at work—every man appeared just as composed as if they were at a funeral."[13]

Warren, Young, and their four compatriots, well accustomed to speaking at public events, mounted the courthouse steps to address the throng below them. Oddly, William Cooper and William Molineux argued that Gage had a legal right to take the powder, since it belonged to the king; besides, they pointed out, it was old and wet. When John Bradford, also of the Boston committee, tried to interrupt them, he was pushed away, but he resumed his argument when they finished. Bradford contended that the action was illegal since Gage had not sought the advice of the council, as constituted under the old charter. The farmers listened attentively, although they had been discussing the matter from the very first. Next, the Bostonians asked the people to approve a proposition "that they abhorred and detested all petty Mobs, Riots, Breaking Windows and destroying private Property." Not surprisingly, since they had earlier passed a similar measure, the vote in favor was unanimous.[14]

All this transpired under "the scorching sun of the hottest day we have had this summer," Thomas Young reported. With that sun at its zenith, William Cooper, in magnanimous fashion, proposed that the crowd choose a committee to take refreshments in the cool of Captain Stedman's inn "to confer about the Situation." Again, the crowd had selected its committee hours earlier, and those men had not sought special comforts while leaving their fellow militiamen behind to endure heat and thirst. Historian Dirk Hoerder explains the Bostonians' high-handed demeanor:

> The stratification and deferential character of Bostonian society made them blind to the social implications of the theory of popular sovereignty. They acted as they were accustomed to at celebrations: The gentlemen drank toasts inside Faneuil Hall, and the people huzzahed outside. Now in Cambridge the action had been done by "the people," and elected spokesmen were literally overlooked by the Boston "radicals" because they did not separate from their constituents, because they did not act like the dignified and elevated "better sort." The Boston leaders, on the other hand, attempted at once physically and politically to separate from the people.[15]

The day might have proceeded without further incident had not the unpopular customs commissioner Benjamin Hallowell passed by in a chaise, a mounted servant following in his wake. Harsh words were exchanged. Hallowell later claimed that some men called him a "Tory Son of a Bitch," while some of Hallowell's adversaries accused him of speaking "somewhat contemptuously of them." According to the patriot-leaning press, "The sight of that obnoxious person so inflamed the people, that in a few minutes about one hundred and sixty horsemen were drawn up, and proceeded in pursuit of him on the full gallop." Leaders who had been preaching against all riots admonished them, saying the chase "might introduce confusion into the proceedings of the day" and that they should return to the business at hand, the "resignation of the unconstitutional Counsellors." All abandoned the pursuit except "one gentleman of small stature," a newspaper claimed, though Hallowell maintained that six or eight went after him as he brandished his pistols and that they were joined in short order by "people from the Houses, which were many." When the horse that pulled his chaise faltered, Hallowell mounted his servant's horse and raced toward Boston. Inside its walls, the hard-pressed steed collapsed from exhaustion and its rider dashed on foot to the military camp. Hallowell closed his account by stating he was followed by "not less than one hundred people."[16]

The press account played up Hallowell's histrionics. Claiming he was "pursued by some thousands, who would soon be in Town and destroy all the friends of Government before them," he supposedly "spread consternation" throughout Boston and triggered "motion" in the British military camp. Those movements, in turn, spurred a rumor that British troops "were on the point of marching to Cambridge," and this "set the people in a prodigious ferment (who before were quite calm and collected)," John Andrews remarked. With no orders given, men who had left their arms nearby retrieved them. Earlier, leaving their guns, they had wanted to demonstrate peaceable, law-abiding intentions; now, expecting troops, they wanted to make a show of strength. Andrews revealed how fearful the situation was when he spoke of "combat"—"They had the presence of mind to get matters in readiness to take up the bridge, to prevent their bringing the artillery to bear upon 'em, least the Combat should be too unequal."[17]

Protesters soon learned that Regulars were not coming but, aroused now, they turned on Thomas Oliver. That morning, politely, they had asked him to intervene with the governor on their behalf, but now, contentious, they demanded that he resign from the council, as Lee and Danforth had done. Although they did not dispute the constitutionality of the position he held as lieutenant governor, they insisted he not sit on a body that was in clear violation of the 1691 charter. In their eyes one office was legitimate, the other illegitimate. Nuanced or not, the demand offended Oliver. Like any government official, he did not expect inferiors to dictate the rules, and after all that he had done to avert a confrontation, he thought them "unkind." He held his ground by arguing a technicality: "as Lieutenant-Governor, I stood in a particular relation to the Province in general, and therefore could not hear anything upon the matter from a particular county." When pushed on this count, he promised he would resign "if it appeared to be the sense of the Province," but he could not do so upon the application of citizens from only one region. The committee appointed to speak with Oliver, thinking this was a reasonable compromise, voted its agreement "by a very great majority," Oliver stated publicly a few days later. In his view, that settled the matter. He expected "no further application made to me on that head."[18]

The lieutenant governor was mistaken. His account continues:

> I observed large companies pouring in from different parts; I then began to apprehend they would become unmanageable, and that it was expedient to go out of their way. I was just going into my carriage when a great crowd advanced, and in a short time my house was surrounded by three or four thousand people, and one quarter in arms. I went to the front door, where I was met by five persons, who acquainted me they were a Committee from the people to demand a resignation of my seat at the Board. I was shocked at their ingratitude and false dealings, and reproached them with it. They excused themselves by saying the people were dissatisfied with the vote of the Committee, and insisted on my signing a paper they had prepared for that purpose.

In that paper, Oliver would be forced to call the Massachusetts Government Act "an oppressive Plan of Government" and "a manifest Infringement of the Charter Rights and Privileges of this People" and afterward "solemnly renounce and resign my seat" on the "unconstitutional" council. Admitting that he feared "the power of the people," Oliver agreed to sign, but he insisted on appending an explanatory note: "My house at Cambridge being surrounded by four thousand people, in compliance with their commands, I sign my name, THOMAS OLIVER."[19]

The Connecticut traveler Mr. McNeil arrived in Cambridge in the early afternoon and "mixt with the Multitude, who were formed & standing before Lt. Gov. Oliver's House." Like Oliver, he commented on the change in the crowd's behavior. At first, "there was no Tumult, but an awful Stillness, Silence thro' the lines and among the surrounding Body of the People." Later, though, "a weighty Spirit began to shew itself." Some men pressed through the gate and into the yard with "Marks of Earnestness & Importunity," but not as yet seeking "Violence." That is when Oliver agreed to sign his paper.

McNeil carefully noted the crowd's chain of command. "All was negotiated by the Committee, but in the presence of the Body, the Committee communicating by the Officers Information thro' the Lines, so that all knew what was transpiring." Following protocol, after Oliver composed his statement, it "was immediately handed along the Lines & read publickly at proper Distances till the whole Body of the people were made to hear it." Many objected to Oliver's defiant disclaimer. The people debated the issue, but in the end they let the matter stand. They would show they were acting reasonably and open to concession, the underpinnings of fruitful politics. Despite their internal differences, they would join as one to defend their charter, the overarching intent of all the day's proceedings.[20]

Late in the afternoon, fanned by wind, clouds crossed the sky, and as the day cooled so did tempers. Readying for departure, companies gathered, but not before being offered "refreshment"—a drink for the road. "The Gentlemen from Boston, Charlestown and Cambridge having provided some refreshment for their greatly fatigued Brethren, they cheerfully accepted it, took leave and departed, in high good humour and well satisfied," the Boston newspapers reported. Soon after, it stormed. "At 5 p.m. came on hard Thunder & Lightning with a great Shower," William Tudor wrote in his diary. The heavens provided a finale.[21]

On September 2, John Andrews estimated that ten thousand were heading to Boston. Four days later, after hearing from distant towns, he revised the figure: "Its allowed, by the best calculations, that at least a hundred thousand men were equipt with arms, and moving towards us from different parts of the country." They came from all around New England. Israel Putnam, Connecticut's celebrated hero from the French and Indian War, "was at the head of fifteen thousand, and its said that five and twenty thousand more were in a body a day's march behind him." In time, this unprecedented mobilization acquired a name: the Powder Alarm.[22]

Although in the space of hours men geared up for battle—shoeing horses, cleaning muskets, rolling cartridges, listing their names, choosing leaders—most of those who mustered did not reach Cambridge Commons. Men who learned of the facts before departing stayed in place, and men already on the road reversed direction as the truth-tellers they met repudiated rumors. But all had imagined engagement and would imagine engagement hereafter, sensing it would come soon now that it had come so close. This fed their sense of resolve, and Governor Gage took note. "The Flames of Sedition," he reported to Dartmouth, had "spread universally throughout the Country beyond Conception."[23]

In the wake of the Powder Alarm, Boston was a world apart, removed in every essential way from the rest of Massachusetts. Even nearby Charlestown and Cambridge were beyond the reach of British authority. "The first, and only step now to take," Gage confessed, was "to secure the friends of Government in *Boston*, and reinforce the troops here with as many more as could possibly be collected, and to act as opportunities and exigencies shall offer."[24]

8

WORCESTER COUNTY: MILITIA

Late in August, Governor Gage complained to Secretary of State Dartmouth of the "general Phrensy" that consumed the province. His troops could not extinguish the mayhem that was surfacing everywhere at once, and there was no way to keep towns from meeting or protect the mandamus councilors from mobs. Success depended on deploying the soldiers under his command systematically, and for that Gage looked to the county courts. Although under constant attack, the courts convened one at a time according to a precise, prearranged schedule. This meant that the attacks themselves would undoubtedly come on schedule and that his troops could repress insurrection on distinct dates in distinct places. It was the best response to an impossible situation.[1]

Gage considered the options and formulated a plan. Although the first court closure in Berkshire County had taken him by surprise, he did have time to prepare a defense for other courts. Hampshire County was next on the docket, but Springfield, the county seat, was over one hundred miles distant; the extended march would leave his troops dangerously exposed. Worcester, however, was less than half as far from Boston and slated to convene on September 6. A show of force there would deter all subsequent attempts to close county courts.

Calculations made, Gage informed Dartmouth, "I apprehend that I shall soon be obliged to march a Body of Troops into that Township." But this would not be easy, he admitted. "In Worcester, they keep no Terms, openly threaten Resistance by Arms, have been purchasing Arms, preparing them, casting Ball, and providing Powder, and threaten to attack any Troops who dare to oppose them. Mr. Ruggles of the new Council is afraid to take his Seat as Judge of the inferior Court."[2]

Gage had accurate intelligence sources. He knew that, early on, Worcester County's political activists had set their sights on the September 6 court session. Worcester, too, had intelligence sources, and these told them that British soldiers would appear as courts convened. With each side expecting the other to show up, both prepared for a showdown.

Worcester had not always been as truculent as it was when Thomas Gage governed. In 1731, when the town became the seat of government for the newly formed Worcester County, it seemed as law abiding as any other. Then and for decades following, a conservative Chandler dynasty held sway. John Chandler II, his son John Chandler III, and grandson John Chandler IV, along with various close relations, commandeered the lion's share of public offices. In one year alone, four of this clan served as Massachusetts councilman, town representative to the assembly, chief justice of the Court of Common Pleas, clerk for that court, probate judge, register of probate, register of deeds, assessor, county sheriff, county treasurer, town treasurer, town clerk, moderator of the town meeting, town selectman, and colonel of the county militia. Chandlers had numbers as well as standing. In 1774 there were John Chandler IV and his fifteen adult offspring; John's younger brother Gardiner, the sheriff, with his six offspring; the

Chandlers' brother-in-law Timothy Paine, with his ten offspring; and others. These people endorsed a status quo that nourished their own ambitions, and no one of them was in a hurry to see official policies challenged.[3]

Yet since the Stamp Act crisis, Chandlers had had to contend with a new breed of upstarts, men who might not be particularly wealthy or well connected but who were solid citizens and commanded the community's respect. These parvenus challenged the status quo and in some years even elected one of their own to the assembly, but despite their encroachment, the system of patronage prevailed for several more years. Only in 1773 did the balance of power begin to swing; defying the will of the Chandler faction, the March town meeting in that year established a committee of correspondence. The following January a group of radicals founded a caucus, the American Political Society (APS), whose declared mission was to oppose "the machinations of some designing persons in this Province, who are grasping at power and the property of their neighbors"—Chandlers and their ilk, of course, and any who were known as government men. This caucus reposed "special trust and confidence in every other member of the society," and as they intended to transact serious business, they limited their liquor expenses, and accordingly their intake, to sixpence per man at monthly meetings and two shillings per man at quarterly ones. The APS met in advance of town meetings to strategize, determine agendas, and put forward candidates for public office. While the committee of correspondence, as a public body, reported back to the town as a whole, this group was avowedly partisan from the outset. It answered to no one and could do and act as it pleased.[4]

Through the spring of 1774, the American Political Society presented the town meeting with sweeping resolutions and proposals for action that the Chandlers opposed, and each time it emerged victorious, if only by a narrow margin. In June, frustrated by a string of defeats, the government men drafted a dissenting statement of their own, which the town clerk, Clark Chandler, entered in the official record and published in the Boston press. With a contemptuous manner that contributed to their own undoing, men who had once wielded power groused that uneducated militants were "spending their time in discoursing of matters they do not understand" while "neglecting their own proper business and occupation, in which they ought to be employed for the support of their families." These agitators were "enemies to our King and Country, violators of all law and civil liberty, the malevolent disturbers of the peace of society, subverters of the established constitution, and enemies of mankind." Liberty men might command a slim majority in town, but defiant and unrepentant government men refused to concede.[5]

That is how matters stood when news of the Massachusetts Government Act, in an instant, altered the terms of political engagement. How could self-respecting citizens support a regime that disenfranchised them? Die-hard friends of government found themselves isolated, unable to muster support from those of moderate persuasion, and from that moment onward the American Political Society ruled. Its membership swelled to seventy-one, almost one-third of the enfranchised citizenry. Its impassioned adherents attended every town meeting, thereby ensuring majority votes for the society. Through the summer and fall of 1774, the American Political Society was in effect the town's shadow government.[6]

Openly combative, the society began to prepare for a military confrontation with British troops. At its July 4 meeting, it declared "that each, and every, member of our Society, be forth with provided, with two pounds of gun powder each 12 flints and led answerable thereunto." While public bodies still eschewed violence, the APS, a private group, saw no need to show restraint.[7]

During this time, the blacksmith Timothy Bigelow came to occupy a central position in the workaday world of Worcester, as blacksmiths often did. No town or hamlet could sustain itself without the nails or the scythes, plow blades, latches, or axes that such an artisan made. He not only shoed horses but supplied the hardware for a harness, bridle, or wagon, propping up the era's sole transport system. Bigelow served everyone, and anyone could pick him out in a crowd—he was six feet tall, some five inches taller than the average adult male, and powerfully built. Inevitably men gathered at his shop, across the street from the county courthouse, where he had lived and worked since 1762. It was an ongoing attraction—the mighty forge and anvil, the hammer striking red-hot iron, the waft of smoke from burning charcoal, the smith's boy working the bellows. There men gossiped about local concerns and discoursed on the looming imperial crisis.[8]

The quality of any man's work served as a measure of his character, and Bigelow's was careful and exact. He could engineer a fix if someone brought in an ordinary hinge that was broken or execute an elaborate design for a wealthy customer's door knocker. He garnered respect and made his mark, and over time he was appointed hogreave, tything man, surveyor of highways and collector of highway taxes, and fence viewer. Serving in these modest but indispensable posts, he spoke up in town meetings with authority and style. By 1773 Bigelow was so well regarded that the town selected him, along with four others, to draft Worcester's response to the *Boston Pamphlet* and to serve, along with two others, on its committee of correspondence. It seemed a tall order for a man with no college degree or formal education, but even though he had not moved up through ranks that a Chandler might recognize, common people credited his ascent. As discord intensified, Bigelow took another far-reaching step upward, as one of the founders of the American Political Society. Again he was at the center of it all, its meetings often held in his house.[9]

On July 4, 1774, Bigelow volunteered to supply more than the minimal share of powder commandeered by the APS and, working alongside another man, "to equally divide and proportion" powder among the members. His workshop became an armaments factory, where he mended guns and cast bullets; other orders could wait. The shop was also an armory of sorts, as British spies duly noted. Two months before Lexington and Concord, they reported that Worcester activists had accumulated fifteen tons of powder and thirteen small cannon, which were poorly mounted but proudly displayed in front of the meetinghouse. The record, written in French, also revealed that a merchant named Salisbury and "un grand chef" named Bigelow had various munitions in their possession.[10]

Again and again the APS tapped Bigelow for his leadership abilities. On August 18, meeting at a tavern run by the widow Mary Stearns, members asked him, his cousin Joshua Bigelow, and five others to suggest "something that they shall think proper for the town to act upon at our next town meeting." This committee settled on a devilish plan. They would round up the fifty-two Tories who in their scathing dissent at the end of June had accused APS members of meddling in politics. Now that they had the upper hand, patriots would compel these men to sign a statement admitting they had "given the good people of this Province in general, and the inhabitants of the town of Worcester in particular, just cause to be offended with each of us . . . and we hereby beg their forgiveness, and all others we may have offended." Six days later, the town approved the plan and ordered each of the miscreants, in full public view, to strike out his signature on the actual physical document that Clark Chandler, John Chandler's son and the town clerk, had entered in the official record. Then the meeting ordered Clark Chandler to "obliterate, erase or otherwise deface the said recorded protest . . . in the presence of the town," first by a scratch of the pen through each and every line he had entered, and then, since some words could still be deciphered, by a series of tightly looped spirals. Finally, townsmen commanded him to dip his own fingers in a well of ink and drag them over the first page of the offending document. Humiliation was now complete. The original town record book reveals short, irregular changes of direction in the defacements, suggesting that Chandler's hand was forced.[11]

The battle with local government men was over but the battle against imperial abuse was only beginning. Previously, on August 9, twenty-two committees of correspondence from across Worcester County had assembled in Stearns's tavern, determining to enlist all townships in the county as combatants. Allied as one, they would prevent the Massachusetts Government Act from taking effect. The convention's resolves closed with a sweeping entreaty:

> Voted, That we most earnestly recommend it to the several towns in this county, (and if it should not be thought too arrogant,) to every town in the province, to meet and adopt some wise, prudent, and spirited measures, in order to prevent the execution of those most alarming acts of parliament, respecting our constitution.

On behalf of the convention, Timothy Bigelow signed a letter to every Worcester County town not present, asking each to send representatives to a convention three weeks hence, on August 30. The timing was no accident. That would be one week prior to the scheduled session of the county courts.[12]

The second gathering, several times larger than the first, could not be contained under Mary Stearns's roof. En masse, attendees trudged one quarter mile north along Main Street to the county courthouse, a stately two-story Georgian structure that served as the official outpost of the British Empire in Worcester County. That seat of government, they assumed, was already theirs for the taking. Three weeks earlier, in their first assembly, delegates had stated "that we bear all true allegiance to his majesty king George the third, and that we will, to the utmost of our power, defend his person, crown, and dignity." Such was the custom of the times, even among Boston's radicals. But the mood of the Worcester

Convention of August 30 and 31 was not so reverent. Their revolutionary agenda was straightforward. Not only did they state
that "It is the indispensable duty of the inhabitants of this county,
by the best ways and means, to prevent the sitting of the respective
courts," they also declared that if any town faced a "danger of
invasion" other towns should "all come properly armed and accoutred to protect and defend the place invaded." Since delegates
knew that Gage had pledged to send troops to protect the courts,
they were, in effect, telling men to appear in the town of Worcester on September 6 with their arms, prepared to fight.[13]

The citizenry of Worcester County responded. Before dawn on
September 6, a small body occupied the courthouse and boarded
the doors to prevent officials from entering. As day broke and
through the morning, thousands more filled the town, intent on
shutting down a government they regarded as oppressive. This
assemblage was not some amorphous crowd but a disciplined
cadre of militiamen from thirty-seven distinct companies, organized by township. Breck Parkman, one of the participants, recorded the turnout for each: 45 from Winchendon on the New
Hampshire border, 156 from Uxbridge on the Rhode Island line,
and so on, for a total of 4,622 men.[14]

Half the adult male population of this sprawling rural county
mustered, walking or riding through the night to reach Worcester, located at the county's center. Some of these travelers were inhabitants of small villages scattered across the county, separated
from one another by only a half dozen miles or so, each containing
its portion of gray, weathered houses, a tavern, a crossroads store,
a schoolhouse, a few artisan shops, and a church. Others farmed
the rocky, inhospitable land surrounding these unprepossessing
centers, which, when persuaded, offered up flax, potatoes, corn,
wheat, or oats. For the most part these were not an affluent people,
but they knew how to make do with what they had. They also

knew how to mend and repair and put things to right, and on this day, joining forces with all others, they intended to do that.[15]

Militia companies at that time were the military embodiments of the people, consisting of all able-bodied men ages sixteen to sixty. Although organized independently from town meetings, they served a parallel purpose. Town meetings *expressed* the collective will of the people, while militia *enforced* it. Some of the so-called mobs that forced councilors to resign were in fact militia, and when tens of thousands responded to the Powder Alarm, they acted not as individuals but as militia companies.

As a town meeting elected civil officials, a town's militia elected its officers, so from the outset a captain would have his company's respect. Worcester, for instance, elected the strapping blacksmith Timothy Bigelow, no stranger to political debate but plainly spoken. Such a man could advance the lively exchanges of ordinary militiamen who drilled on the commons or regrouped later in the tavern. Thoroughly committed, more an activist than a politician, he was a true citizen-soldier, as were his men.

On this day, many of the companies marched "with staves and fife" rather than the guns and powder they had been gathering for the occasion. Although earlier intelligence had led them to expect a confrontation with British Regulars, the latest word was that Gage had changed his mind. On August 31, in Boston, Governor Gage had asked his diminished council "whether they would advise to the sending of any troops into the County of Worcester, or any other County in the Province, for the protection of the Judges and other officers of the Courts of Justice." Council members, who knew firsthand of the fury of the people, answered "that inasmuch as the opposition to the execution of any part of the late Acts of Parliament relating to this Province, was so general, they apprehended it would not be for His Majesty's service to send any Troops into the interior parts of the Province." Two days later, as thousands upon thousands mustered for the Powder Alarm, Gage told Dartmouth that although he had intended "to send a Body of Troops to Worcester, to protect the Courts there," he would not dispatch any troops. "Disturbance being so general, and not confined to any particular Spot," he did not know "where to send them to be of Use." Sending soldiers to quell every "disturbance" would require "dividing them in small Detachments, and tempt Numbers to fall upon them, which was reported to be the Scheme of the Directors of these Operations."[16]

The American Political Society learned of Gage's change of heart before meeting at Mary Stearns's tavern on September 5 and revised their plans, voting "not to bring our fire-arms into town the 6 day of Sept." Guns were now unnecessary, and a chance firing could taint the day's events. Only a few companies, coming from afar and ignorant of the new policy, arrived with their weapons.[17]

The once tense mood turned festive, and attention centered on staging the event in the theatrical fashion colonials favored. This was to be the largest gathering ever to assemble in Worcester, and the first consideration was simply finding a venue large enough. The town common quickly filled with the first companies to arrive. At midmorning, the militia marched north along Main Street to an open expanse behind Stephen Salisbury's store, catercorner to the courthouse. Timothy Bigelow's house was close by, and there the committees of correspondence assembled to coordinate the event, but they soon moved their proceedings outside "to attend the body of the people," the only legitimate source of authority.[18]

In Boston, "the body of the people" assembled in a single, and sizable, group. Here "the body" was a composite of thirty-seven discrete units—each an individual town's militia company. This arrangement complicated the proceedings. Each company had to elect a special representative, distinct from the military captain it had already elected, "to wait on the judges." This ad hoc committee then walked down Main Street to Daniel Heywood's tavern,

to which, after being barred from the courthouse, the court officials had retreated. The committee and the officials hammered out
the terms of surrender: a formal recantation, which Breck Parkman characterized as "a paper . . . signifying that they would
endeavor &c." The draft was then taken back to the separate companies for their approval, or disapproval. The judges' statement,
in Parkman's words, "was not satisfying," no more than an empty
promise. Told to devise a stringent, binding contract, representatives returned to Heywood's tavern. The process was democratic
but cumbersome and time-consuming, and when some militiamen grew impatient, the committees of correspondence appointed
three men to inquire about the delay.[19]

Finally, in the midafternoon, militiamen arranged themselves
along Main Street, half on the Mill Brook side and the other half
under the embankment to the west. The lines stretched for a quarter mile, each company in formation, Uxbridge in front of the
courthouse, Westborough next, and so on, down to Upton and
Templeton, stationed outside Heywood's tavern. When all were
in place, two dozen court officials emerged from the tavern—
judges, justices of the peace, court attorneys, and any whose
power had been sanctioned by the Crown. Hat in hand, signaling
deference, each in turn recanted before the first company of militiamen. The rest, however, could not hear, so each made his way
through the gauntlet, repeating his recantation over thirty times.
The officials pledged "that all judicial proceeding be stayed . . .
on account of the unconstitutional act of Parliament . . . which,
if effected, will reduce the inhabitants to mere arbitrary power."[20]

That should have sufficed, but it did not. The militiamen then
demanded that those who had signed the Tory dissent back in
June, and inked through their signatures to that document in
August, walk through the lines, reciting their own recantations.
Throughout, militiamen kept good order, although High Sheriff
Gardiner Chandler required an extra guard of four men to ensure

he would not be abused. He was John Chandler IV's brother, and years later, exiled in England, John complained bitterly to the British government:

> In September A.D. 1774 a mob of several thousands of Armed People drawn from the neighboring Towns assembled at Worcester for the purpose of Stopping the Courts of Justice then to be held there which having accomplished they seized your memorialist who in order to save himself from immediate death was obliged to renounce the aforesaid Protest and Subscribe to a very Treasonable League and Covenant.[21]

After this daylong display of the people's power, climaxed by humiliating submissions, officials sanctioned by the British government would never again exert authority over Worcester County.

Inadvertently, in rejecting British rule, the people of Worcester County placed themselves in a "state of nature," a common term in an eighteenth-century lexicon. Without government, anarchy reigns: bands of outlaws plunder at will, and one man steals from another with no consequence. Now that the citizenry had dismantled local government, what body could prevent disorder?

Nobody had a firm plan, but the Worcester County Convention of the committees of correspondence, the only countywide public body, stepped in to fill the vacuum. On September 7, with delegates still in town, this convention addressed routine matters of governance, voting, for example, "to put the laws in execution respecting pedlars and chapmen." Surprisingly, it pressed into service most of the former justices of the peace, sheriffs, coroners, and probate judges "till further provision can be made." Some later commentators have concluded that since so many continued in office, the court closure had no authentic revolutionary impact. The larger issue, though, was not *who* held office, but under *whose authority* officers served. That the Worcester County Convention presumed it could appoint men to government posts, although it possessed no legal claim to do so, was in and of itself revolutionary.[22]

Further, those who returned to office served under new restraints. They had to reject authority based on the unconstitutional laws recently passed by Parliament. If Governor Gage contested this arrangement and issued any "proclamation designed to prevent them from holding and exercising their said offices" in the manner prescribed by the committees of correspondence, they were not to comply. Accordingly, any official who had not recanted could not serve. Cast out of office were Timothy Ruggles and John Murray, who refused to resign from the council, and John Adams's former law tutor James Putnam, who had refused to walk the gauntlet the day before.[23]

Others served under the new provisos, some willingly, the majority grudgingly. Artemas Ward was more amenable than most. At first glance, Ward fit the profile of a Chandler or a Worthington. The son of a prominent founder of the town of Shrewsbury, he had received both a BA and an MA from Harvard, was granted a colonel's commission in the militia, and became a judge for the Worcester County Court of Common Pleas in 1762. During the Stamp Act crisis, however, he had sided with the protesters, for which then-governor Francis Bernard revoked his colonelcy. Ward did manage to keep his judgeship on the Court of Common Pleas, but he was hardly a typical government man. He even represented Shrewsbury for all sessions of the Worcester County Convention of the committee of correspondence, including the one that placed him back in office.

John Chandler, his power entirely shattered, agreed to the terms only with the greatest reluctance. Four years hence he would be banished, but for the moment he bent with the wind. If he were to remain in the town he half owned and had formerly controlled, he had no other choice.

Somewhere in between these two was Timothy Paine. He had walked the gauntlet twice, first as a mandamus councilor and now as a justice of the peace, but Paine had never been as firmly fixed on pro-government positions as were others in the Chandler bloc. He had not signed their dissent in June, although he had joined other justices of the peace in complaining to Governor Gage that "certain persons, calling themselves a committee of correspondence of the town of Worcester," were "stimulating the people to break off all connexion with Great Britain." Even-tempered, disinclined to rub people the wrong way, and an expert fence sitter, Paine survived the tumult. By 1778 he was serving on town committees once more, and at the close of the war, in 1783, the town asked Paine and Timothy Bigelow to ferret out counterfeiters, a new, cutting-edge assignment. Paine prospered. When local farmers fell into debt in the mid-1780s, he was among their creditors. Starting in 1788 he represented Worcester in the state assembly, and late that year he almost became a member of the First Federal Congress, losing narrowly on the third ballot.[24]

Paine's sons did not navigate the troubled waters as well as their father. One, William, would soon be banished. Another, Samuel, at the tender age of twenty, had been appointed clerk of the county courts in 1773, a position that his father had long held. In that capacity, he dutifully summoned prospective jurors to appear in court, even after the great majority of townsmen vowed to oppose the Government Act in every possible way. When asked to recant, he said he was "acting merely officially" and "had no right to judge of the propriety of the act of parliament." This won him no friends among those who were in the habit of judging acts of Parliament. The convention resolved, "The letter appears to have been written by a young man, who, by his connections, has lately started into the office of clerk of the sessions and inferior court, through the indulgence of the bench of justices. The letter is affrontive to the convention, and in no respect answers their reasonable requisitions. Considering the person who wrote it," the delegates added, Samuel's feeble recantation was "of too small importance to be noticed any further." Henceforth, Samuel Paine was to be "treated with all neglect."[25]

Not trusting the officials continuing in office, the committees of correspondence placed them under the oversight of a nine-person committee that included Timothy Bigelow and other leading radicals. Justices could act only "as single justices" in simple affairs. Courts that had operated with pomp and circumstance under authority of the Crown were to remain closed. In their absence, the Worcester committees of correspondence called upon "every inhabitant of this county, to pay his just debts as soon as possible, without any dispute or litigation." This was a command, not a plea: "If any disputes concerning debts or trespasses should arise, which cannot be settled by the parties, we recommend to them to submit all such causes to arbitration; and if the parties, or either of them, shall refuse to do so, they ought to be considered as co-operating with the enemies of the country." That last clause indicated that measures would be enforced and offenders punished—if not in the courts, then through the effective extra-legal channels.[26]

Although they had won the day, delegates to the Worcester Convention did not expect their victory to go unchallenged. Commander in chief Gage, on behalf of the Crown, would certainly retaliate, and if he decided to launch an armed attack, it would fall upon the county's militia to put up a defense.

Colonial militia differed markedly from regular armies. In the words of historian Fred Anderson, "The militia was defined . . . not as an army per se, but as an all-purpose military infrastructure: a combination home guard, draft board, and rear-echelon supply network." Most significantly, although militiamen trained in military arts, they were not professionals. By law, companies were required to drill only four times a year. Even if called upon for service, they turned out for a day or a week at a time and then went home. Men who fought longer than that, as many did during the French and Indian War and prior conflicts, would sign up with the Massachusetts Provincial Army—but now there was no war and no Massachusetts army to join. How would these civilians, who played the part of soldiers only briefly and sporadically, match up against true professionals?[27]

This was the question the Worcester Convention of committees of correspondence asked when they reconvened to address military preparedness on September 20 and 21. Building on a militia structure that had varied only slightly since 1693, the convention increased the number of regiments in the county from three to seven. If it had not already done so, each town was to elect a new captain and a "sufficient number" of lower officers, depending on the size of its militia. Before October 10 all such regimental officers would gather to "choose their field officers to command the militia." This manner of selecting field officers was not new, but in the past, no choice would be final until the governor granted a commission. Now, elected officers would serve without commissions until they could be "constitutionally appointed"—a troublesome requirement, since provincials had yet to figure out what "constitutional" might mean now that Parliament had altered their charter in a manner they could not accept.[28]

In addition to ordinary militia composed of all able-bodied men, officers from each militia company were urged "to enlist one-third of the men of their respective towns, between sixteen and sixty years of age, to be ready to act at a minute's warning." This elite crew, presumably the sturdiest and most mobile, would form an organizational structure parallel to that of the militia, but smaller so it could act more swiftly and efficiently. Men in towns everywhere would soon sign covenants such as this one:

> We whose Names are hereunto subscribed, do voluntarily
> Inlist our selves, as Minute Men, to be ready for military

operation, upon the shortest notice. And we hereby Promise & engage, that we will immediately, each of us, provide for & equip himself, with an effective fire arm, Bayonet, Pouch, Knapsack, & Thirty rounds of Cartridges ready made. And that we may obtain the skill of compleat Soldiers, We promise to Convene for exercise in the Art Military, at least twice every week.

Minutemen also promised to obey orders as "practiced by any well regulated Troops," and agreed to "forfeit & pay the sum of two shillings Lawfull money for the use of ye Company" if they failed "to attend the time & place of exercise."[29]

The convention stipulated that "company officers of the minute men" from throughout the county, again elected, were to "meet at Worcester, on the 17th of October next, at ten o'clock in the forenoon, to proportion their own regiments, and choose as many field officers as they shall think necessary." Never has there been a more democratically constituted fighting force, from bottom to top.[30]

Although militia had been part and parcel of New England society since the early days of colonization, they were taking on a role normally assigned to an actual army. Gone were the convivial militia days of old, where children ran about and women sought each other's company while men drilled and drank. Men now drilled believing they might soon march to war.

If and when militia did march, the Worcester Convention wanted to ensure they had sufficient arms and provisions. It asked each town to procure "one or more field pieces, mounted and fitted for use, and also, a sufficient quantity of ammunition for the same," with "a suitable number of men, out of their respective companies, to manage such field pieces." Since men called to duty in an instant would require guns, powder, ammunition, food, blankets, tents, and other supplies, the convention asked each town to "choose a sufficient number of men as a committee to supply and support those troops that shall move on any emergency." Men could not be sent to fight without the means to sustain themselves in prolonged battles.[31]

Following on the heels of the Powder Alarm's massive turnout on September 2 and Worcester's victorious court closure four days later, the convention's avid attention to military detail evidenced the rebellion's new, warlike phase. Governor Gage, now wary of igniting an armed confrontation, made no further attempt to protect courts scheduled to convene in other insubordinate county seats. This did not mean he surrendered, however, nor that patriots would be able to control the genie they had unleashed. Rebel activists from throughout the province would try to figure out where they were heading with all this. Citizens in other colonies would have to decide whether to support the revolution in Massachusetts and, if so, to what extent. General Gage, meanwhile, would send to London for more soldiers.

Nobody knew how all this would turn out, yet all sensed that reconciliation, though not impossible, was becoming less and less likely.

PART III

DEFENDING THE REVOLUTION

Our Military Preparation here for our own Defense is not only excusable but justified in the Eyes of the impartial World: nay, for should we neglect to defend ourselves by military Preparation, we never could answer it to God and to our own Consciences or the rising [generations].

—Concord's Reverend William Emerson,
sermon of March 13, 1775

9

PHILADELPHIA AND CAMBRIDGE: TWO CONGRESSES

Britain assumed that the harsh regime imposed on the province of Massachusetts Bay would ward off defiance in all other colonies. Forewarned by the strict, punishing measures in the Coercive Acts, they would be less insolent and more compliant, deferring to imperial authority and shunning Massachusetts. Colonial activists turned the Parliamentary assumption on its head. Yes, Massachusetts *did* serve as an example to all others, but only because every colony was as vulnerable to ill use at the hands of the Crown. It was imperative, they concluded, to mount a swift, assertive, and unified defense. Virginia's Richard Henry Lee, railing against the Coercive Acts, warned "of immense danger to America when the dirty ministerial stomach is daily ejecting its contents upon us." Although the language others used was less scathing, all were in fact thinking of Lee's "America" and of joint resistance.[1]

But what might that entail? The Boston committee of correspondence thought a sweeping nonimportation and nonconsumption agreement would convince British merchants to push for repeal of the new acts, but its "Solemn League and Covenant" met stiff resistance from merchants there and in other colonial ports whose businesses would suffer. Philadelphia's committee of correspondence, influenced by the city's many merchants, rejected Boston's covenant, calling in its turn for "a general Congress of Deputies from the different Colonies, clearly to state what we conceive our rights and to make claim or petition of them to his Majesty, in firm, but decent and dutiful terms." In late May and June 1774, other colonies issued similar calls. After Virginia's Governor Dunmore dissolved the House of Burgesses because it proclaimed a day of fasting and prayer, 89 of the 103 members moved to the nearby Raleigh Tavern and issued their own appeal for a general congress.[2]

In Salem on June 17, the Massachusetts Assembly, defying Governor Gage's order to disband, met behind locked doors to endorse "a meeting of Committees, from the several Colonies on this Continent . . . to consult upon the present state of the Colonies, and the miseries, to which they are, and must be reduced, by the operation of certain Acts of Parliament respecting *America*; and to deliberate and determine upon wise and proper measures to be by them recommended to all the Colonies, for the recovery and establishment of their just rights and liberties." This notable gathering would soon become known as the "Continental Congress."[3]

The rump Massachusetts Assembly specified time and place: the first week of September in Philadelphia, the largest city on the continent and midway between northern and southern colonies. It then selected its delegates—John Adams, Samuel Adams, James Bowdoin, Thomas Cushing, and Robert Treat Paine. Their mission, unique to delegates from Massachusetts, was to garner support for their province, which had been singled out for punishment and was then in active revolt.

From the very start, and continually, John Adams chronicled his experiences as a delegate. Shortly after learning he would go to Philadelphia, Adams envisioned meeting "the wisest Men upon the Continent," yet he harbored doubts, which he disclosed in his diary. "What will such Consultations avail?" he asked. Perhaps delegates would propose petitions, but previous petitions had been "neglected and despized." What else could they possibly try? "Some are for Resolves—Spirited Resolves—and some are for bolder Councils. . . . The Ideas of the People, are as various, as their Faces." Adams remained unsettled, writing days later, "I muse, I mope, I ruminate.—I am often In Reveries and Brown Studies. The objects before me, are too grand, and multifarious for my Comprehension. We have not Men, fit for the Times. . . . I feel unutterable Anxiety."[4]

And yet, on August 10, at eleven in the morning, John Adams set off in a four-horse coach with his cousin Samuel, Cushing, Paine, and four servants. (James Bowdoin stayed home because his wife was ill.) On some days, they took off at five in the morning and endured hours of travel over dusty, hot roads, but they often found relief when they supped with coteries of gentlemen who applauded the congress and its undertaking. Not all did, however. During their five-day stay in New York, Alexander McDougall, whom Adams found sensible but talkative, cautioned him that certain parties in that colony opposed the Massachusetts delegates. One was "intimidated by Fears of a Civil War," and another "intimidated least the leveling Spirit of the New England Colonies should propagate itself into N. York." Another was made up of merchants, who feared "Non Importation, Non Consumption and Non Exportation Agreements." Then, as always, there were "those who are looking up to Government for Favours"; loyalty might secure an appointment or some economic or political advantage, as it could in any era or place.[5]

McDougall's comments were an omen of what was to come. When delegates met, there would be parties of every stripe and factions appearing from colonies with their own allegiances, geographies, populations, social structures, customs, crops, manufactures, or exports. In this eighteenth-century world the sense of union, aroused by transitory events, was generally fleeting while the sense of local identity was constant. Yet only if they acted in concert could they combat Britain's incursions. Their ideas were as various as their faces, to use John Adams's expression, but they had to close ranks.

Three days after leaving New York at midday on August 29, the delegation stopped to dine five miles from Philadelphia. There, Adams reported, "a number of carriages and gentlemen came out to meet us." Such men were rarely in face-to-face contact and they met eagerly. "We then rode into town, and Dirty, dusty and fatigued as we were, we could not resist the Importunity, to go to the Tavern, the most genteel one in America," Adams wrote. The recently erected City Tavern, three stories high, held lodging rooms, club rooms, a coffee room, and a large dining chamber and was standing proof of Philadelphia's advancement and possibility. Here Adams and company ate a meal "as elegant as ever was laid upon a Table," and one that was prepared in basement kitchens, where dogs trudged in circular cages, turning huge spits that held fowl and cuts of beef and venison. The Massachusetts men did not retire until eleven.[6]

The coming days and evenings were as sociable as the first. In New York Adams had complained that "I have not seen one real Gentleman, one well bred Man since I came to Town." Here, well-bred people were plentiful, and they entertained delegates in stately homes. As men awaited the arrival of the entire body, they took each other's measure during conversations that consumed hours. The prelude was worthwhile, but a week after the Massachusetts delegates arrived, on September 5, the real business began.[7]

Forty-four gentlemen from eleven colonies gathered that Monday morning at City Tavern. Their first task was to choose a suitable location for a "Grand Council of America," as many called it. Walking along streets that ran in perfectly straight lines and formed right angles at each corner—unlike streets in Boston— the delegates soon arrived at a building that had recently been built by and for the city's artisans. Named for them, it was called Carpenter's Hall. Would this suffice? A few delegates, including Joseph Galloway, speaker of the Pennsylvania Assembly, preferred the assembly chamber of the Pennsylvania State House, which was the provincial seat of British authority, but the majority thought they might be challenging that authority, so Carpenter's Hall was the better choice. "The General Cry was, that it was a good Room," John Adams noted. The delegates, gentlemen all, then took their seats in chairs that had been crafted specially for the occasion by Philadelphia artisans.[8]

If people did not know quite what to expect from this "general Congress," merely assembling was a positive, collective first step. But soon there was contention. Since this body was without precedent, delegates needed to settle on rules of operation. Should each colony have a vote, giving small and large colonies an equal say, or should votes be apportioned according to respective populations or property holdings? Debate was active, lengthy, and dictated by self-interest. Thirteen years later, the framers of the United States Constitution would haggle over the same troublesome issue.[9]

The next day, at about two in the afternoon, delegates were at work again when alarming news arrived from the north, carried by an express rider: British artillery had bombarded Boston and killed six patriots. This, of course, was the same rumor that triggered the Powder Alarm throughout the New England countryside. John Adams wrote worriedly to his wife, Abigail, who was still at home in Braintree, not far from the supposed conflict: "When or where this Letter will find you, I know not. In what Scenes of Distress and Terror, I cannot foresee.—We have received a confused Account from Boston, of a dreadfull Catastrophy. The Particulars, We have not heard. We are waiting with the Utmost Anxiety and Impatience, for further Intelligence. . . . Our Deliberations are grave and serious indeed." Silas Deane, a delegate from Connecticut, told his wife, "This City is in the utmost Confusion, all The Bells toll muffled, & the most un-feigned marks of sorrow appear in every Countenance."[10]

News of the Powder Alarm electrified Christopher Gadsden, the gadfly from South Carolina who had been crying *"Aut Mors Aut Libertas"*—"either death or liberty" in Latin—ever since the Stamp Act crisis. A colleague reported that Gadsden was "for tak-ing up his firelock, & marching direct to Boston, nay he affirmed this morning, that were his wife, and all his children in Boston, & they were there to perish, by the sword, it would not alter his sen-timent or proceeding, for American Liberty, by which you may judge of the man." Even moderate delegates, ever intent on rec-onciliation with Britain, recognized that a British assault on Bos-ton required the colonies to unite in defense of that city. "Every Gentleman seems to consider the Bombardment of Boston, as the Bombardment of the Capital of his own Province," John Adams wrote to Abigail. Days later, after the rumor was discounted, he wrote her once again: "War! War! War! was the Cry, and it was pronounced in a Tone, which would have done Honour to the Or-atory of a Briton or a Roman. . . . If it had proved true, you would have heard the Thunder of an American Congress."[11]

Not long after, on September 16, Paul Revere rode into town with an easily authenticated report: Massachusetts was in a virtual state of rebellion. Delegates learned how citizens there obstructed Parliament's Massachusetts Government Act, disabling it entirely. They paralyzed the legislature by forcing Crown-appointed council members to stand down. Jurors refused to serve, and amid great fanfare, swarms of militiamen closed the courts. The only court not closed was in Boston, the seat of government for Suffolk County, but even there, citizens joined the rest of the province in condemning the unconstitutional acts. In Dedham, less than ten miles from Boston, committees of correspondence from through-out the county had unanimously declared, point-blank, that "no obedience is due from this province" to any of Parliament's Co-ercive Acts. Unless the acts were repealed, taxes should not be paid to the provincial treasury, nor should the Crown's militia commissions be honored. Militiamen were to elect new officers and "use their utmost diligence to acquaint themselves with the art of war as soon as possible, and . . . appear under arms at least once every week." Other Massachusetts counties had made similar declarations, but these "Suffolk Resolves," the handiwork of Harvard-educated Joseph Warren, were the most cleanly crafted and stood for all the rest.[12]

Revere handed the resolves to his congressional delegation, which presented them to Congress. This forced the hands of delegates who wanted to avoid any breach with Britain. Although these moderates did not approve their radical tone, they could hardly oppose the resolves without seeming to abandon the people of Massachusetts. Congress unanimously endorsed them:

> This assembly deeply feels the suffering of their countrymen in the Massachusetts-Bay, under the operation of the late unjust, cruel, and oppressive acts of the British Parliament—that they most thoroughly approve the wisdom and fortitude, with which opposition to these wicked ministerial measures has hitherto been conducted, and they earnestly recommend to their brethren, a perseverance in the same firm and temperate conduct as expressed in the resolutions . . . trusting that the effect[s] of the united efforts of North America in their behalf, will carry such conviction to the British nation, of the unwise, unjust, and ruinous policy of the present administration.[13]

John Adams celebrated. He wrote in his diary: "This was one of the happiest days of my life. In Congress we had generous, noble sentiments, and manly eloquence. This day convinced me that America will support the Massachusetts or perish with her."[14]

Still, there was a limit. Massachusetts delegates knew they could not push too hard. A few congressional radicals wanted to engage the British Army right away, but not John Adams or Samuel Adams. Leading the militant charge were South Carolina's tendentious Christopher Gadsden and Virginia's firebrands Richard Henry Lee and Patrick Henry. "Mr. Gadsden, leaves all N England Sons of Liberty, farr behind," Connecticut's Silas Deane wrote to his wife. Pennsylvania's Joseph Reed reported that compared to Virginians like Lee and Henry, "the Bostonians are mere milkstops." But when Lee moved that "the free citizens of Boston" should "quit the place" so insurgents could launch an attack on the city's garrisoned soldiers, he was summarily defeated. Moderates, alarmed by the possibility of war, wanted to prevent the obstreperous Massachusetts colony from starting one.[15]

When agreeing to back the resolves, moderate delegates pointed to the clause in the document that called for restraint. Massachusetts citizens, the resolves stated, were "to act merely on the defensive" and within "reason." Congress ended its endorsement by underscoring this. It advised "the people of Boston and the Massachusetts-bay . . . still to conduct themselves peaceably towards his excellency General Gage, and his majesty's troops now stationed in the town of Boston, as far as can possibly be consistent with their immediate safety, and the security of the town; avoiding & discountenancing every violation of his Majesty's property, or any insult to his troops, and that they peaceably and firmly persevere in the line they are now conducting themselves, on the defensive." "Peaceably" was the operative notion. In a letter to Governor Gage, Congress explained that it was "deliberating on the most peaceable means for restoring American liberty, and that harmony and intercourse, which subsisted between us and the parent kingdom." The Continental Congress, shying from an immediate war, urged both sides to proceed with care.[16]

Even Samuel Adams, often proclaimed the leader of radicals in Congress, urged caution. He sent a letter off to Plymouth's James Warren, a key ally:

I beseech you to implore every Friend in Boston by every thing dear and sacred to Men of Sense and Virtue to avoid Blood and Tumult. They will have time enough to dye. Let them give the other Provinces opportunity to think and resolve. Rash Spirits that would by their Impetuosity involve us in unsurmountable Difficulties will be left to perish by themselves despisd by their Enemies, and almost detested by their Friends. Nothing can ruin us but our Violence.[17]

He wrote also to Joseph Warren, lead author of the Suffolk Resolves: "I have been assured, in private conversation with individuals, that, if you should be driven to the necessity of acting in the defence of your lives or liberty, you would be justified by their constituents, and openly supported by all the means in their power; but whether they will ever be prevailed upon to think it necessary for you to set up another form of government, I very much question." Another form of government? If Massachusetts attempted that, it would in effect be declaring independence, and Congress would not even entertain the concept, let alone support it.[18]

Joining in the fray, alongside his cousin Samuel, John Adams issued warnings. "The Proposal of Setting up a new Form of Government of our own" and "absolute Independency" were "Ideas which Startle People here," he cautioned a friend in Massachusetts. He then detailed the fears of many delegates:

I have had opportunities enough both public and private, to learn with Certainty, the decisive Sentiments of the Delegates and others, upon this Point. They will not at this Session vote to raise Men or Money, or Arms or Ammunition. Their opinions are fixed against Hostilities and Ruptures, except they should become absolutely necessary, and this Necessity they do not yet See. They dread the Thoughts

of an Action because, it would make a Wound which could
never be healed. It would fix and establish a Rancour, which
would descend to the latest Generations: It would render
all Hopes of a Reconciliation with Great Britain desperate. It would light up the Flames of War, perhaps through
the whole Continent, which might rage for twenty year,
and End, in the Subduction of America, as likely as in her
Liberation.[19]

Among the delegates startled by the notion of "absolute Independency" was Virginia's George Washington. When he heard
from a friend that the "fixed aim" of Massachusetts patriots was
"total independence," Washington rushed to "the Boston gentn.
[gentlemen]" in Congress and asked them if this were true. It was
not true, John Adams and Samuel Adams told him, even though
their own contacts had reported that there was much talk of "independency" among country radicals. Misled but duly satisfied,
Washington told his informant that he had learned "the real sentiments of the people" from their "leaders." He could now affirm
"with a degree of confidence & boldness . . . that it is not the wish,
or the interest of the government, or any other upon this continent, separately or collectively, to set up for independency. . . .
[N]o such thing is desired by any thinking man in all North
America."[20]

In truth, no so-called "leader" in Massachusetts could represent
"the real sentiments of the people" because there was no central
leadership. Command was dispersed through the various local
committees of correspondence, and, as the revolution progressed,
the county conventions of these local committees. Although the
Boston committee was a hub of information, its influence was
increasingly limited. When the Boston committee suggested a
"Solemn League and Covenant" in response to the port closure,

other committees designed alternate versions. Although Boston had played a key role in establishing the committees of correspondence throughout the province late in 1772 and in 1773, those committees were now setting the agenda. Committees from Berkshire initiated the court closures, and it was the committee of correspondence from the town of Worcester that first promoted a "plan of operation . . . which in all probability will run through the Province."[21]

Worcester's proactive move came in mid-August, and it was motivated by self-preservation. On August 13, William Henshaw of Leicester received intelligence that Gage was planning to send a regiment of troops to protect the Worcester courts on September 6. Worcester did not want to face British Regulars on its own and at once sought support. Two days later, the town of Worcester's committee of correspondence wrote to its Boston counterpart:

> As we think it necessary the Counties through the Province should adopt as near as possible one form of procedure we take the liberty to propose if you think best that you appoint a meeting of your committee on the 26th day of this month at 2 o'clock PM and request the attendance of the committees of Charlestown, Cambridge and as many more of the neighboring towns in that County as will be Convenient and we will depute one or more of our committee to attend. By that means we think there may be a plan of operation agreed upon that will easily be adopted by the Counties of Suffolk, Middlesex and Worcester which in all probability will run through the Province.[22]

Boston agreed to host the meeting and added towns in Essex County to the list of invitees. So on August 26, as Worcester stipulated, representatives from the province's most populous counties convened at Faneuil Hall, a hallowed meeting place. On the six-man committee chosen to draft resolutions was Worcester's blacksmith Timothy Bigelow, who now rubbed shoulders with prominent Boston activists.[23]

The document these men hammered out called upon the towns to select representatives to a "Provincial Congress" and to "resolutely execute" whatever measures it adopted. It also urged all counties to shut down their courts, as Berkshire had done. "Every officer belonging to the courts" who acted under the authority of the Massachusetts Government Act was to be considered "a traitor cloaked with the pretext of law," and noncompliant officials "ought to be held in the highest detestations by the people, as common plunderers." Knowing the British would not sit idly by, the plan then advised "the People of this Province" to learn "the military art . . . as necessary means to secure their liberties against the designs of enemies whether foreign or domestick." The province as a whole was moving toward coordinated military defense, so Worcester got what it came for—protection. If British troops did march on Worcester, other counties would be prepared to come to its aid.[24]

Through the month of September and into the first week of October, Middlesex, Barnstable, Bristol, and Plymouth Counties closed their courts, and as each one did it endorsed the proposal for a Provincial Congress. Towns selected delegates and often instructed them to pursue a prescribed agenda. Written instructions were common through the late colonial period, but now, with a revolution in the making, the practice allowed voters to comment directly on critical issues.[25]

Citizens spoke their minds and seemed to relish the opportunity. The town meeting in Plymouth "enjoined" its representatives, James Warren and Isaac Lothrop, not to "Cooperate or act in concert with the new sett of Mandamus Councillors whose appointment is founded on the Destruction of our Charter, which we hold sacred and Inviolable in all its parts and no Power on Earth has a right to Disannull it and God forbid that we should Give up the Inheritance of our Fathers or tamely submit to the efforts of Despotism and the loss of Freedom." Such rhetoric was backed by action. Refusing to "tamely submit," some four thousand citizens closed the Plymouth County courts on October 4. To celebrate, they "attempted to remove a Rock (the one on which their fore-fathers first landed, when they came to this country) which lay buried in a wharfe five feet deep, up into the center of the town, near the court house. The way being up hill, they found it impracticable, as after they had dug it up, they found it to weigh ten tons at least."[26]

On October 4, the town of Worcester issued a very particular instruction to its representative, Timothy Bigelow. Unless Parliament revoked the Massachusetts Government Act and fully restored the Charter of 1691 "before the day of your meeting," just one week away, he was

> to consider the people of this province absolved, on their part, from the obligation therein contained [in the 1691 charter], and to all intents and purposes reduced to a state of nature; and you are to exert yourself in devising ways and means to raise from the dissolution of the old constitution, as from the ashes of the Phenix, a new form, wherein all officers shall be dependent on the suffrages of the people, whatever unfavorable constructions our enemies may put upon such procedure.[27]

Exactly twenty-one months before the Continental Congress approved its own Declaration of Independence, the citizens of the town of Worcester decided it was time to form a new government with officers dependent exclusively on "the suffrages of the people." No longer would citizens be bound by a distant Parliament, in which they were not represented, or be subjects of a king or queen, whom they had not elected. This is the earliest known record of a public body in British North America issuing a declaration in favor of a new and independent government.[28]

As towns prepared for the Provincial Congress, they faced a nagging issue: under what legal authority would this new group act? According to the 1691 charter, which towns honored, the lower house of the General Court, the assembly, already represented their interests. But Governor Gage would convene the General Court only under Government Act directives, which liberty men refused to honor. To legitimize the Provincial Congress as the *new* representative body, citizens had to declare an end to the *old* one and concoct a plausible defense for doing such an unheard-of thing.

Fortuitously, Gage had summoned the assembly and the new council to meet in Salem on October 5, but on September 28, due to "the present disorder'd, and unhappy State of the Province," he changed his mind and canceled it. Newly chosen representatives immediately took advantage of the cancellation by flouting it. Knowing full well that Gage and his mandamus councilors would not be in attendance, they appeared on the specified date. From dawn to dusk on October 5, ninety representatives awaited their arrival. By the end of the day, assembly members could claim that, in assembling, they had fulfilled their mandated role under the 1691 charter, but, since the other two arms of the General Court had not, the General Court was defunct. The next day, to fill the vacuum left by its demise, representatives declared themselves a Provincial Congress.[29]

As its first authoritative act, the new Provincial Congress adjourned to the county courthouse in Concord on October 11, the place and date set by county conventions. There, the ninety original delegates were joined by some two hundred others. Altogether, 209 of the 260 towns and districts of Massachusetts sent at least one delegate—a far greater participation than the General Court had ever inspired. Only the smallest and most distant communities failed to attend. The turnout was so large, in fact, that the congress moved to Cambridge, a town that could better accommodate delegates for weeks on end. Through the fall and into the winter, this group and the committees it established convened almost daily in its meetinghouse "to take into consideration the dangerous and alarming situation of public affairs in this province," and "to consult and determine on such measures," as the official minutes stated.[30]

The Provincial Congress faced formidable challenges. First and foremost, it had to prepare for an offensive by British Regulars, a likely prospect now. Although not legally sanctioned, it also needed to assume basic governmental functions of the operationally defunct General Court. Further, it had to referee the factional strife that had emerged among the liberty men. In one corner were those who urged "independency" and who wanted to turn the array of militia companies into an actual army, which would invade Boston before Britain had a chance to dispatch reinforcements. In the other corner were men who hoped, despite all odds, for reconciliation. Standing between these contestants, attempting to broker a truce, strategic moderates counseled the Provincial Congress to prepare for war but not initiate conflict—the approach Samuel Adams and John Adams had been advocating.

This rift had strong regional overtones. Describing Boston's political temperament, Joseph Warren said, "The town of Boston is by far the most moderate part of the province." Warren was a reliable judge, more familiar than most with people of all classes and all political tastes or predilections. A decade earlier he had attended to the poor in public clinics and cared for the suffering during a smallpox epidemic. The inoculation hospital he opened then saved countless lives, and ever after he was so widely regarded that diverse Bostonians came to him for doctoring. John Adams, Paul Revere, and William Dawes were among them, but also government men, such as Thomas Hutchinson.

Governor Gage, certainly an authority on provincial politics, agreed with Warren's characterization. On October 5, as the old assembly was transforming into a Provincial Congress, merchant John Andrews noted that the country people, not Boston's notorious crew, were getting under Gage's skin:

> The Dispositions of the people in the Country are in general so restless, that they are continually sending Committees down upon one errand or other—which has caus'd the Governor to say, that he can do very well with the Boston Selectmen, but the damn'd country committees plague his soul out, as they are very obstinate and hard to be satisfied.[31]

Boston moderates and country radicals found themselves at odds over two contentious issues, one legal and the other military. Legally, now that the Massachusetts Government Act had revoked essential provisions of the 1691 charter, what constitution should the people of Massachusetts heed? "Almost all in the western counties," Joseph Warren wrote to Samuel Adams, "are for taking up the old Form of Government, according to the First Charter." Under that charter, issued to the Massachusetts Bay Company in 1629, *all* officers, even the governor, were elected "by the Freemen of the saide Company." If they opted for the earlier charter, Massachusetts citizens would control their political world absolutely, no longer "obligated to contend with their Rulers, quarrel for their rights every year or two." Warren and the Boston leadership refused to endorse this extreme position: "The resumption of the old charter of this colony is much talked of," Warren wrote, "but I think should be handled very gently and cautiously . . . lest we should be thought of as aiming at more than the colonies are willing to contend." Their solution was to reconstitute the General Court under the broad lines of the 1691 charter, with the council that had been elected the previous spring but without the royal governor.[32]

Perhaps wisely, the Provincial Congress decided to ignore

constitutional matters, at least for the moment. Rather than stipu-late the nature of its authority, it simply acted like a government, without ever claiming that it was one. Rather than pass "laws," it issued "recommendations." No matter the nomenclature, it ex-pected people to heed them.

The military issue could not be so easily sidestepped. War enthusiasts from the interior wanted to initiate offensive opera-tions. As Governor Gage reported to London, "There are vari-ous Reports spread abroad of the Motions made at the Provincial Congress. . . . Some, it's said, moved to attack the Troops in Boston immediately, others to value the Estates in the Town, in order to pay the Proprietors the Loss they might sustain, and to set the Town on Fire." Boston residents found such talk harsh and inhumane. John Andrews, who had been commenting favorably on the resistance, complained that the Provincial Congress was "principally compos'd of spirited, obstinate countrymen, who have *very* little patience to boast of. . . . [T]hey have several times agitated the matter about requesting the inhabitants of this town to leave it: which is as absurd as it is impracticable." James Lovell, a lifetime Bostonian who helped his father run the Boston Latin School, echoed this: "It is become a downright task for the warm-est patriots of our Town [Boston] and County [Suffolk] to confine the spirit of the other Counties."[33]

Having successfully unseated British authority, rural radicals had momentum in their favor, but the political playing field was shifting. Critical decisions were no longer made by isolated town meetings or county committees of correspondence but by a prov-incewide deliberative chamber, where eastern moderates applied restraint. Although they were outnumbered, these gentlemen used their social standing, education, and familiarity with polit-ical infighting to temper the actions of the Provincial Congress. Historian L. Kinvin Wroth calculates that twenty-three out of the thirty-four men who held multiple assignments or who served on committees that initiated policies came from Boston or other "major trading towns." Even though these gentlemen accounted for only 20 percent of the delegates, they were able to slow the pace of revolution. No army would attack Boston.[34]

If an offensive campaign was ruled out, all delegates were bent on securing defensive positions. While they did not bury their differences, they did work through them. They had an urgent job ahead of them, laying the groundwork to resist armed intervention by British Regulars.

Delegates to the Continental Congress had come to Philadelphia to forge a united front and resist the Crown, but like their counterparts in Massachusetts, they too had ruled against an offensive strike. Now they searched for alternatives.

Conservatives clung tenaciously to reconciliation. Joseph Galloway presented an ingenious scheme to create an American "Grand Council," a legislative body of representatives from the various colonies. Any law or tax applicable to Americans would require the approval of both this council and the British Parliament, but shared sovereignty was no longer viable. Politically, its time had passed.[35]

While Galloway and a few other cautious souls favored compromise at all costs, and Gadsden, Lee, and Henry wanted to push resistance to the extreme, most delegates searched for an approach that was forceful but would not drive the colonies over a precipice. How far should they press, they wondered.

They started by doing what public bodies at local and provincial levels had been doing since the Stamp Act crisis nine years earlier: passing resolutions and submitting petitions. Resolutions were strongly worded lists of grievances and demands that could arouse the citizenry; petitions, submitted to the Crown, contained similar grievances and demands but also conspicuous displays of deference and professions of submission. Congress tussled over the wording of a series of resolutions, which it passed on October 14. Eleven days later it submitted a petition to King George III, which closed with this: "That your Majesty may enjoy every felicity through a long and glorious Reign, over loyal and happy subjects, and that your descendants may inherit your prosperity and dominions till time shall be no more, is, and always will be, our sincere and fervent prayer." Whether such a declaration of loyalty, following a rancorous list of complaints, would ever soften the king's heart was questionable. Even more to the point, how many delegates seriously believed it would?[36]

The October 14 resolutions did conclude with a concrete proposal: "Resolved, unanimously, That from and after the first day of December next, there be no importation into British America, from Great Britain or Ireland of any goods, wares or merchandize whatsoever, or from any other place of any such goods, wares or merchandize." This too was standard fare—nonimportation agreements had contributed to the repeal of the Stamp Act and most Townshend duties—but the Continental Congress would elevate the strategy to new heights. Six days later, on October 20, delegates approved what they called the "Association." Previous agreements had been local, with groups of individuals pledging compliance, but this one was continental, applicable to residents of all colonies from New Hampshire to South Carolina. (Georgia did not send representatives to the First Continental Congress.) Delegates pledged, "We do, for ourselves, and the inhabitants of the several colonies, whom we represent, firmly agree and associate, under the sacred ties of virtue, honour and love of our country," to abide by the agreement.[37]

Many prior agreements were limited to nonimportation, but this one, in the words of Congress, would be a "nonimportation, nonconsumption, and nonexportation agreement," which, "faithfully adhered to," would cause Parliament to repeal the Coercive Acts. The addition of nonconsumption and nonexportation strengthened the Association considerably. Since all citizens, through their representatives, were pledging not to consume goods imported from Britain, American merchants who tried to elude the agreement would find no market for their wares—and with no market, they would see no gain in subverting the agreement by ordering British imports. This, in turn, would lead British merchants to lobby for repeal of the Coercive Acts.

Nonexportation would affect consumers in England. Threatened with the loss of staples from America like rice, wheat, and tobacco, they too would push for repeal. Prohibiting exports, however, created concerns for those colonists dependent on the sale of commodities. Delegates from South Carolina literally walked away from Congress for a short period until they got their way: rice was exempted from the agreement. Virginia's tobacco planters forced a delay in the implementation of the agreement so planters had time to sell their current crop, and in fact the anticipated shortage drove up the price in Britain and provided planters with handsome profits. Although these concessions weakened the agreement, they did not destroy it; the very threat of losing basic colonial imports worried consumers in the British Isles.

The assertive enforcement mechanisms elucidated in section 11 ensured the Association's effectiveness:

> That a committee be chosen in every county, city, and town, by those who are qualified to vote for representatives in the legislature, whose business it shall be attentively to observe the conduct of all personals touching this association; and when it shall be made to appear, to the satisfaction of a majority of any such committee, that any person . . . has violated this association, that such majority do forthwith cause the truth of the case to be published in the gazette; to the end, that all such foes to the rights of British-America may be publicly known, and universally contemned as the enemies of American liberty; and thenceforth we respectively will break off all dealings with him or her.[38]

With this provision, the Continental Congress added a critical component to the emerging revolutionary infrastructure. If in the past, prosecution of those who ignored nonimportation compacts in various locales was scattershot, now it was systematic. Congress drafted Americans of all regions and classes into an economic war that could be waged in every port, at every shop, and on every hearth. Everywhere citizens chose committees of safety or inspection, universally called simply "The Committee," for each jurisdiction. These committees assumed police, legislative, and judicial powers in all matters pertaining to political conduct—and in those times, nearly everything *did* pertain to politics, not only what people said, but what they produced or consumed. Committees wielded a potent weapon: the threat of social and commercial ostracism at the hands of a populace that did not easily forgive transgressions.

Through the Association, power circled from the Continental Congress, the highest intercolonial structure, back to each colony's local inhabitants. Earlier in 1774, as unrest deepened and broadened, local communities had dispatched delegates to county and provincial conventions, congresses, or assemblies, and these in turn had created this "general Congress of Deputies from the different Colonies" to devise a coordinated response to imperial usurpations. Now that body, not incognizant of its local roots, established revolutionary institutions within each community. While the Massachusetts Provincial Congress kept the revolution in that colony from proceeding too quickly, the Continental Congress, through the Association and its enforcement mechanisms, fostered the radicalization of its constituent colonies, helping them to keep pace with the revolution under way in Massachusetts.

10

NEW ENGLAND: ARMS RACE

In Boston on October 5, "a deputation of twelve," one of those "damned country committees" that so bothered Governor Gage, delivered "a *very* spirited remonstrance from the *body* of Worcester County." Moving quickly past the obligatory deferential salutation ("May it please your Excellency"), Worcester's citizenry protested Gage's "formidable hostile preparations making on the [Boston] Neck leading to our distressed capitol." He was "fortifying the only Avenue to the Town, . . . bringing into the Town a number of Cannon from Castle William, . . . sending for a further reinforcement of Troops"—all these actions "strongly indicating some dangerous design." The body of the people of a rural Massachusetts town then ordered the royal governor "to desist from any hostile preparations" and threatened that if he did not, he would be "held accountable for all the Blood and Carnage made in consequence thereof."[1]

The governor was fully aware that even as his accusers chastised him for *his* "hostile preparations," *they* were actively preparing for war. This was common knowledge. John Andrews reported, correctly, that Worcester County had expanded its militia and formed "*seven regiments* consisting of a thousand men each," each one choosing its own officers and training "twice a week to perfect themselves in the military art."[2]

"The Maxim in time of peace prepair for war, (if this may be call'd a time of peace) resounds throughout the Country," Abigail Adams, writing from what she called the "Boston Garison," reported to her husband, John. Both sides honored that maxim. Each diligently noted the military headway of the other, then pointed to those actions to justify its own militarization. It was the classic dynamic of an arms race.[3]

Worcester had been preparing for armed resistance since the July 4 meeting of the American Political Society, which instructed its members to secure flints and powder for their muskets. Six weeks later merchant Stephen Salisbury told his brother Samuel that he was completely out of gunpowder; the demand was so great, in fact, that he was thinking of building his own powder-house. On August 20 he wrote, "Guns are in good demand as well as powder. I would therefore have you send me all the Longest guns that you have." On August 25 he asked Samuel to send him, along with chocolate, pepper, and Spanish indigo, some "Barr Lead," "Gun Locks," and "Bullets—25 to the pound." Worcester's sudden interest in armaments was not unique. The second week in September, Boston merchant John Andrews wrote, "Every man in the country not possess'd of a firelock makes it a point to procure one, so that I suppose for a month past, or more, not a day has pass'd, but a hundred or more are carried out of town by 'em." Also writing from Boston, in mid-September, William Tudor reported to John Adams, "It is thought that within a Month there has been sold out of this Town 5000 small Arms."[4]

Gage countered on September 1 by seizing gunpowder stored in the magazine at Quarry Hill, and that maneuver inspired tens of thousands of provincials to march under arms toward Boston—the so-called Powder Alarm. In response, Gage prepared to defend his stronghold against a possible invasion. From

a military point of view, securing Boston was relatively elemen-
tary. The peninsula connecting it to the mainland, the "Neck,"
was only forty yards across at its narrowest spot. In the earliest
days of the town, the Neck featured an earthen wall that spanned
the peninsula. A wooden gate permitted entry, and just outside
the gate stood a gallows, exhorting newcomers by its very presence to obey the laws and norms within. Early in the eighteenth
century, passage was enhanced, with one gate used for foot traffic
and a second for carriages. Now, Gage wanted to restrict passage.
Strengthening the wall at the Neck would not only keep country
people from storming into Boston but also keep arms from flood-
ing out of the city and into their hands.[5]

Although the demand for armaments was high, supplies were
limited. Militia companies could and did purchase muskets, flints,
powder, and even cannons on the open market, where military
wares were much in demand and purchase competitive; merchants
like Stephen Salisbury in Worcester and his brother Samuel in
Boston made considerable money selling them. Commercial exchange was perfectly legal, but late in the summer of 1774 local inventories ran low. Replenishing stock took time and required two
transatlantic crossings—one heading eastward to place a merchant's order, the other returning with the merchandise. Towns
and ad hoc groups of activists purchased what they could, but they
also set their sights on British army stockpiles within Boston.

The day after the Powder Alarm, anticipating raids, Governor Gage ordered soldiers under his command to drag "four large
field-pieces" from the town common to the Boston Neck. By September 9, eighteen artillery pieces stood by the gate. Andrews reported that on the mainland side of the gate, British officers "have a
guard patrole Roxbury streets at all hours of the night," while Regulars camping on the Neck "keep so many and such strict guards
of nights, that the soldiers don't get but one undisturb'd night's
sleep out of four." To smuggle arms out of Boston by land, patriots
would have to sneak by artillery and elude two sets of guards.[6]

The Neck was well defended, and following Gage's instructions Admiral Samuel Graves ordered HMS *Lively*, with its twenty cannons, to police the route of the Charlestown ferry, Boston's northern access. British vessels also anchored at all other crossing routes on the Charles. "They have haul'd the Men of War close in upon the town at all quarters," John Andrews wrote. The British Navy, the best and largest in the world, knew how to defend vulnerable peninsulas from foreign enemies; in this case, it protected the Boston peninsula from the rest of Massachusetts.[7]

Meanwhile, Gage coveted armaments that already had fallen into the hands of rebellious militia. On September 7, he learned that Charlestown's had pilfered and buried some "ammunition, such as shot, &ca., belonging to the battery there." After an officer confirmed the report, Gage dispatched a "*formidable* expedition" to secure what was left. Men-of-war stationed in the harbor transported soldiers across the Charles River "with orders to dismantle the fort and bring off all the Ordnance, Stores, &ca." By then, as John Andrews reported, residents of Charlestown had removed not only the "reposit of shot" but also the cannons that comprised the battery, which they hitched to "teams, such as carry ship timbers," and hauled "up country."[8]

Gage pursued the hijacked arsenal. On September 11 he sent out "a number of officers and soldiers . . . who were employ'd . . . in traversing the streets and by-ways, and tampering with the children, to get out of them where the cannon were hid." Two days later an informant revealed the location, but before Gage could muster another expedition a local workforce "of about three thousand," again assisted by their beasts of burden, hauled the battery—cannons, shot, and all—"about ten or a dozen miles further up." Some of the cannons, Andrews reported, "weigh'd between two and three ton apiece."[9]

After that, a frustrated governor took extra steps to protect artillery lodged in Boston itself—but to little avail. On September 16,

Andrews reported, "Ever since ye cannon were taken away from Charlestown, the General has order'd a double guard to ye new and old gun houses, where ye brass field pieces belonging to our militia are lodg'd: notwithstanding which, the vigilance and temerity of our people has entirely disconcerted him, for We'n'sday evening, or rather night, they took these from the Old house (by opening the side of the house) and carried away through Frank Johonnot's Garden."[10]

Outflanked by rebel trickery, Gage again tightened security. He "gave it in orders the next day to the officer on guard to remove those from the New house . . . sometime the next night into the camp; and to place a guard at each end, or rather at both doors, till then." Yet even this proved inadequate. "At the fixed hour the Officer went with a number of Mattrosses to execute his orders, but behold, the guns were gone! He swore the *Devil* must have help'd them to get 'em away." John Andrews, in recounting the tale, was astonished, as Gage must have been and as historians are to this day: "Its amazing to me how our people manag'd to carry off the guns, as they weigh near seven hundred weight apiece; more especially that they should do it, and not alarm the centinels."[11]

Artillery such as these were a hallmark of organized warfare in the late eighteenth century. Citizens had scrambled for muskets, flints, and powder ever since the Massachusetts Government Act set the province on edge, but their pursuit of field pieces in the late summer and early fall indicated that they anticipated an outright war. On September 6, the day Worcester shut down its courts, the county convention there issued a bellicose directive:

> That it be recommended to the several towns and districts of this county, that they provide themselves, immediately, with one or more field pieces, mounted and fitted for use; and also a sufficient quantity of ammunition for the same; and that officers appoint a suitable number of men, out of their respective companies, to manage said field pieces.[12]

Worcester rebels could mount a defense against attack with such weaponry, or, potentially, mount a military offensive on Boston— a thing Gage suspected and cautious citizens feared. No longer was the last option idle talk.[13]

Provincials had stolen several cannons but wanted many more. Fortuitously, Boston merchants possessed stock left unsold after the French and Indian War as well as newly acquired items intended to protect vessels against piracy. Local militia could purchase these, and skilled artisans could then construct carriages to move them about battlefields—but first they had to be smuggled out of Boston. Cannons were not easily concealed in wagons, so getting past British guards on the Neck was nearly impossible. Conveying them across the Charles River on boats was more realistic, but that too was risky business. One contraband load of "six good pieces of large cannon" wound up stranded by low tide in what Bostonians called "the Mill Pond," the shallows of the Charles River just west of town. Others, though, must have made it through. "There is said to be fifty Cannon in the upper Part of the County of Middlesex completely fitted for Service," William Tudor reported to John Adams. "About 20 pieces of cannon" had found their way to Worcester, according to British intelligence.[14]

Increasingly, the provincial force resembled an army. Militiamen trained more frequently and earnestly, and companies increased their supplies of muskets, flint, powder, and artillery. Until mid-October, however, town militia operated with only minimal coordination by the committees of correspondence of the respective counties. The Provincial Congress changed that. On October 20, acting extralegally as the de facto provincial assembly, this new body appointed a committee "to consider what is necessary to be now done for the defence and safety of the province." When this committee produced a draft four days later, the body of the whole discussed it behind closed doors and then appointed another committee to figure out "the most proper time for this province to provide a stock of powder, ordnance, and ordnance stores."[15]

According to official records, the second committee returned that same afternoon and "reported, as their opinion, that *now* was the proper time for the province to procure a stock of powder, ordnance, and ordnance stores"—the emphasis on "now" was theirs. This triggered the immediate formation of yet another committee to "determine what number of ordnance, what quantity of powder, and ordinance stores will be now necessary for the province stock, and estimate the expense thereof." The following afternoon, in short order, this third committee submitted an exacting list of armaments the province should acquire:

16 field pieces, 3 pounders, with carriages, irons, &c.; wheels for ditto, irons, sponges, ladles, &c., @ £30	£480
4 ditto, 6 pounders, with ditto, @ £38	£152
Carriages, irons, &c., for 12 battering cannon, @ £30	£360
4 mortars, and appurtenances, viz: 2 8-inch and 2 13-inch, @ £20	£80
20 tons grape and round shot, from 3 to 24 lb., @ £15	£300
10 tons bomb-shells, @ £20	£200
5 tons lead balls, @ £33	£165
1,000 barrels of powder, @ £8	£8,000
5,000 arms and bayonets, @ £2	£10,000
And 75,000 flints	£100
Contingent charges	£1,000
In the whole	£20,837[16]

This shopping list, a sensitive military matter, prompted another call for secrecy. Little did delegates know that at least one well-placed informer, Dr. Benjamin Church, reported the details of their military preparations to Governor Gage.

Two days later, the Provincial Congress established a committee of safety and granted it the power of the purse. The committee could dispense "twenty thousand eight hundred and thirty-seven pounds," enough to fulfill the congress's order exactly. Further, the committee could actually *pay* the men it mobilized.[17]

There was one problem, however. The congress so far had no money for any of this. In dire need of funds, it appointed its own receiver-general, Henry Gardner, and "recommended" that sheriffs, constables, and collectors for each town and district transfer whatever tax monies they had in their possession to Gardner instead of to Harrison Gray, the official receiver-general for Massachusetts. It "earnestly recommended" that towns continue to collect funds according to the old warrants and "strongly recommended" that inhabitants honor their financial obligations, with all funds funneled to Gardner. But the congress was not an actual government, and its committee could not erect a legally binding system of taxation. Individuals and towns might, or might not, take its "recommendations" to heart and pay up. Recognizing this, the congress authorized the committee of safety to make its purchases "upon the credit" of funds it hoped to receive. Presumptive taxation and deficit spending—there was no other way to finance an extralegal army.[18]

Clearly, the Provincial Congress was engaging in "warlike preparations of every sort," its primary complaint against British officials. In addition to stockpiling armaments, it chose five "commissaries." The word clarified its intent: such officials supply soldiers who go to war, not men who stay home and train. Beyond that, the Provincial Congress appointed three commanding "general officers" to head an army that was yet to be: Jedediah Preble of Falmouth, Artemas Ward of Shrewsbury, and Seth Pomeroy of Northampton, in that order. When Preble declined because of ill health, Ward assumed top command and held that position until

George Washington replaced him the following June. By that time, the consortium of Massachusetts militia had evolved into the Continental Army.[19]

The Provincial Congress also called for companies of minutemen "who shall equip and hold themselves in readiness on the shortest notice from the said committee of safety." Duplicating the bottom-up structure used in Worcester, each company was to appoint a captain and two lieutenants. These officers would then organize battalions composed of nine companies and choose field officers for each. Additionally, the congress settled on a province-wide plan for discipline and military drill in all militia companies, "placing them in every respect on such a permanent footing as shall render them effectual for the preservation and defense of the good people of this province." Citizens were expected to drill *as if* they were soldiers, which they might soon be but were not yet.[20]

On October 29, Boston's John Andrews related word-of-mouth scuttlebutt from the closeted congressional meetings. "Several times since their sitting it is likewise been reported, that they were about establishing a standing army to be compos'd of fifteen thousand men: a scheme not only ridiculous, but fraught with a degree of madness at this juncture." Colonials had long objected to the Crown's standing armies, and many were as perturbed as Andrews at the prospect of creating one. If radicals in the Provincial Congress, during the heated debates over militarization, had succeeded in establishing a standing army, they would have torn apart the thin alliance that bound Massachusetts citizens of almost all stripes. Placing well-organized militia on a "permanent footing" was a serviceable compromise.[21]

General Gage understood full well that he might soon be facing a large fighting force and pressed Britain to reinforce his own army. As early as September 12, in the wake of the Powder Alarm, he told Lord Dartmouth, "Nothing less than the Conquest of almost all the New England Provinces will procure Obedience to the late Acts of Parliament for regulating the Government of Massachusetts Bay." On October 3 he explained to Lord Barrington, the secretary of war, how such a conquest might be accomplished: "You should have an Army near twenty Thousand strong, composed of Regulars, a large Body of good Irregulars such as the German Huntsmen, picked, Canadians &ca, and three or four Regiments of light Horse, these exclusive of a good and sufficient Field Artillery." When Gage inventoried the forces he had on hand, he counted only 1,766 men "under Arms" and ready for battle. That was dangerously insufficient:

> Resistance should be effectual at the Beginning. If you think ten Thousand Men sufficient, send Twenty, if one Million [pounds] is thought enough, give two; you will save both Blood and Treasure in the End. A large force will terrify, and engage many to join you, a middling one will encourage Resistance, and gain no Friends. [22]

But London had already decided on a far smaller number, which even Lord Dartmouth called "very embarrassing." There was nothing to do about it, he informed Gage. "The State of this Kingdom will not admit of our sending more Troops," neither from Great Britain nor from "our distant Garrisons." Two regiments posted in Ireland "might be spared," but not immediately. In the meantime, the British command would muster "as many men as can be spared from the different quarters" and load them on three vessels headed to Boston, but these would amount to no more than six hundred—not twenty thousand or even ten thousand. [23]

Only in late October and early November, as Gage's letters and other dispatches from early September reached London, did King George III and his administration begin to understand the scale of the resistance. Their reaction was combative. On November 18, King George III told Prime Minister Lord North:

"The New England Governments are in a State of Rebellion, blows must decide whether they are to be subject to this Country or independent. . . . We must either master them or totally leave them to themselves and treat them as Aliens." North agreed. The following day he told Thomas Hutchinson, who was then in London, that "it was to no purpose any longer to think of expedients; the Province was in actual rebellion, and must be subdued."[24]

If the king and his like-minded prime minister were to "master" and "subdue" the "New England Governments," they would need a solid majority in Parliament, whose Whig members too often defended American colonists. Hoping to bolster his support, King George had prorogued Parliament in June, and the elections held in October and November yielded favorable returns. On November 30, in his welcoming speech to the reconstituted and more compliant body, he signaled his intention to clamp down. "A most daring spirit of resistance and disobedience to the law still unhappily prevails in the Province of the Massachusetts-Bay," he announced. "I have taken such measures, and given such orders as I judged most proper and effectual for carrying into execution the laws which were passed in the last session of the late Parliament." Newly elected members and those who had voted for the Coercive Acts applauded the message. The minority, their number reduced, complained and introduced various conciliatory measures that were soundly trounced, suffering the same fate such measures had the previous spring.[25]

King George had already initiated one bold move to interrupt the buildup of arms in Massachusetts. On October 17 he had received intelligence that "a Ship-load of Canon" had left Amsterdam and was headed toward America "on board a vessell from Rhode Island." Two days later, with his Privy Council, he prohibited the export of "Gunpowder, or any Sort of Arms or Ammunition" from Britain to the colonies and the carrying of any "Military Stores" from Europe to America. If "blows must decide" the conflict in Massachusetts, the British Army would certainly be able to stamp out a rebellion that lacked arms.[26]

When Gage received official notice of the order in early December, he issued enforcement instructions to his customs officials and dispatched the circular letters that Dartmouth had prepared for all colonial governors. Crown-appointed governors waited until effective procedures were in place before divulging news of the ban, but governors from the charter colonies of Rhode Island and Connecticut, who had been elected rather than appointed, did not feel so constrained. Rhode Island's Governor Joseph Wanton shared the news with his assembly, which responded by approving the purchase of three hundred barrels of gunpowder, three tons of lead, forty thousand flints, and four brass field pieces. It also voted to remove arms held at Fort George, in Newport Harbor, to Providence, beyond the reach of British naval forces. Similarly, militia in New London, Connecticut, moved their cannon "into the Country" for safekeeping.[27]

On December 10 the *Providence Gazette* published the exact wording of the official ban, which it must have received through Governor Wanton. Two days later, the *Boston Gazette* also publicized it. Word was out. With an international supply denied them, provincials looked to any and all domestic reserves. The arms race within the colonies immediately intensified.[28]

Right at this moment a rumor floated around Boston: HMS *Somerset* was headed toward Portsmouth, New Hampshire, bearing two regiments of Regulars who were to reinforce Fort William and Mary, which guarded the harbor and housed a large stockpile of powder and weaponry.

A small cadre from Boston's committee of correspondence, acting without sanction of the committee's required quorum, dispatched a seasoned courier, Paul Revere, to alert compatriots in Portsmouth. Departing on the evening of December 12, Revere spurred his horse on, riding over fifty miles of frozen, rutted roads. Upon his arrival the following afternoon, he alerted the local committee of correspondence to the *Somerset*'s imminent arrival and delivered a copy of the December 12 *Boston Gazette*, which publicized the ban on arms importation. Portsmouth patriots knew that if they wished to seize the fort's rich store of armaments, they had to act swiftly, before the *Somerset* landed.

Hearing of the designs against the fort, New Hampshire governor John Wentworth dispatched his own courier to Boston to plead for reinforcements, but it was too late. At three o'clock in the afternoon of December 14, "upwards of four hundred men" charged Fort William and Mary. Captain John Cochran and the five soldiers who watched over the fort were taken unawares. Cochran later testified that he "ordered three four pounders to be fired on them and then the small arms, and before we could be ready to fire again, we were stormed on all quarters." The insurgents, Wentworth reported, carried away "upwards of 100 barrels of powder belonging to the King." According to the tally of two customs officials stationed at Portsmouth there were 234 "whole Barrells Powder" stored in the fort, "all of which were taken but one." Whatever the total, the raiders hauled away as much powder as they could on the barges they pressed into service.[29]

That evening Wentworth vented to General Gage: "This event too plainly proves the imbecility of this government to carry into execution his Majesty's order in Council, for seizing and detaining arms and ammunition imported into this Province, without some strong ships of war in this harbor." Gage understood this all too well. He too had pleaded for reinforcements to no avail.[30]

The following day over one thousand men from the surrounding area gathered in town. Wentworth beat the drums to call out the militia, but militiamen had already mustered to raid the fort, not protect it. "Not one man appeared to assist in executing the law," he complained. "It was impossible for me, with four Councillors, two Justices, one Sheriff, Mr. Macdonough, and Mr. Benning Wentworth, to subdue such multitudes, for not one other man would come forth. Not even the Revenue officers—all chose to shrink in safety from the storm, and suffered me to remain exposed to the folly and madness of an enraged multitude, daily and hourly increasing in numbers and delusion." These raiders completed the work begun the night before, carrying off every musket they could locate and sixteen cannon, leaving only those too heavy to transport. By the time British ships arrived from Boston to take back the fort, all guns and powder had been hidden deep in the rebel-controlled interior.[31]

Many say, with some justification, that the assault on Fort William and Mary was the opening skirmish of the Revolutionary War. British soldiers did fire four-pound balls from cannons and managed a volley of musketry before they were overrun. Though brief and one-sided, the raid added significantly to the insurgents' arsenal—half a year later, at Bunker Hill, rebels would make full use of ammunition and powder they had seized. It also confirmed what Gage had already told officials back in London: to reestablish rule, Britain would need to conquer not just Massachusetts but all of New England.

11

SALEM, WORCESTER, OR CONCORD: WHERE WILL THE BRITISH STRIKE?

Governor Gage had asked for "an Army near twenty Thousand strong." King George III, Prime Minister North, Secretary of State Dartmouth, and Secretary of War Barrington thought the request exorbitant. In their minds, if Gage only cracked down, using the forces at his disposal, colonials in Massachusetts could be brought into line.[1]

In fact, Gage had good reasons *not* to attack. As the man-on-the-ground, he understood that a British offensive, if it were not immediately conclusive, would only unify American colonials, who, once attacked, would in all likelihood rise up in arms. If they did, he lacked the military strength to launch a campaign into what today would be called "rebel-held territory"— anywhere outside of Boston, that is. Urged on by Massachusetts insurgents, twelve colonies had agreed to respond as one against any British strike. Choosing to bide his time, Gage simply waited for the promised reinforcements, insufficient as their numbers were to be.

By now, the governor perceived that the Coercive Acts were at the root of the escalating rebellion and that the Government

Act, in particular, was unenforceable. Writing to Dartmouth, he dared to propose "a Suspension of the Execution of the late Acts" until he possessed the military strength to enforce them. At first glance, and that was the only glance the communication received in London, this notion appeared preposterous. King George told Lord North, "His idea of suspending the Acts appears to me the most absurd that can be suggested." If colonials saw the "mother-country" so fearful as to suspend "the measures she has thought necessary," they would take heart. It was this sort of weakness that "prompts them to their present violence," he pronounced. North agreed. In private conversation with Thomas Hutchinson, he confessed that he did not know "what General Gage meant by suspending the Acts; there was no suspending an Act of Parliament."[2]

In retrospect the proposal that Gage put forward was not unreasonable. Suspension might have dampened enthusiasm for the rebellion and allowed colonial moderates to gain the upper hand in their dispute with radicals. Alternately, if the Crown opted for enforcement, it would be "expedient . . . to be better prepared," as Gage told Dartmouth. The Crown could either affirm British superiority with a show of overwhelming military might or grant concessions. The current policy, passing harsh acts without the ability to execute them, made little sense.[3]

Deep into the winter of 1774–75, both sides played a waiting game. The British did not take the offensive because they lacked sufficient military strength; Massachusetts provincials refrained because they did not yet possess ample political capital in other colonies. From the actual combatants' point of view, this was just as well. Sustained military expeditions in the dead of winter were rare in the eighteenth century, and with good reason. Although soldiers might set off on occasional forays to acquire and secure arms, they did not relish tramping through inhospitable country in snow or bitter winds, their hands so numb that they could barely prime a musket.

Time worked in the provincials' favor. On January 29, 1775, William Emerson, Concord's young minister and one of the "black regiment" of preachers who supported the revolution, made a matter-of-fact note in his diary: "Extraordinary Weather for warlike Preparation. Much time spent in military Manoeuvres." With their fields fallow, farmers could focus on drills. The Provincial Congress accumulated not only muskets and cannons, powder and projectiles, but the various accouterments that soldiers in the field required—food, cookware, blankets, and tents. Men showing up "at a minute's warning" would need, within minutes, all of war's necessary trappings. Provisioning fell to the committee of safety and its workhorse partner, the committee of supplies. A home had its hearth, an army its mess, as any soldier, then or now, would contend. At its first meeting, on November 2, the committee of safety recommended that the committee of supplies procure 355 barrels of pork (200 to be stored at Worcester, the remainder at Concord), 700 barrels of flour (400 for Worcester, 300 for Concord), and 300 bushels of peas (split evenly). The pork, of course, was salted, but still, such a quantity would not keep indefinitely. The committees must have believed that farmers-turned-soldiers would be consuming it within months if not weeks, and that war itself was as close as that.[4]

In subsequent meetings the committees continued to attend to the nuts-and-bolts needs of wartime. Their diligence in requisitioning supplies reflected as strongly as any patriot oratory a readiness to commit to war if colonials were first attacked. They ordered food (20 casks of raisins, 20 bushels of oatmeal), drink (20 hogsheads of rum, 6 casks of Malaga wine, 9 casks of Lisbon wine), kitchen and dining wares (1,000 quart iron pots, 1,000 wooden mess bowls, "a suitable supply of wooden spoons"), tools for building earthen fortifications (200 spades, 150 iron shovels, 150 pickaxes, 50 wheelbarrows), and surgeon's stores. As for military wares, they tried to procure "all the arms and ammunition" they could from neighboring provinces. They purchased cannon in Boston, to be smuggled out of town "to some place in the country." They voted "to purchase all the powder they can, upon the best terms they can," and to "procure ten tons of brimstone" for the manufacture of yet more gunpowder. The "best terms," for the most part, turned out to be credit. Backed by community pressure, the committee was able to lean on suppliers to place goods at the disposal of the province. If used, the province would pay; if not, goods would be returned.[5]

The committees also considered where to position their stores. On January 25 they ordered that "all the cannon, mortars, cannon balls and shells, be deposited at the towns of Worcester and Concord, in the same proportion as the provisions are to be provided." This army-to-be was to have two base stations, one a night's march from Boston, the other deep in the hinterlands and more secure.[6]

When the Provincial Congress recessed for a month on February 16, the committees of safety and supplies continued to meet daily. On February 21 the committee of safety "voted, unanimously . . . that the committee of supplies purchase all kinds of warlike stores, sufficient for an army of fifteen thousand men to take the field." Details followed the next day: "one thousand field tents complete," "ten tons of lead balls, in addition to what were formerly ordered," "cartridges for fifteen thousand men, for thirty rounds," plus more food—molasses and salt fish. Further, "on certain intelligence" of "the arrival of the reinforcements coming to General Gage," the provincial arms were to be removed to Worcester, the safest place, and the Provincial Congress was to reconvene instantly.[7]

The day after that, February 23, the committees ordered "the commanding officers of the minute men through the province, to assemble one fourth part of the militia." They also moved "to form an artillery company when the constitutional army of the province shall take the field." Not *if*, but *when*. The following day, the committees appointed a "wagon master for the army." *The* army, as if it already existed. The body of the Provincial Congress, despite a push by radicals, had not yet voted to create an actual army, but the committees of safety and supplies, on their own, were setting the agenda.[8]

Governor Gage knew about all of this. Benjamin Church was present at most committee of safety meetings. He worked with the congress while working with Gage, taking full advantage of his pivotal position. Later, in his own defense, Church claimed he had only wanted to prevent a showdown, but in fact he made conflict more likely by alerting Gage to the extraordinary advances in rebel planning. Church was not Gage's sole source of information. As commander in chief, Gage dispatched spies from the ranks of his army and paid close attention to the secret reports of Tories; taking all intelligence seriously, he forwarded some accounts to London.[9]

On February 24, Gage received an intriguing state-of-the-enemy report. The committee of safety was to "observe the motions of the Army, and if they attempt to penetrate into the Country, imedietly to communicate the intelligence" to five militia leaders. Three of these—Artemas Ward, Joseph Henshaw, and Timothy Bigelow—lived "in or near the towns of Worcester, and Leicester," focal points for militia in the interior of the province; the others—James Warren of Plymouth and Jeremiah Lee of Marblehead—represented coastal communities south and north of Boston. Upon receiving notice, these men were "to send express's round the Country to collect the Minute Men who are to oppose the troops. These Minute Men amount to about 15,000 and are the picked Men of the whole body of Militia, and all properly armed."[10]

Most of this, save for the names, was general knowledge, but the report continued:

There are in the Country thirty-eight Field pieces and Nine-teen Companies of Artillery most of which are at Worcester, a few at Concord, and a few at Watertown.

Their whole Magazine of Powder consisting of between Ninety and an Hundred Barrells is at Concord.

There are eight Field pieces in an old Store or Barn, near the landing place at Salem, they are to be removed in a few days, the Seizure of them would greatly disconcert their schemes.

Colo. Lee, Colo. Orme, Mr. Devons, Mr. Chever, Mr. Watson, and Moses Gill, are appointed a Commit-tee of supply, who are to purchase all military stores, to be deposited at Concord and Worcester.[11]

Gage weighed his alternatives. He could either wait for reinforce-ments or try to disrupt the military buildup by immediately con-fiscating provincial arms or powder. If he chose to act, should he go after Worcester, Concord, or Salem? Worcester, which housed most of the artillery, was distant and primed for defense. Concord was nearer, but an expedition there might trigger a mobilization reminiscent of the Powder Alarm, and the hordes this time would be better trained and better armed.

That left Salem. It was farther from the heartland of the prov-ince, where the rebels held sway, and British ships could reach it easily. Three days earlier, Gage had spotted this item in a spy re-port: "Twelve pieces of Brass Cannon mounted, are att Salem and lodged near the North River, on the back of the Town." Whether there were twelve "Brass Cannon" or eight "Field pieces" at Salem, it was a tempting target. He decided upon a quick, surgical strike: find the weaponry and leave.[12]

On Sunday, February 26, Colonel Alexander Leslie and a con-tingent of 240 troops boarded a boat to Marblehead, as ordered. From there, they were to march overland toward Salem, just a few miles away. It promised to be a brief and straightforward expedition, but Gage made three mistakes. He ordered the march for Sunday, when Salem's inhabitants collected in the church and could respond quickly and in great numbers. He chose a route that was guarded by a drawbridge at the approach to the town. Finally, he trusted reports with misleading intelligence. A week later, Gage confessed to Dartmouth:

> The Circumstance of the Eight Field Pieces at Salem led us into a Mistake, for supposing them to be brass Guns brought from Holland, or some of the foreign Islands, which Report had also given Reasons to suspect; a detachment of two hundred men under Lieut. Col. Leslie was sent privately off by Water to seize them. The Places they were said to be concealed in were strictly searched, but no Artillery could be found. And we have since discovered, that there had been only some old Ship Guns which had been carried away from Salem some time ago.[13]

In his account, Gage reported that "the people assembled in great Numbers with Threats and abuse." Town residents, after lifting the drawbridge, perched on its open leaf and gleefully hurled taunts as the Regulars lined up on the opposite bank: "Soldiers, red-jackets, lobster-coats, cowards, damnation to your government!" Into the nineteenth century, locals celebrated their triumph in a rich heroic folklore, rooted in fact but probably embellished. Captain John Felt, it was said, intended to cross the river, "grapple with Col. Leslie," swim back, and if British troops fired on him, so be it. "I would willingly be drowned myself to be the death of one Englishman," Felt later pronounced. Joseph Whicher, who found himself on the Regulars' side of the river, scuttled a gondola so the troops could not use it for a crossing, and when "the soldiers ordered him to desist, and threatened to stab him with their bayonets if he did not," he refused to back down and supposedly "opened his breast and dared them to strike. They pricked his breast so as to draw blood." Sarah Tarrant, a nurse, reportedly yelled from her window as the Regulars passed by: "Go home and tell your master he has sent you on a fool's errand and broken the peace of our Sabbath. What, do you think we were born in the woods, to be frightened by owls?" When a soldier then pointed his musket at her, she further exclaimed, "Fire if you have the courage, but I doubt it."[14]

The rebuff at Salem, embarrassing enough in any case, gave Gage further cause for concern. He had chosen Salem rather than Worcester or Concord to avert another mass mobilization, but even that had foundered. Two days later the *Essex Gazette* reported that accounts of the redcoats' march on Salem "flew like lightning . . . so that great numbers were in arms." The following week the *Gazette* elaborated:

> Col. Leslie's ridiculous expedition, on the 26th ult., occasioned such an alarm, that the people of all the neighboring towns, as well as those at 30 or 40 miles distance were mustering, and great numbers actually on their march for this place; so that it is thought not less than 12 or 15,000 men would have been assembled in this town within 24 hours after the alarm, had not the precipitate retreat of the troops from the drawn-bridge prevented it.[15]

What happened at Salem demonstrated that *any* offensive maneuver would precipitate a massive response from provincials. Gage knew that London expected him to act once reinforcements arrived, but he also knew that a successful outcome was far from guaranteed. He would have to consider his plan carefully and cautiously, yet strike boldly—a difficult combination.

•   •   •

Spring approached. With more British Regulars expected, the question on everybody's mind was not *whether* General Gage would initiate a vigorous assault, but *where* he would and *when*. Gage himself pondered this as weeks passed, weighing risks against potential gains. Foremost candidates were, of course, Worcester and Concord, where most armaments were stored.

Before making a final determination, Gage wanted to examine the logistical particulars, knowing, as any general does, that they influence a campaign's outcome. It was critical to ascertain beforehand where his troops, or an enemy's, might make a stand, or if the land could support thousands of advancing soldiers. He started with Worcester, where "the Provincial grand magazine of provisions and warlike stores is kept." On February 22 he dispatched two spies, Captain William Brown and Ensign Henry De Berniere. "You will go through the Counties of *Suffolk* and *Worcester*, taking a sketch of the country as you pass," Gage told them. He made no mention of Lexington, a village of little military importance, nor of Concord, neither of which lay on the way to Worcester. Suffolk, on the other hand, was of great interest, for the routes to Worcester went through that county. Brown and De Berniere were to "mark out" roads, distances between towns, heights and the difficulty of their ascents, passes, and the breadth and depth of rivers, together with fording places. Gage's detailed instructions testified to his interest in a prolonged expedition, little like Colonel Leslie's raid on Salem:

> The nature of the country to be particularly noticed, whether enclosed or open; if the former, what kind of enclosures, and whether the country admits of making Roads for Troops on the right or left of the main Road, or on the sides.
>
> You will notice the situation of the Towns and Villages, their Churches, and Church-yards, whether they are advantageous spots to take post in, and capable of being made defencible.

If any places strike you as proper for encampments, or appear strong by nature, you will remark them particularly, and give reasons for your opinions.

It would be useful if you could inform yourselves of the necessaries their different Counties could supply, such as Provisions, Forage, Straw, &c., the number of Cattle, Horses, &c., in the several Townships.[16]

On their first night out, Brown and De Berniere were discovered by a black woman who served them dinner. The spies confessed that she eyed the papers they carried, deciphered a few words, and surmised their task. She also recognized that Captain Brown was a soldier, despite his disguise of "brown clothes and reddish handkerchiefs," the dress of "countrymen." "When we observed to her that it was a fine country," they reported, "she answered so it is, and we have got brave fellows to defend it, and if you go any higher you will find it so."[17]

In Worcester the spies thought they escaped notice, but on their departure, a "horseman" followed, looked them over, and then rode past, presumably to warn others. They escaped "ill usage" by altering their route, but barely escaped even so. After returning to Boston, they received a communication from their host in Marlborough, who said that the "Committee of Correspondence" had come to his house immediately after they left. They had searched it "from top to bottom, looked under the beds, and in their cellars, and when they found we were gone, they told him if they had caught us in his house they would have pulled it about his ears." If two men traveling incognito were so easily discovered, Gage must have grasped that an army would be, too. There could be no surprise attack.[18]

Brown and De Berniere produced sketches for a fortress and encampment on Worcester's Chandler Hill, a location that was conceivably defensible, but thousands upon thousands of insurgents could besiege supply trains heading there, and that alone might spell defeat. Even though an informer embedded within the Provincial Congress revealed on March 8 that "the greatest magazine of provisions and ammunition is at Worcester," and even though, three days later, a report written in French said that Worcester housed fifteen tons of powder, thirteen small cannons by the meetinghouse, and smaller arms in the homes of merchant Stephen Salisbury and "un grand Chef" named Bigelow, Gage apparently took Worcester off the table.[19]

The other main storehouse of rebel arms and supplies was at Concord. On March 9 Gage received a report, again written in French, that detailed the quantity and whereabouts of military wares and provisions housed in that town: four brass cannon stored "chez Monsr. Barret" (James Barrett), several iron cannon of various calibers, an unspecified quantity "des Fusils et autres armes a feu" (rifles and other firearms, some with "Bayonets"), seven tons of "poudre a feu" (gunpowder), one hundred barrels of flour, and a considerable quantity of lard. Seizing any significant portion of these would impact the military effectiveness of the rebels and perhaps weaken their resolve, Gage reasoned.[20]

On March 20, Gage dispatched Brown and De Berniere to Concord. They were to "examine the road and situation of that town" and "to get what information we could relative to what quantity of artillery and provisions" that might be seized. The spies' report this time was short and to the point. Hidden in the woods outside of town were ten iron cannons, poorly mounted, and four valuable brass cannons, possibly the ones smuggled out of Boston the previous fall. Also in Concord was "a store of flour, fish, salt and rice; and a magazine of powder and cartridges." As Brown and De Berniere were returning to Boston, a friendly countryman showed them an alternate route from Boston to Concord that passed through Lexington. It was shorter than the most frequently traveled road, and, with the exception of a single "bad place," in very good condition—obviously a preferable route.[21]

By the last week of March, Gage was at least leaning toward

Concord, and he might even have settled on it. Fortuitously, that town was also hosting the Provincial Congress, which had reconvened on March 22. Not only could his troops disrupt the burgeoning rebel military, but they could also wreak havoc on the upstart pseudogovernment.

Rebels easily surmised that Gage would target Concord. The committee of safety, in preparation, ordered the removal of "all the Cannon Stores &c. from Concord to the Town of Leicester," a spy reported on March 26. The committee's intent at that point was to secure the stores from British troops, but in time members changed their minds, thinking that cannons could be useful in defending the entire cache. On April 14 they ordered that Concord's cannons remain hidden nearby and that the "cannon powder now at Leicester [in Worcester County] be removed, one load at a time, to this town [Concord], and made into cartridges." With the location of arms, powder, and food in constant flux, who knew where the goods would be if and when rebels needed them or British Regulars attempted to capture them.[22]

Concord's Reverend Emerson felt a conflagration was at hand and tried as best he could to prepare the men in his congregation. "In all Probability you will be called to real Service," he warned. "The clouds hang thick over our Heads. Indications of an approaching Storm of War and Bloodshed." Like many New England ministers, Emerson regarded royal transgressions as sin and railed against them. Concord's militiamen would not "be innocent and stand unconvicted in the Eye of Heaven . . . if you dropped your Weapons and submitted to the late Bill for the Alteration of our Constitution," he told them. "Arise my injured Countrymen, and plead with your Arms, the Birthright of Englishmen the dearly purchased Legacy left by your never to be forgotten Ancestors." That legacy meant much to Emerson, a fifth-generation colonist and the twelfth of thirteen children. Two generations later, Ralph Waldo Emerson, William's grandson, would coin the phrase "the shot heard round the world."[23]

Even Emerson, however, insisted that the patriots apply restraint: "But then, let me drop this one Word—Let every single Step taken in this most intricate Affair, be upon the Defensive. God Forbid that we should give our Enemies the Opportunity of saying justly that we have brought a civil War upon ourselves, by the smallest offensive Action." Only if the enemy attacked could they engage. It was a moral matter, preached by ministers everywhere, and, politically, a pragmatic consideration.[24]

Emerson did not sermonize lightly. He would follow men into the field after war broke out, serving as chaplain to troops. Two years later he wrote to his wife of the "seasoning of new Soldiers" and of camp disease that "strikes at the very Life and Spirit of a Soldier," revealing that he himself was now beset by a "mongrel Feaver & Ague." By September William Emerson was so ill that he resigned as chaplain and was unable to travel. On the 23rd of the month, in another of his continual letters home, he told his wife, "I desire to leave You and our dear little Ones, to a kind and gracious Providence." Four weeks later, at age thirty-three, he died.[25]

Although provincials could now establish, with reasonable certainty, *where* Gage would attack, they still had no idea *when* he would. On March 14, the committee of safety told its members from Charlestown, Cambridge, and Roxbury, the towns rimming Boston, to "procure at least two men for a watch every night." Watches were also to be "kept constantly at places where the provincial magazines are kept." If watchmen detected "sallies" out of Boston by British troops, committee members would "send couriers forward to the towns where the magazines are placed." Any five members of the eleven-man committee of safety were empowered by the Provincial Congress "to alarm, muster and cause to be assembled, with the utmost expedition, and completely armed, accoutred, and supplied with provisions . . . so many of the militia of this province, as they shall judge necessary."[26]

That five men could instigate a war troubled some delegates. Joseph Hawley, who had broken from fellow "river gods" in Hampshire County and supported resistance, argued, "If we, by order of our committee of safety, should begin the attack, and so bring on hostilities before the general express consent of the colonies that hostilities are altogether unavoidable, . . . I conceive . . . that the other governments will say, that we have unnecessarily and madly plunged into war, and therefore, must get out of the scrape as we can, and we shall have no other aid from them." He perceived a "danger" that "our people," once mustered, would "rashly and headily rush into hostilities before they can be upheld and supported." That had been the constant refrain in September and October when men like Samuel Adams and John Adams warned against Massachusetts becoming the aggressor.[27]

While moderates balked, radicals worried that the militia, seeing no action, were showing signs of internal dissent. "Ambitious men" were "Indeavouring to Break our Companys to pieces in order to get Promotion," Ephraim Doolittle, who was working closely with Timothy Bigelow, protested to the Provincial Congress. "A Number of Companys in my Regiment are now in such Circumstances and I fear if we are not soon Called to action we shall be Like a Rope of Sand and have no more Strength."[28]

With little to do, equally restless British soldiers in Boston began to "behave more like a parcel of children, of late, than men," John Andrews reported. One Sunday, outside a meetinghouse, "An officer, with men from the 4th Regiment in Barracks at West Boston, erected a couple of tents . . . and conducted a parcel of fifes and drums there, which play'd and beat Yankee Doodle the whole forenoon service time, to the great interruption of the congregation." This taunting band vowed to repeat the performance during afternoon service, but Gage shut it down. At Old

South Meeting House, an army captain heckled Joseph Warren, who was delivering the annual oration on the anniversary of the Boston Massacre, but the captain was heckled in turn when a woman "attack'd him and threatened to wring his nose." A group of officers, mimicking Warren's oration, put on a farcical skit on King Street that "contain'd the most scurrilous abuse upon the characters of the principal patriots here," but again Gage ordered them to desist.[29]

Boston's citizenry, in Gage's thinking, was as continually vexed as the woman who assailed the army captain. They were as easily affronted, as quick to react, and as oblivious to rank and authority. He feared that any prank or jibe might set off the multitudes in this town, so he reined in his men. They bridled. "The officers and soldiers are a good deal disaffected towards the Governor," Andrews wrote. "Thinking, I suppose, that he is partial to the inhabitants," they started calling him "*Old Woman*."[30]

In truth, as the winter's waiting game drew to a close, Gage had good reason to curb his soldiers while placating Boston's inhabitants. As he prepared for an assault, he saw provincials for what they now were, near enemies, and he guessed that, very probably, war was at hand. The Crown would order it. Acting for the Crown, he would unleash it. Until that precise moment, he must restrain these people and his own.

12

MASSACHUSETTS:
SIXTEEN DAYS

After six weeks at sea, the schooner *Hawke* set anchor in the port of Marblehead on April 2, 1775. On board as a passenger was John Davis, a ship captain from Boston, who carried with him a "London Print of the 11th of February." Without delay, Davis delivered his paper to Benjamin Edes and John Gill, publishers of the *Boston Gazette*. Type was set through the night, and the next day the *Gazette* published breaking news: King George III had dispatched four additional regiments from Ireland to help suppress the insurrection in Massachusetts. Further, to counter the Continental Congress's ban on trade with Britain, Lord North, on behalf of the king, had asked Parliament to prohibit New England from trading with any country *but* "Great Britain, Ireland, or the West-Indies." As a final blow, North proposed to close Newfoundland's vast fisheries to New Englanders. To support these restrictions, the Crown would send a "proper number of frigates" and two thousand seamen to assist the Royal Navy in America. Taken together, these new measures put more soldiers on the ground and more sailors and ships on the seas. "We are no longer at a loss what is intended us by our dear Mother," James Warren wrote to his wife, Mercy. "We have ask'd for bread and she gives us a stone, and a serpent for a fish."[1]

More than two weeks before Paul Revere's celebrated ride, another galloper appeared in Concord announcing the imminent troop arrivals. Fact and rumor mixed as usual, and on April 3, Reverend William Emerson recorded exaggerated totals in his diary: "This month is ushered in with the alarming News of 15 Regiments more of british Troops, on their Way to Boston which with 11 already in the Town would amount to 10,000." General Gage would in reality command two thousand additional soldiers, expanding the size of the Boston garrison to almost seven thousand.[2]

The Provincial Congress, which had reconvened in Concord on March 22, immediately instructed the committee of the state of the province "to collect all the late intelligence from Great Britain relative to their sending reenforcement to General Gage." It also dispatched express riders to call in delegates from outlying counties who had not yet showed up. Off they rode to Worcester, Hampshire, and Berkshire in the west, to Bristol in the south, and to Essex in the northeast. Meanwhile, post riders carried the news to neighboring colonies. While it had taken six weeks for the London paper to make its way to Boston, it took only one day for the *Boston Gazette* to travel to New Haven, Connecticut. There, on April 4, Ezra Stiles, president of Yale College, wrote of his town's response in his diary: "In general the Friends of Liberty are hereby exasperated & declare themselves ready for the Combat, & nothing is now talked of but immediately forming an American Army at Worcester & taking the Field with undaunted Resolution."[3]

Though many, undaunted, wanted to take to the field immediately, others clung to what were by now time-honored reservations. One of Governor Gage's spies—likely Benjamin Church, since he was fully cognizant of the inner workings of the Provincial Congress—reported that "the people without doors are clamorous for an immediate commencement of hostilities but the moderate thinking people within wish to ward off that period till hostilities shall commence on the part of Government which would prevent their being censured for their rashness by the other Colonies." If censure was at issue, so too was dread of war and of all that war entailed. Delegates from coastal towns like Salem feared that seaports would be "burnt and plundered," the agent said.[4]

Although most did not want the province to initiate war, another course of action that had been defeated repeatedly found new purchase: turning the network of militia into an actual army. According to Gage's well-placed informer, "several members" from inland communities were "positively required by their Constituents to urge the immediate raising of an army." Again, the West led the way while the East moved cautiously. "Upon the whole a spirit of irresolution appears throughout all their transactions," the spy concluded.[5]

Radical delegates ceded to moderates only slightly. On April 5 the body resolved that since "the great law of self-preservation may suddenly require our raising and keeping an army of observation and defence," it would elucidate fifty-three "articles, rules, and regulations" for the army that "may be raised." Moderates, who now fought a rearguard action, inserted the qualifiers—" 'may' suddenly require" and " 'may' be raised." Technically, the army was hypothetical, its sole assignment "observation and defence," but radicals didn't quibble. They held a winning hand and knew it. Across Massachusetts, militia were at this point well armed, provisioned, trained, and properly structured. At the first sounding of an alarm they would be fully operational, and in that moment the province would task itself, according to the agreed-upon provisions, with "Keeping an army." An army so kept was a standing army—and that had been the radicals' objective for months.[6]

In its detailed rules and regulations, the Provincial Congress insisted on the strict behavior of the men who would soon take to the field. They were not to transgress devotional norms, as soldiers often were inclined to do, or belittle military discipline, as freeholders and autonomous commoners might be tempted to do. They must "diligently frequent divine service and sermon." Any commissioned officer "found drunk upon his guard, or other duty under arms" would "be cashiered for it." Any officer or soldier "who shall shamefully abandon any post committed to his charge, or induce others to do the like, in time of engagement, shall suffer death immediately."[7]

Politically on the defensive, moderates still hoped to delay a direct confrontation with British Regulars. Asserting that delegates must consult their constituents before committing blood and treasure to the cause, they pushed for a recess. Here was an argument they could win. Delegates could hardly refute a request couched in democratic terms like these, no matter their political persuasions.

Indirectly, Governor Gage might have played a role in securing a recess. On April 7 the congress appointed Dr. Joseph Warren and Dr. Benjamin Church to its critical committee on the state of the province, which drafted key resolutions, such as the rules and regulations for the army. Shortly after, Gage received a curious report from an inside informant. Some delegates called for the "immediate raising of an Army," the spy reported, but others favored "a recess to consult their Constituents." In his estimate, the second option, by buying time, would provide the opportunity for a decisive British strike: "A sudden blow struck now or immediately on the arrival of the reinforcements from England should they come within a fortnight would oversett all their plans." The agent then stated, "A recess at this time could be easily brought about" and asked for "the Genl. [General's] opinion and his directions to act." Only a man of great influence within the congress could claim such influence over its proceedings. It was later revealed that Dr. Church was an informant for Gage, and it is likely that Gage did tell Church to push for a delay.[8]

Delegates would not recess, however, until April 15. Understanding that an attack was imminent, they needed first to conclude critical business. On April 8, the committee on the state of the province submitted a sweeping resolution:

> *Resolved,* That the present dangerous and alarming situation of our public affairs, renders it necessary for this colony to make preparations for their security and defence, by raising and establishing an army, and that delegates be appointed forthwith to repair to Connecticut, Rhode Island and New-Hampshire, informing them that we are contemplating upon, and are determined to take effectual measures for that purpose; and for the more effective security of the New England colonies and the continent, to request them to co-operate with us, by furnishing their respective quotas for general defence.

Gone was the word "may," which moderates had inserted in the April 5 resolution. Instead, an army was "necessary." If radicals managed to carry this resolution in the Body of the Whole, a standing army would appear in all of New England, not only in Massachusetts. According to Gage's informer, most delegates had come to believe "that the N. England Colonies are of themselves sufficiently populous to raise an Army superior to any that G.B. can send against them." The Provincial Congress determined that Massachusetts could contribute eight thousand soldiers, Connecticut and New Hampshire three thousand each, and Rhode Island two thousand.[9]

Despite their apprehension, moderates did not dare to oppose the recommendations and appear unpatriotic. Ninety-six of the 103 members present voted to create a New England army. The congress then dispatched Timothy Danielson to Connecticut, Elbridge Gerry to New Hampshire, and James Warren to Rhode Island to seek the approval of these colonies and request their support.[10]

At this juncture, on April 12, the Provincial Congress also decided to "check on the state of the conduct of the towns and districts with respect to their having executed the continental and provincial plans." Each town was expected to enforce the Association initiated by the Continental Congress, arm and train its minutemen, and pay tax monies into "the public treasury of the colony" to support the emerging army. "Whereas some towns and districts in this colony may be destitute of so excellent an institution as committees of correspondence," the congress stated, those with no committees should immediately form them. Originally appendages to the town meetings, the committees of correspondence were to assume oversight of local governments. If they discovered any "neglect," dereliction of duty should be "speedily and effectually remedied." To ensure compliance, local committees would report to a newly created committee of correspondence for each county, and these, in turn, "are hereby required to render their account quarterly, to this Congress." "Required" meant that towns and local committees were answerable to a higher authority. Technically, the Provincial Congress did not declare itself to be a true government, but it talked like a government and acted like a government.[11]

The following day, returning to military concerns, the congress created six artillery companies that were to "constantly be in readiness to enter the service of the colony, when an army shall be raised." Again, "when" was replacing "if" or "may" in the congressional lexicon. These artillerymen answered directly to the province and would be paid, as soldiers were in any professional army.[12]

The day after that, the congress opened the application process for field officers. These, once selected, would in turn work with a committee to select "such subaltern officers, as may be necessary for each regiment, when an army shall be raised." All armies seek officers, but in this one, "preference" was to be given "to persons who have been chosen officers in the regiments of minute men."

If, in Britain, well-connected functionaries looked to pools of well-connected gentry like themselves when foraging for officers, in Massachusetts candidates were to be vetted from below by the minutemen they led.[13]

Also on April 14, with a climax looming, the Massachusetts Provincial Congress took stock of "warlike stores" amassed over the previous half year. In the province's armory were 21,549 "firearms," 10,108 bayonets, 17,444 pounds of powder, and 22,101 pounds of lead balls. In addition, towns had stockpiled 66,781 pounds of lead balls and 357 barrels of powder. Provincial and town stocks included almost a quarter million flints. (The report did not list artillery, much of which was sequestered in hidden locations.)[14]

By the time the Provincial Congress finally adjourned on April 15, civil, military, and informational infrastructures were in place or in the works. Towns were at the ready. Other New England colonies were being recruited. Military stores were at hand, but stored in diverse locations to ensure against all-embracing seizure. Last, "considering the great uncertainty of the present times, and that important unforeseen events may take place, from whence it may be absolutely necessary that this Congress should meet sooner than the day above said [May 10]," members from Charlestown, Cambridge, Brookline, Roxbury, and Dorchester—the communities rimming Boston—would keep watch and would reconvene the body immediately "in case they should judge it necessary." If Regulars went on the march during the recess, congressional delegates from the rest of the province would at once be instructed to return.[15]

With communities on edge, residents had been keeping watch for weeks. On March 27 William Emerson stated in his diary, "Greatly alarmed by a Report that 1200 of the Troops were on their march out of Boston. Under apprehension coming to

Concord." What triggered that report remains a mystery, but three days later, at dawn, the first brigade of General Gage's army crossed the Boston Neck. This procession "excited the Curiosity of some and the fear of Others," Samuel Swift reported to John Adams. "Our worthy fellow Citizen Paul Revere was posted away it is said to Concord—&c." The soldiers in this instance had no direct military target. Perhaps Gage ordered the maneuver to create a decoy so any upcoming, genuine expedition would not excite much notice. In any case, troops returned to Boston by ten that morning after marching without purpose. In mocking tones, Swift pointed out that they had only made a spectacle of themselves: "They marched it seems as far as Jamaica-plain, and there the light Infantry display'd their Military Genius to the Admiration of Stumps and Alderbushes, . . . manfully lay'd Siege to a Certain Swamp, Surrounding the Same, [and] traversed all the Thickets, swamps, meadows and deserts between Jamaica plain and . . . the Tavern at Roxbury."[16]

On April 7 Boston activists noted inordinate activity in the harbor, which meant, they guessed, that preparations were under way for the expected assault. Dr. Warren, often the one to dispatch messengers when Boston's committee of correspondence sensed danger, sent Paul Revere to Concord for a second time. "There came up a post to Concord [on] Saturday night [April 8] which informs that the regulars are coming up to Concord the next day," Jonathan Hosmer, a local resident, wrote. No one was surprised. "We daily expect a Tumult," Hosmer said. "If they come I believe there will be bloody work." Two days earlier, James Warren, who was attending the Provincial Congress, had informed his wife, Mercy Otis Warren: "This town [Concord] is full of cannon, ammunition, stores, etc., and the [British] Army long for them and they want nothing but strength to induce an attempt on them. The people are ready and determine to defend this country inch by inch."[17]

Within Boston, resistance leaders known to British authorities feared they might soon be arrested. "The Inhabitants of Boston are on the move," James Warren wrote on April 7. "H [John Hancock] and A [Samuel Adams] go no more into that Garrison." Hancock's "female Connections," Warren continued, had left Boston that morning, and Adams's family was to follow shortly.[18]

The thought of impending conflict terrified Bostonians. If British troops set upon the countryside, provincials might fire on the British garrison and turn their town into a battlefield. Residents fled in droves, taking what they could and locking up what they left, even if no barred door or window could deter rampaging British soldiers who sought entry. On April 10 a Boston newspaper reported, "A number of Families are moving themselves and their most valuable Effects from this Town into the Country, in Consequence of the late Advices from England." The following day Boston merchant John Andrews noted "the streets and neck lin'd with waggons carrying off the effects of the inhabitants . . . imagining to themselves that they shall be liable to every evil that can be enumerated, if they tarry in town." Four days later, the Provincial Congress recommended that donations intended for relief of the poor in Boston be used to help evacuate Boston.[19]

By mid-April, on the seaward side of the Neck, Boston was largely populated by soldiers in red uniforms who were much on their guard and friends of government who sought their protection. Transient sailors wandered the half-deserted streets. Inside houses, some still prepared to go or had nowhere to go or were simply unsure and waited to see what might befall them. Others determined to stay. Reverend Andrew Eliot, having sent away his eight children and his wife, was set on remaining to minister and preach. A few resolute activists, no matter the personal risk, lingered to keep a close eye on British movements.[20]

As tension intensified, General Gage awaited instructions. Lord Dartmouth's letter containing them had been sent from London on January 27, but in that bitterly cold winter, ice in the waters kept ships in harbor for weeks. The original did not arrive until April 16, although two days earlier Gage perused a facsimile. Dispatched on February 22, that copy had overtaken the original.[21]

Gage could not have been happy reading one ill-informed line after the next. Dartmouth told Gage that he could thwart the rebellion by simply arresting the "principal actors and abbettors"—the rest, he said, were no more than "a tumultuous Rabble, without any appearance of general Concert, or without any Head to advise, or Leader to conduct." Seizing the leaders could "hardly fail of Success, and will perhaps be accomplished without bloodshed. . . . Any efforts of the People, unprepared to encounter with a regular force, cannot be very formidable." In a self-assured and accusatory tone, Dartmouth not only instructed the governor but censured him: "I have already said, in more Letters than one, that the Authority of this Kingdom must be supported, & the Execution of its Laws inforced. . . . The King's Dignity, & the Honor and Safety of the Empire, require that, in such a Situation, Force should be repelled by Force." Yet instead of applying force, Gage had requested twenty thousand additional troops, whose deployment to Boston would only weaken the empire elsewhere. By gathering soldiers that could be spared "from other parts of America," Gage should already have almost four thousand "effective Men" at his command. The exasperated secretary was "unwilling to believe" that with these men, and the few regiments he was sending, the governor could not suppress a colonial revolt.[22]

However harsh, Dartmouth concluded his letter with a caveat: "the Expedience and Propriety of adopting such a Measure must depend upon your own Discretion under many Circumstances that can only be judged of upon the Spot." This disclaimer shifted all accountability to Gage should the plan fail, but, on the other hand, it gave him room to maneuver, and he did. He decided not to arrest rebel leaders, which in his view would do very little to hinder the pervasive, firmly entrenched uprising. Instead, since he must act, he would seize their arms, hampering their defensive capabilities and, perhaps, their offensive schemes.

Just hours after the Provincial Congress had recessed in Concord on April 15, General Gage sent out orders. His grenadier and light infantry companies were to be relieved of their normal duties so they might learn "new evolutions"—or drill routines. Neither British soldiers nor observant civilians accepted the cover story. "This I suppose is by way of a blind," Lieutenant John Barker of the Fourth Regiment wrote in his diary. "I dare say they have something for them to do." Merchant John Andrews reported, "Orders were sent to the several regiments quartered here not to let their Grenadiers or Light Infantry do any duty till further orders, upon which the inhabitants conjectured that some secret expedition was on foot."[23]

The following morning, April 16, Paul Revere made a third ride westward, this time to confer with Samuel Adams and John Hancock in Lexington. An assault was at hand, a plan necessary. Returning, Revere stopped in Cambridge and at Charlestown to consult with local committees and fine tune an intelligence and communication network that had been in place since March 14, its lines stretching from the towns neighboring Boston to those far distant that stockpiled arms and provisions. In Charlestown, Revere and his comrades settled on a legendary scheme. Nightly, a watchman on the Charlestown shore would fix his eyes on the steeple of Boston's North Church. If he spotted the light of a single lantern in the tower, the Regulars were leaving town by the Boston Neck, but if he saw two, they were preparing to cross the Charles River.[24]

That same evening, other men engineered a covert enterprise that was critical to the rebellion. War was fought with firearms, but also with words, and printing presses were as prized as cannon. Presses were few in number, and at this point, if a press was in rebel hands it was in jeopardy. One such piece of machinery belonged to Isaiah Thomas, the radical publisher of the *Massachusetts Spy*, and rumor had it that the British would come for it at any moment. Patriots resolved to transport the machinery from Boston to a place of safety.

Not surprisingly, the intrepid Timothy Bigelow took command of the clandestine operation. He was returning to Worcester from the Provincial Congress and offered to take the press to a safe haven there: his own home, which already storehoused some of the Provincial Congress's military wares. Bigelow and a handful of cohorts first broke the bulky wooden machine into its separate components—the large hunks of elm, white oak, and chestnut that constituted the body itself, and the carriage, plank, coffin, cheeks, cap, head, winter, and so on. They piled these into a wagon, together with several cases of heavy lead type and a massive stone table on which type was laid out. In the end, the load resembled a printing press very little, and nobody was likely to immediately identify it. At a landing along the Charles, the smugglers transferred their weighty cargo onto a vessel that carried it across the river. Watchmen aboard HMS *Somerset*, placed strategically in the Charles to interfere with the movement of arms, had no idea that a printing press floated by them. Less than three weeks later, Thomas's press would print the Provincial Congress's official narrative of events at Lexington and Concord.[25]

The following morning, April 17, while the Provincial Congress was recessed, the committees of safety and supplies met in Concord. Those present sent an urgent summons to Timothy Bigelow, who was heading toward Worcester, forty miles distant, and much occupied with the rescue of the printing press. He was to return by April 19 to confer "on business of great importance." Bigelow was coordinating the mobilization of the western counties and was also in charge of Worcester County's newly authorized artillery company. The "business of great importance" concerned both mobilization and artillery, and he was needed on both counts. The committees were considering whether the cannon at Concord should be mounted and whether artillery companies who had not yet been trained should actually use the weaponry. Instead of keeping the deadly guns in or near Concord, where they could be quickly activated, might it be better to remove them to a remote and safe site? In the end, the committees ordered that "four six pounders" be sent to Groton and "two seven inch brass mortars" to Acton, but also that "two four pounders" be mounted in Concord. They charged Colonel James Barrett, who had been storing cannons at his Concord farm, to form a seventh artillery unit there.[26]

Unable to finalize a coordinated plan, committee members reconvened the next morning at the Black Horse Tavern in Menotomy (now Arlington). They conducted their business at a breakneck pace, suspecting that a British incursion was almost upon them. Four days earlier, the committees had ordered that all the cannon powder stored at Leicester, in Worcester County, be "made into cartridges" and shipped to Concord to supply its cannons. Now, the committees reversed that call: "Voted, that the vote of the fourteenth instant, relating to powder being removed from Leicester to Concord, be reconsidered, and that the clerk be directed to write to Col. Barrett, accordingly, and to desire he would not proceed in making it up into cartridges." They feared that makeshift artillery companies, such as Barrett's, might perform poorly and hamper the movements of minutemen. Instead, they would secure the cannon so they could be used at a later date.[27]

To confuse and confound British troops, the committees continued to shuffle their stores. Cannon that belonged to the province, along with shot and powder, were apportioned between Worcester, Concord, Stow, and Lancaster. Ammunition was divided among nine towns: Worcester, Lancaster, Concord, Groton, Stoughtonham, Stow, Mendon, Leicester, and Sudbury. Precise quantities of cannonballs and grapeshot were moved from Stoughtonham, well south of Boston, to Sudbury, closer

to Concord and accessible in case of sustained conflict. The vast
quantities of supplies in Worcester would stay where they were,
safe from British hands, but two-thirds of Concord's "spades,
pick-axes, bill hooks, shovels, axes, hatchets, crows, and wheelbarrows" were transferred to nearby Stow and Sudbury. Concord would also release fifty barrels of beef, one hundred barrels
of flour, twenty casks of rice, fifteen hogsheads of molasses, ten
hogsheads of rum, and five hundred candles to Sudbury. And so
it went—pots, bowls, and canteens were dispersed. Tents were
divied up "in equal parts in Worcester, Lancaster, Groton, Stow,
Mendon, Leicester, and Sudbury," which meant, as is evident
when the towns are plotted on a map, that minutemen coming to
Concord from anywhere in central and western Massachusetts
could find shelter. Rebels also could stage defensive operations in
base camps on these same routes if British Regulars invaded the
interior.[28]

All this was dictated in exact detail on a single day, the coop-
erative effort of committee members appointed by the Provincial Congress, an elective body. Lord Dartmouth could scarcely
have imagined this, accustomed as he was to military strategizing
being the sole province of decisive military commanders. He had
assured Gage that there could be no "general Concert" among the
insurgents "without any Head to advise, or Leader to conduct."
The Crown faced an enemy it simply could not envision and one
that accomplished much before the sun set on April 18. Yet there
was much left to do. The committees agreed to convene the following morning at 9:00, an hour earlier than usual. Gage might
advance on Concord any day.

Any day turned out to be that very day. Two members—Richard
Devens of Charlestown and Abraham Watson of Cambridge—
suspected as much soon after leaving the meeting. "Mr. Watson
and myself came off in my chaise at sunset," Devens reported.

"On the road we met a great number of B.O. [British officers] and their servants on horseback." Devens and Watson quickly returned to the Black Horse Tavern, where the delegation from Marblehead—Elbridge Gerry, Azor Orne, and Jeremiah Lee—was lodging for the evening. After a brief consultation, Gerry penned a short note to warn Samuel Adams and John Hancock that a contingent of officers was headed their way. When that message reached Lexington around 8:00 that evening, some militiamen collected at Buckman's Tavern to await further developments while others gathered around the home of the minister Jonas Clarke, where Hancock and Adams were staying. "It was suspected they [the officers] were out upon some evil design," Clarke later recalled.[29]

And there *was* a British design. Early that afternoon, an unusually high number of British seamen descended from their ships to the Boston waterfront. In a stable nearby, a hostler overheard officers whispering of plans as they prepared their horses for riding, unable to contain their excitement. Later in the afternoon, a light infantryman was spotted "with his accoutrements on." By early evening, when alert civilians saw that longboats utilized for transporting troops were floating in the bay by the HMS *Boyne*, they realized that the Regulars would march that night. Lieutenant Frederick Mackenzie, adjutant for the Twenty-Third Royal Welsh Fusiliers, noted in his diary that night: "The town was a good deal agitated and alarmed at this Movement, as it was pretty generally known, by means of the Seamen who came on shore from the Ships, about 2 O'Clock, that the boats were ordered to be in readiness."[30]

Gage suspected that adversaries in Boston would take notice and try to alert the countryside. "To stop all advice" of the expedition from reaching Concord, he ordered twenty officers to patrol the roads and halt horsemen at points not easily circumvented.[31]

At around 8:00, as militiamen started to gather in Lexington, patriots in Boston observed that troops were gathering on the shore of the Charles River in Back Bay. Joseph Warren orchestrated yet another alarm. Paul Revere, one of the riders Warren hurriedly called into service that night, later recalled that he was "to go to Lexington, and inform Mr. Samuel Adams, and the Hon. John Hancock Esq. that there was a number of Soldiers, composed of Light troops, & Grenadiers, marching to the bottom of the Common, where there was a number of Boats to receive them; it was supposed that they were going to Lexington, by the way of Cambridge River, to take them, or go to Concord, to destroy the Colony Stores."[32]

The alarm traveled several pathways, the first by line of sight. The young sexton of North Church, Robert Newman, aided by two friends, lit two lanterns. The prearranged signal indicated that Regulars would cross the Charles River and march to Concord along the road leading through Menotomy and Lexington. Immediately Richard Devens, one of a multitude of the night's conspirators, dispatched a rider with the warning, but that is where this story ends. Perhaps British officers detained this man, whose identity is unknown, for there is no record that this express reached Lexington or Concord.

William Dawes carried the message by land, heading south over the Boston Neck before looping back to the northwest. By some combination of stealth, luck, and British negligence, he managed to elude Gage's patrols and make it all the way to Lexington.

Taking a more direct route, Revere boarded a small boat on a North End shore and slipped past the HMS *Somerset*, anchored in the Charles River. At Charlestown he disembarked, mounted a horse, and charged off toward Cambridge. The committee of safety's Richard Devens, who helped to procure Revere's horse, had warned him of British patrols, and before Revere even reached Cambridge two of the officers Gage had dispatched tried to stop him. The messenger eluded his would-be captors by detouring on a network of roads familiar to him and "proceeded to Lexington, through Mistick, and alarmed Mr. Adams and Col. Hancock," as he stated in a deposition taken a few days later. This was all Revere said at the time about the "Midnight Ride" that Henry Wadsworth Longfellow would immortalize eighty-five years later. Although Longfellow had Revere warning "every Middlesex village and farm," the famed rider never did reach Concord, his destination and the seat of government for Middlesex County. British officers captured both Revere and Dawes on the final leg of their course, as well as a rider who had joined them, Dr. Samuel Prescott. It was Prescott who escaped and reached Concord with the warning.[33]

Whatever happened to any single rider was immaterial, however. Once alerted by Revere or any other, towns sent out gallopers of their own, who tore along the crisscrossing roads to other towns that in turn unleashed riders. Some crossed the borders of Massachusetts and entered other colonies. Like Revere, they had no interest in single farms; instead they activated a network many months in the making, seeking out foremost men in the committees of correspondence, who knew exactly what to do. Nothing done was single or solitary; all was the work of congregate townspeople and committees and militia. Everything occurred within an ever-expanding matrix. A flaming bonfire on a hill set another aflame; each sounding bell caused another to sound.[34]

Alerted, militia everywhere mustered at meetinghouses, on town commons, or at any prearranged "alarm post." Afterward, men recounted how they had immediately taken up arms that they had kept close at hand for months, anticipating this moment. They jammed personal essentials into knapsacks. Wives packed in biscuits and dried beef and filled canteens and watched them go, just as for months they had imagined them going. Militia had ready access to weaponry collected over weeks and months. They set out on routes that men had selected in advance.

All had geared up for an engagement, but before this night no man knew exactly when it would transpire. No man knew whether his militia company would face mobile troops, intent on a quick strike to seize weapons, or a sizable force armed with artillery that could level Concord or any other town. Most critically, no one knew beforehand how things would turn out. Would there be an actual battle or only a standoff? Would the encounter end in immediate defeat or mark the start of the civil war that Abigail Adams had forecast sixteen months earlier during the tea crisis? "The flame is kindled," she had written, "and like lightening it catches from soul to soul." She had imagined men spending their lives in the cause and heroes dying. This might be the work of a night or the work of years, no one knew. As prepared as they were, all were apprehensive.[35]

13

LEXINGTON AND CONCORD: WAR

G eneral Gage did not want to start a war. All along he had said that Britain could only conquer New England with a force of twenty thousand men, and even once his promised reinforcements arrived, the Boston garrison would have only one-third that number. Secretary of State Dartmouth said he should deploy this meager force in arresting the rebellion's leaders, but Gage knew that a handful of arrests would gain him little. Instead, as he had determined weeks earlier, he hoped to weaken the rebels' military capacity by seizing armaments and supplies in Concord.

Secrecy was key. Warned in time, rebels would remove their cache of weaponry and roust their own forces as they had during the Powder Alarm and, more recently, during Colonel Leslie's raid on Salem. Cognizant of these pitfalls, Gage took precautionary measures. An advance patrol would intercept messengers. Troops would make no moves until nighttime. They would not exit Boston in either of the usual manners—by land across the Neck or by water at the Charlestown Ferry. They would travel lightly, bearing haversacks for rations but no knapsacks. Unencumbered by any supply wagons, an elite corps of light infantry would lead the way.[1]

Gage supplied Lieutenant Colonel Francis Smith, the expedition's commander, with a map and an exacting list of weaponry, gleaned from intelligence reports that included the location of specific items:

Four Brass Cannon and two Mortars or Cohorns with a Number of small arms in the Cellar or out Houses of Mr. Barrett a little on the other side of the Bridge where is also lodged a Quantity of Powder & Lead.

Ten Iron Cannon before the Town-House and two within it which Town-House is in the Center of Town. The ammunition for said Guns within the House.

Three Guns 24 Pounders, lodged in the Prison yard with a Quantity of Cartridges and Provisions.

Several individuals housed additional ammunition and provisions, including "Mr. Whitneys who lives on the Right Hand near the Entrance of the Town, at a House plaistered white a small yard in Front and a railed Fence." Gage also told Smith how to deal with items his soldiers found:

You will seize and destroy all the Ammunition, Provision, Artillery, Tents, Small Arms, and all Military Stores whatever. . . . You will order a Trunion [the cylindrical projections on each side of a cannon that support it on its carriage] to be knocked off each Cut, but if it's found impracticable on any, they must be spiked, and the Carriages destroyed. The Powder and flower [flour], must be shook out of the Barrells into the River, the Tents burnt, Pork or Beef destroyed. . . . Men may put Balls or lead in their pockets, throwing them by degrees into Ponds, Ditches &c., but no Quantity together, so that they may be recovered afterwards. If you meet with any Brass Artillery, you will order their Muzzles to be beat in so as to render them useless.

It would be a search and destroy mission, but only that. "You will take care that the Soldiers do not plunder the Inhabitants, or hurt private property," Gage directed. "You will open your business, and return with the Troops, as soon as possible, which I must leave to your own Judgment and Discretion."[2]

At eight that evening, after sundown, General Gage ordered approximately eight hundred grenadiers, light infantry, and marines "to parade quietly at their respective Barracks, and to march to the place of Rendezvous in small parties," Lieutenant Frederick Mackenzie wrote in his diary. From Back Bay's isolated shore, at ten p.m., the first contingent clambered aboard longboats that sank dangerously low under their weight. Crossing the Charles was cumbersome and slow. Three or four boats were tied together so that no single one would be carried off in fast-moving tidal currents and lost in darkness. The boats wedged in place in the shallows of the bay in Cambridge at Lechmere Point, an uninhabited marsh. Scrambling off, the men found themselves in knee-high water. Chilled through, they made their way to what there was of a beach, near Phips's farm. Leaving them there, the longboats returned to Back Bay, where the remaining troops waited. The mile-long crossing needed repeating.[3]

It was midnight when the last of the soldiers stood on land, the grenadiers in their tall bearskin caps and splendidly adorned coats and the light infantry in black leather helmets, decked out with plumes or horsehair crests. They wore regalia, but muck spattered their white broadcloth breeches. The twenty-one companies, drawn from various regiments, had not drilled together or been told where they were off to or why, and even the junior officers were not briefed on the mission. They milled about, the scene confused, the moon bright overhead.

An hour passed as officers tried to muster their companies. Formed at long last into properly ordered regimental lines by Lieutenant Colonel Smith, the Regulars tramped across boggy ground that gave way at every step. Ooze clung to the heavy shoes they wore, the left a perfect replica of the right, and the two inter-changeable. They crossed beneath a bridge through the ice-cold waist-high water rather than over it, their commander having de-termined that marching feet on wooden planks would broadcast troop movements.[4]

At close to three o'clock in the morning, as the troops proceeded on their twenty-mile trek, they heard a perplexing noise, consid-ering the hour: gunshots. Soldiers surmised the reason for the shots. "The Country people began to fire their alarm guns [and] light their Beacons, to raise the Country," Ensign Jeremy Lister recounted. Lieutenant William Sutherland offered more detail. "We heared several shots being then between 3 & 4 in the Morn-ing (a very unusual time for firing)," he reported eight days after-ward to Gage's secretary. Shortly, a party of British soldiers on horseback sped toward them from the west, where the expedition was headed. These were some of the riders Gage had dispatched earlier in the day to intercept messengers. They had done this—in fact, they captured "Paul Revierre" on his way from Lexington to Concord—but to little avail. "The whole Country was alarmed," the officers reported. They had just "Galloped for their lives" to escape militiamen who were gathering in Lexington.[5]

The officers Gage dispatched to prevent an alarm had created one. The mounted riders whom Richard Devens and Abraham Watson noticed when leaving their meeting in Charlestown at sunset were heading westward, away from Boston, when nor-mally at that hour officers would be returning to their garrison. This irregularity triggered the note to Adams and Hancock, which arrived in Lexington two hours *before* the first wave of Smith's expedition embarked from Boston's Back Bay.[6]

Others also encountered British scouts. Three young residents of Lexington—Solomon Brown, Jonathan Loring, and Elijah Sanderson—testified to the Provincial Congress a week later that at around ten o'clock in the evening, on the road between Lex-ington and Concord, nine officers stopped them and kept them captive for four hours. In a deposition taken soon after, Paul Revere focused on his detention, when his life was threatened, but paid only scant attention to the ride that would make him famous.[7]

By 3:00 a.m. residents in Sudbury, ten miles southwest of Lexington, and Dracut, ten miles to the north, were put on their guard, and by 5:00 a.m. the eastern half of sprawling Middlesex County had been alerted. Lexington's John Parker, giving testimony to the congress, described his town's response to the alarm:[8]

> I, John Parker, of lawful Age, and Commander of the Militia in Lexington, do testify and declare, that on the 19th instant, in the morning about one of the clock, being informed there were a Number of Regular Officers, riding up and down the Road, stopping and insulting People as they passed the Road; and also was informed that a Number of Regular Troops were on their March from Boston in order to take the Province Stores at Concord, ordered our Militia to meet on the Common in said Lexington to consult what to do.[9]

Even under cover of darkness, eight hundred soldiers marching on a public road were bound to be discovered, and Gage's secret had become an open secret. All along their route, they attracted onlookers, whose memories are enfolded in rich country lore. Widow Elizabeth Rand left her house in a nightdress, thinking the noise of the soldiers was the noise of a thief trying to steal the butchered hog that hung in her yard, and she saw them. So did young men at cards, dairymen carrying fresh milk to market, an innkeeper, a wife who was up with a husband while he melted down the household pewter to make bullets—all told their stories over the years.[10]

The futile attempts at disguise came at great expense. The route Gage had chosen was perhaps the least visible but disastrous by any other measure. Time was squandered in the slow crossing of the Charles and during the confusion on landing at Lechmere Point. There were unwarranted hardships for troops, who were marched at a rapid clip to make up for the loss. A few exhausted soldiers broke from the line in search of wells and drinking water, having emptied their canteens close to the start. Sent ahead of the grenadiers to secure the two bridges in Concord, companies of light infantry were pressed particularly hard.

As the first wave of soldiers neared Lexington, they heard worrisome reports from travelers. "A very genteel man riding in a Carriage they call a Sulky assured me there were 600 men assembled at Lexington with a view of opposing us," Lieutenant Sutherland recalled. A little later, at the first signs of dawn, "some men with a Waggon of wood" told the Regulars "there were odds of 1000 men in Arms at Lexington & added they would fight us." Sutherland and a small party took the lead to scout. Moving ahead, Sutherland spotted "a vast number of the Country Militia going over the Hill with their Arms to Lexington." Within a thousand yards of the village, he and his men "saw shots fired to the right & left of us, but as we heard no Whissing of Balls I concluded they were to Alarm the body that was there of our Approach."[11]

Major John Pitcairn, who commanded the marines and light infantrymen in the lead contingent, did not anticipate such a response. He had stated in December, "I have so despicable opinion of the people in this country that I would not hesitate to march with the Marines I have with me to any part of the country, and do whatever I was inclined. I am satisfied they will never attack Regular troops." In March he called provincials "those foolish bad people," and said, "I am satisfied that one active campaign, a smart action, and burning two or three of their towns, will set everything to rights." Pitcairn now found himself in the advance of a "smart action," and his claim that country people would never attack Regulars would be put to the test.[12]

Lexington militiamen were better prepared than British officers had imagined. More than five months earlier, on November 10, the town meeting had met for the express purpose of deciding "what method the Town will take to promote Military Discipline and to put themselves in a posture of defence against their Enemies." The body determined that "defence" required armaments—two more "half Barrells of Powder," a "Sufficiency of Ball for Said Powder," and a "suitable Quantity of Flints . . . if there be found a deficiency." At its next meeting, on November 28, the town appropriated funds for buying and mounting two cannon, acquiring ammunition, and purchasing "a Pair of Drums for the use of the Alarm Band of this Town, and for the Carriage and Harness, for Burying the Dead." Practical-minded New Englanders considered every detail. Ironically, the town also voted "to have no Liberty Pole," deciding instead that "the Training Band and alarm," at their next drill, should take another survey of the town's usable "arms and ammunition." The time for symbolic gestures had passed.[13]

On the night of April 18, Lexington's militiamen knew the British troops would vastly outnumber their own. Jonas Clarke reported one year later that "1200 or 1500 was the number we then supposed the Brigade to consist of." Meanwhile, only about half of the 141 men listed on Lexington's militia roll were present on the Lexington common at dawn; militias elsewhere were either still mustering or on their way to Concord, the expected target of the British expedition. Captain Parker called militiamen together "to consult what to do," as he would soon testify. They could not prevail over such a formidable opponent, yet they refused to cower. According to Parker, they decided "not to meddle or make with said regular troops (if they should approach) unless they should insult or molest us," but at the same time they would take their stand on the town common, openly declaring themselves.[14]

On their heads were cocked or uncocked hats or caps. Dressed in everyday coats, waistcoats, and breeches, with neckerchiefs or neckstocks at the throat and socks that rode below the knee, they were entirely respectable, but no two men looked alike and they barely looked like soldiers. Assembled in formation, and each man armed, they waited for the meticulously uniformed redcoats who would pass Buckman's Tavern and the meetinghouse and see them.

What happened next remains unclear, shrouded by contradictory accounts. Many dozens were deposed in the immediate aftermath or interviewed decades later, when recollections were often less reliable, memory faltering. Even immediate reports varied as to the particulars, as naturally they might. In the chaos of battle, it isn't always possible to calculate the trajectory of bullets or accurately note the position of distant soldiers or their numbers.

One of the Lexington militiamen, John Robbins, gave his deposition five days after the engagement:

> I, John Robbins, being of lawful Age, do Testifye and say, that on the Nineteenth Instant, the Company . . . being drawn up (sometime before sun Rise) on the Green or Common, and I being in the front Rank, there suddenly appear'd a Number of the Kings troops, about a Thousand, as I thought, at the distance of about 60 or 70 yards from us Huzzaing, and on a quick pace towards us, with three Officers in their front on Horse Back, and on full Gallop towards us, the foremost of which cryed, throw down your Arms ye Villains, ye Rebels! Upon which said Company Dispersing, the foremost of the three Officers order'd their Men, saying, fire, by God, fire! At which Moment we received a very heavy and close fire from them, at which Instant, being wounded, I fell, and several of our men were shot Dead by one volley. Captain Parker's men I believe had not then fired a Gun. And further the Deponent saith not.[15]

Robbins's tally of the opposing force was too high—in fact, the lead contingent that had arrived in Lexington comprised fewer than three hundred men. Yet the miscalculation carried truth on its back. The soldiers were fearsome and the militiamen edgy, not knowing if this would be a standoff, as had happened before, or if the British would actually fire. Robbins's count was an accurate measure of the militiamen's apprehension.[16]

Militiamen and local onlookers agreed that British horsemen had opened fire. Thomas Fessenden, viewing the scene from a nearby pasture, stated that three officers on horseback charged toward the militiamen while yelling "Disperse, you Rebels, immediately." One "Brandished his sword over his head three times," another "fired a Pistol, pointed at said Militia," and finally "the Regulars fired a Volley at the Militia." Much later, in 1824, Elijah Sanderson stated that "the commander," who was Major Pitcairn, "said 'Fire!' and he fired his own pistol, and the other officers soon fired, and with that the main body came up and fired."[17]

Captain Parker, like the others, stated emphatically that the men in his company bore no blame. "Upon their sudden approach, I immediately ordered our militia to disperse and not to fire," he stated, yet the Regulars, "rushing furiously, fired upon us and killed eight of our party, without receiving any provocation therefor from us." Half a century later, more heroic renditions of Parker's orders appeared. He was made to say, "Stand your ground! Don't fire unless fired upon! But if they want to have a war let it begin here!" and "The first man who offers to run shall be shot down." Only in retrospect could people imagine that a militia captain in 1775, faced with insurmountable odds, would speak offhandedly of beginning a war or threaten to execute the men who had elected him. The concurrent record, including Parker's own rendition, is more credible.[18]

Not surprisingly, British accounts contradicted provincial accusations. They said that the first shot came from behind a hedge or from the meetinghouse at the edge of the common or from Buckman's Tavern or from nearby houses—testimony varying but all exonerating British soldiers and officers. Lieutenant Sutherland stated that "Gentlemen" faced "Villains" in Lexington, and, mirroring John Robbins, he exaggerated the enemy's numbers.

Perhaps he mistook onlookers for militiamen or had in mind the reports he received earlier that one thousand were mustering and ready to fight. Anxiety has a multiplier effect, and Sutherland, like Robbins, had reason to be anxious. Throughout the night he had marched deeper and deeper into hostile territory. Officers who disparaged provincials from a distance might still fear the unseen "Villains" who lurked in the woods throughout this unwelcoming countryside. When Sutherland came face-to-face with armed men in Lexington, seventy men may have seemed to be four hundred and more:

> When we came up to the main body which appeared to me to Exceed 400 in & about the Village who were drawn up in a plain opposite to the Church, several Officers Called out throw down your Arms & you shall come to no harm, or words to that Effect, which they refusing to do, instantaneously the Gentlemen who were on horseback rode in amongst them of which I was one, at which instant I heard Major Pitcairns voice Call out Soldiers dont fire, keep your Ranks, form & surround them, instantly some of the Villains who got over the hedge fired at us which our men for the first time returned.[19]

If testimony was inconsistent, the facts were not. Seven militiamen died running, as did a Woburn man the patriots had captured, the eighth victim. Two lay where the company had stood, one pierced by a bayonet; the others were shot while dispersing. Nine were wounded. Spectators who had come to the common fled. British soldiers, momentarily under nobody's command but their own, fired in one direction or another and charged toward houses or Buckman's Tavern and the meetinghouse, where powder they knew nothing about was stored in a loft.

Only the arrival of Lieutenant Colonel Francis Smith with the main body of the troops ended the melee. Perhaps Smith had in mind General Gage's directive not "to plunder the inhabitants, or hurt private property." In Lexington Smith saw much worse, the bodies of provincials lying on the field and his own rampaging troops. The light infantry, he noted, were "much enraged at the treatment they had received and having been Fired on from the Houses, were going to Break them open and come at those within." If that continued, "none within could well be saved" and he would be held responsible. Immediately Smith put a "stop to all further Slaughter of those deluded People." Perhaps reluctantly, the Regulars formed up in disciplined lines. Provincials later reported that Smith permitted a victory volley and three huzzahs, and if he did, the people of Lexington undoubtedly heard the reverberating shots and piercing, triumphant cries. Who but an enemy would celebrate the carnage, they must have asked themselves as they looked about. Grief and fury fed their sense of purpose. No matter who shoots first, this is how wars begin.[20]

Lieutenant Colonel Smith considered the skirmish in Lexington an unwanted delay, not a victory of any kind. In broad daylight his men were fully exposed, yet their destination was still six miles distant. To pull back might have been wise, but it would not be honorable. In his diary, Lieutenant Mackenzie remarked on the contention that arose: "Several of the Officers advised Colo Smith to give up the idea of prosecuting his march, and to return to Boston, as from what they had seen, and the certainty of the Country being alarmed and assembling, they imagined it would be impracticable to advance to Concord and execute their orders." Most of the weary soldiers would undoubtedly have agreed, but "Colo Smith determined to obey the orders he had received, and accordingly pursued his march, and arrived at Concord without further interruption." Once the Regulars left, militiamen gathered a second time on the Lexington green. Joined now by men from outlying farms, their body twice as large as before, they too set out for Concord.[21]

The people of Concord had long anticipated a day like this. The preceding September, after the Powder Alarm, they had formed a company of minutemen. By April 1775 this special group had drilled for months, as had the rest of the town's militiamen, including the "alarm list" of older men assumed to be less mobile. Beyond the common drill, Concord's militiamen faced the unique task of guarding the huge storehouse of military wares and supplies in and about their town. The Provincial Congress had placed sixty-four-year-old James Barrett in charge of these goods. A prosperous farmer and miller, Barrett had served as selectman, moderator of the town meeting, militia captain, and representative to the assembly. He did not have a radical temperament; until the Coercive Acts widened the rift, he had helped supply the British Army in Boston even as he, with his townsmen, objected to British policies. Recently, though, he helped draft the minutemen's oath, and he currently served as a delegate to the Provincial Congress and colonel of the Middlesex County militia. James Barrett was, all in all, the town's leading citizen and a steadfast patriot.[22]

Ever meticulous, the colonel carefully compiled a list of "the provincial stores sent to Colonel Barrett of Concord" during the month of March. These were "partly in his own custody, and partly elsewhere," but "all under his care." Charlestown's David Cheever, member of the committee of supplies, had sent twenty wagonloads containing "20,000 pounds of musket-balls and cartridges" along with tents, axes, harnesses, candles, matches, and other items, goods enough to stock a general store. From Boston's Moses Gill came eleven loads of butter, beef, tents, axes, spades, dishes, spoons, and canteens. And so it went, scores of wagonloads containing everything from gunpowder to chests of medicine. ("Don't so much as mention the name of powder, lest our enemies should take advantage of it," Marblehead's Jeremiah Lee

cautioned Barrett when he sent thirty-five half-barrels of powder.) Listed, too, were the homes where these items were stored—
Willoughby Prescott's, Ephraim Potter's, and a score of private
houses, including Elisha Jones's, where "7 loads of salt fish, containing 17,000 pounds" were stored. All these goods and more,
those that had arrived in April and items of local manufacture,
were secured from British troops in thirty different households or
businesses.[23]

In March, the committees of safety and supplies had directed
Barrett "to engage a sufficient number of faithful men to guard
the colony magazines in that town, to keep a suitable number
of teams in constant readiness, by day and night, on the shortest notice, to remove the stores." But in April the committees had
vacillated, not certain whether the armaments in Concord should
be hidden from British troops or used to repel a British advance.
Just hours before Smith's expedition departed Boston, the committees of safety and supplies, at their meeting in Cambridge, ordered "the muskets balls under the care of Col. Barrett, be buried
under ground, in some safe place, that he be desired to do it, and
to let the commissary only be informed thereof." Additionally,
the committees stopped the shipment of powder from Leicester to
Concord and ordered Barrett to cease making cartridges.[24]

Upon receiving the initial alarm, militiamen living in town
gathered at Amos Wright's tavern. Their first order of business
was to dispatch "a considerable number . . . to assist the citizens
who were actively engaged in removing and secreting cannon,
military stores, and provisions." They also dispatched scouts to
assess enemy numbers and determine when they might arrive.
The first to return was Reuben Brown, who had witnessed the initial gunfire on Lexington common. Having departed immediately
after, Brown could not tell the men congregating on the Concord
town common whether the British had actually discharged shot
or simply set off powder to unnerve the militiamen. But the dis-
tinction was critical. If no blood had been shed in Lexington, and

if the Concord men opened fire on the Regulars, they would be accused of starting a civil war.[25]

Young, hot-blooded minutemen urged an immediate encounter with the redcoats, before they even reached the town. Older militiamen wanted to hold back until reinforcements appeared or at least until they were fully informed. The body settled on a multipronged strategy. The minutemen, along with men who had just arrived from nearby Lincoln, would march toward the invading enemy. If their numbers were small, and if these companies felt they could gain the upper hand, they would engage them. If not, they would distract the redcoats while townspeople did what they could to protect the invaluable military cache. Other militiamen, including the alarm company, would establish an outpost on a hill just above town, by its Liberty Pole.[26]

The ground the minutemen tramped over was still damp with rain that had fallen the day before, but overhead the new sun was bright and the sky clear. A mile or two to the southeast of the town (historians still debate the exact location), they mounted a hill above the road. From that vantage point they first caught sight of the formidable British cortege. When Lieutenant Colonel Smith ordered some of his light infantry to ascend the hill and confront the rebels, the minutemen retreated. Half a century later one of their number, Amos Barrett, recalled that they had done so proudly and defiantly, in confident parade, with their own "Droms and fifes agoing, and all so the [British]. We had grand Musick." Defiance aside, the retreat was also strategic, siphoning off a contingent of British soldiers and delaying their arrival in Concord.[27]

The minutemen followed the ridge until they met up with the alarm company just above the town. Reverend William Emerson was there with these older men when the advance company arrived with fearful news. "We must retreat," the minutemen said, "as their number was more than treble ours." In his diary that evening, Emerson chronicled the subsequent movements of the provincials. Thinking themselves vulnerable, the minute companies and regular militiamen from Concord and Lincoln, together with Concord's alarm company, "retreated from the hill near the Liberty Pole, and took a new post back of the town, upon an eminence, where we formed into two battalions and waited the arrival of the enemy."[28]

In Lexington, armed provincials and Regulars had faced one another on a plain. That topography gave British troops the upper hand, but in Concord topography favored the rebels. Ensign De Berniere, one of Gage's spies, had observed earlier that the town "lies between two hills, that command it entirely." Moving from one hill to the next, the militiamen and minutemen kept a close eye on the British position while constantly adjusting their own. From their new position, momentarily safe, they observed the enemy "glittering in arms, advancing towards us with the greatest celerity." On the spot, men held another of their continual, ad hoc consultations. Emerson's narrative continues:

> Some were for making a stand, notwithstanding the superiority of their number; but others, more prudent, thought best to retreat, till our strength should be equal to the enemy's by recruits from neighboring towns that were continually coming to our assistance. Accordingly we retreated over ye Bridge.[29]

Many years later, in 1832, an aging witness has Emerson declaring, "Let us stand our ground. If we die, let us die here!" Emerson's own diary gives evidence of his own prudence and, undoubtedly, of his wisdom; dying had no strategic value, but waiting did. Even as conflict seemed imminent, Emerson continued to counsel against initiating it. "We were more careful to prevent a rupture with the King's troops," Emerson explained, "as we were uncertain what had happened at Lexington, and knew [not] they had begun the quarrel there by firing upon our people, and killing eight men upon the spot."[30]

Unopposed, British troops marched into a village that was almost deserted. The grenadiers, under Lieutenant Colonel Smith's strict command, searched for goods listed in the spy reports. Their methods varied. In one instance, they put a pistol to an innkeeper's head until he showed them the place in his yard where three large cannon were buried; in another, they let the miller Timothy Wheeler keep hold of provincial flour after he claimed, lying, that it was his own. Elsewhere, they broke apart five dozen barrels of precious provisions and threw a hidden cache of lead bullets into a millpond, which the townspeople would recover the next day. They burnt carriage wheels and barrels of wooden spoons and plates, throwing the Liberty Pole into the flames for good measure.[31]

Some in their number adhered to Gage's orders forbidding plunder and the destruction of personal property, even offering to pay for the food they downed, their appetites voracious by now. Roaming here and there, others took advantage of the opportunity to enter any house and apparently pilfered at will. Afterward, residents compiled lists of the various items of no military value that "Ministerial Troops" had taken. Losses from Martha Hartshorn's household included, among many other objects, an iron candlestick, two pewter porringers, two spoons, four knives, four forks, a coffee mill, one pair of gold sleeve buttons, a gold ring, a scarlet broadcloth cloak, fourteen yards of "Irish Linnen," a "Singing Book," a black handkerchief, and one thimble, plus three pounds of butter and two dozen eggs.[32]

As the grenadiers did their work, seven companies of light infantry filed out of town and crossed the North Bridge, a mile to the west. They were closely watched by retreating militiamen who had already crossed the bridge and mounted Punkatasset Hill, a promontory that provided a commanding view of the river below. Four companies of infantrymen marched on toward James

Barrett's farm, where they would destroy cannon carriages but never discover the cannons that Barrett and others, working feverishly that morning, had moved to outlying farms or to nearby Stow and Acton. The Concord men had also either dispersed supplies or concealed them, hiding some in the woods and the rest under straw and ample quantities of aromatic manure.[33]

Meanwhile, on Punkatasset Hill, the rebel force swelled with the arrival of other militia companies. Scarcely one hundred redcoats had been left behind to guard the return passage across the bridge, while provincials soon numbered around five hundred. For the first time that day they enjoyed a distinct military advantage.

Colonel Barrett, who had resumed command after securing the stores at his farm, held counsel with other officers. As they contemplated whether to take the offensive, smoke spiraled high into the air above the town of Concord. Many thought the British were deliberately setting fire to the town, and their anger settled the issue. There would be no holding back. No one realized that the fire's spread was due to an accident and that British soldiers had taken their place in the bucket brigade.[34]

The provincials started down the hill, with minute companies in the lead. Marching side by side in twos, a fifer leading their procession, relentless and numerous, they were formidable. British soldiers were stunned by the audacity of this ragtag army. "They began to march by Divisions down upon us . . . in a very Military manner," Lieutenant William Sutherland reported. Ensign Lister also evidenced surprise: "The Rebels begun their March from the Hill . . . with as much order as the best disciplined Troops." Both immediately recognized the precarious position they and their men were in. "I looked up to my right & saw a large body of men marching almost within Pistol shot of me," Sutherland wrote. "It struck me it would be disgracefull to be taken by such Rascals & I made the best of my way for the Bridge never out of reach of

Musquet shot of this party." Lister noted that to get back to the bridge he had to pass "under the Mussels of the Rebels pieces." With great urgency, officers sent a message to Lieutenant Colonel Smith asking for reinforcements.[35]

The Regulars retreated across the bridge, and to hamper the advance of their pursuers the rearmost soldiers pulled up some of its wooden planks. "I being the last that came over . . . raised the first plank myself," Sutherland wrote. The demolition angered the local men, as thoughts of Concord's fiery destruction had only minutes before. Determined, they continued forward. Threatened, the British officers ordered their men into a firing formation.[36]

To hear minutemen tell it, the Regulars opened fire, and they, in response, returned it. Ensign Lister claimed otherwise: "Before we got one plank [off] they got so near as to begin their Fire which was a very heavy one. . . . Our Comp[ys] [companies] was drawn up in order to fire Street fireing, yet the weight of their fire was such that we was oblidg'd to give way then run with the greatest precipitance." Whether militiamen fired first or not, they certainly took special care not to be perceived as the instigators. Emerson reported that even as the men advanced, they were under "special orders not to fire upon the troops unless fired upon."[37]

Later generations of Americans freely celebrated that first volley. In 1837, Ralph Waldo Emerson, William's grandson, immortalized the event and the place with a poem commissioned by Concord's Battle Monument Committee:

> By the rude bridge that arched the flood,
>   Their flag to April's breeze unfurled,
> Here once the embattled farmers stood,
>   And fired the shot heard round the world.

At Lexington, provincials had confronted a vastly superior force. Shots were fired, each side believing it was fired upon, and havoc followed. At Concord's North Bridge, by contrast, militia-men primed their muskets and deliberately advanced, and when at last they discharged their guns, some shots hit their marks. Bod-ies crumpled. The light infantry fled for Concord, leaving behind their dead and wounded. A civil war was under way. Hours and even minutes earlier, Reverend Emerson and his fellow militia-men had shied from starting it. After that confrontation, they em-braced it.

From above the town center, the victorious militiamen watched the various detachments of Regulars regroup. With the enemy's force steadily growing, Lieutenant Colonel Smith prepared for the long march back to Boston. His men pilfered with great pur-pose now; they commandeered wagons, chaises, and carriages to carry the wounded, one belonging to the morning scout and a harness maker, Reuben Brown. Around noon the weary soldiers finally departed.[38]

For the first mile, the line encountered little resistance, but at an intersection called Merriam's Corner, Regulars began to receive serious fire from the north side of the road. The militia force had doubled once more, to a thousand, and before the British reached Bloody Curve, two miles farther on, it had doubled again. At times a single militiaman in this multitude took cover behind a stone wall or a tree and fired and felled a redcoat. In a call out to individual might and will, isolated actions like this are often commemorated. But for months these "embattled farmers" had trained within their townships, braced by the fervor of each town's meetings, committees, congregations, and training bands. Even now, with a barrage of gunfire and the smoke and the screams, they moved through the woods and fields in disciplined units, led sometimes by combat veterans from the French and Indian War. They engaged the enemy in open combat and joined in military formation as many as eight times before the day was done.[39]

As they retreated through Lexington, the harried British troops at last met up with twelve hundred men from Lord Percy's

First Brigade, which Governor Gage had sent out to rescue the faltering expedition. Smith's men had by then expended much of their ammunition, and without assistance many more might have been killed and the rest captured. "I had the happiness . . . of saving them from inevitable destruction," Percy reported the next day to his father.[40]

It was almost 4:00 in the afternoon when the last detachment left Lexington, and the troops continued to receive fire all the way to Charlestown. Not until 7:00 did survivors arrive at the shores of the Charles River opposite Boston, bloodied and battered after twenty-one hours of marching and fighting. Official returns listed 65 of their number killed, 180 wounded, and 27 missing.[41]

Lord Percy recognized the competence of the adversaries he had encountered: "You may depend upon it, that as the rebels have now had time to prepare, they are determined to go through with it, nor will the insurrection here turn out so despicable as it is perhaps imagined at home. For my part, I never believed, I confess, that they wd have attacked the King's troops, or have had the perseverance I found in them yesterday."[42]

Having fired on the king's soldiers, these combatants were indeed all rebels now, and Dr. Joseph Warren was as guilty of treason as any other. He had slipped through the woods on the road the redcoats took and, although the wound was slight, he was shot. An ardent patriot, and farsighted, he knew very well that New England militiamen had crossed over a line that day and that their action impelled every colony to cross over now and join them. Speaking for all of America, he said, "The next news from England must be conciliatory, or the connection between us ends."[43]

A tally of enemy dead and wounded provides one measure of rebel victory and is often cited. A survey of military wares and the everyday supplies that remained in their keeping provides another, and those numbers were colossal, Gage's soldiers having destroyed no more than a minuscule fraction. At the end of the day, provincials possessed the wherewithal to create an army.

The very next day, with arms and provisions secured, the Provincial Congress's committee of safety dispatched a circular letter to all Massachusetts towns:

> The barbarous murders committed upon our innocent brethren, on Wednesday, the 19th instant, have made it absolutely necessary, that we immediately raise an army to defend our wives and children from the butchering hands of an inhuman soldiery. . . . Our all is at stake. Death and devastation are the certain consequences of delay. Every moment is infinitely precious. An hour lost may deluge your country in blood, and entail perpetual slavery upon the few of our posterity who may survive the carnage. We beg and entreat, as you will answer to your country, to your own conscience, and above all, as you will answer to God himself, that you will hasten and encourage by all possible means, the enlistment of men to form the army, and send them forward to headquarters at Cambridge.

Recruits signed up in droves for "the Massachusetts service" and pledged to remain in service until "the last day of December next." This fighting force had a commander, Artemas Ward. It had guns, powder, and ammunition, and everyday necessities like food, pots, tents, or wooden spoons, as well as operative rules and regulations. And it had a clear mission: to contain British Regulars within the confines of Boston.[44]

The Massachusetts Army became a New England Army as New Hampshire, Connecticut, and Rhode Island joined. But there was no political organization that represented all of New England, so by default the Massachusetts Provincial Congress continued to administer it. This could not last. On May 16 that body, overwhelmed, asked the Continental Congress to take over. "As the army, collecting from different colonies, is for the general defence of the rights of America," the Provincial Congress explained, "we would beg leave to suggest to your consideration, the propriety of your taking the regulation and general direction of it." The Continental Congress agreed.[45]

In quick succession, provincial militias were subsumed by a Massachusetts Army, a New England Army, and a Continental Army. Local militiamen were now soldiers fighting on behalf of the "United Colonies of North America." Together with fellow New Englanders and riflemen from Pennsylvania, Virginia, and Maryland, they would serve under a common commander, George Washington, whom the Continental Congress chose to succeed Artemas Ward.

And so begins a story we know.

POSTSCRIPT

LOCAL EVENTS, NATIONAL NARRATIVES, AND GLOBAL IMPACT

In Worcester, now the second largest city in New England, a historical plaque tucked back from the sidewalk, across from the exit to the Pearl-Elm Municipal Garage, reads:

On his way to take command of
the Continental Army at Cambridge
GENERAL GEORGE WASHINGTON
was entertained in this spot then
occupied by Stearns' tavern
July 1st 1775
Erected by the Worcester Continentals
April 19, 1915

Such commemorations are common in communities across the thirteen original states, even a brief encounter with George Washington giving cause for celebration. Proud residents lay claim to any and all ancestral participants who can be connected to prominent men or legendary battles. In this accounting, however, local figures do not create or shape the national narrative. They only inhabit it.

By dining with Washington at Mary Stearns's tavern, Worcester's leading citizens did nothing to alter the history of our nation, but in fact matters of great consequence unfolded on this site, events not memorialized on any plaque. Here the American Political Society plotted against local Tories, and here the first Worcester County Convention of committees of correspondence organized the September 6 court closure. Countless unrecorded political discussions echoed from the walls as men drank and let off steam, their sense of purpose intensifying. Those convening here, and thousands of others like them, *did* shape the trajectory of the American Revolution. Using a revolutionary infrastructure of their own creation, they cast off British rule throughout the province—except in Boston, of course. Because they did, the Crown resorted to military measures that impelled other colonies to side with Massachusetts, and war was on. Had local people *not* cast off British authority in 1774, the Revolutionary War might have started somewhere else or under different precipitating circumstances—or there might have been no war at all. Only in hindsight can we say that war was absolutely inevitable.

When people first hear that Massachusetts shed British rule well before Lexington and Concord, some ask, "When did that rebellion join with the American Revolution?" This question presupposes that a national narrative supersedes, and necessarily predates, all others. Such thinking marginalizes regional customs and interests, and worse yet, it blinds us to the driving force of local actions. The Massachusetts Revolution of 1774 did not *join* the American Revolution; it was the very heart of colonial rebellion, and when other colonies entered the fray, as they did in the wake of Lexington and Concord, it *evolved into* the American Revolution. If there was joining to be done, the American Revolution joined it.

•   •   •

When local people staged illegal town meetings, forced council members to resign, and closed their county courts, they triggered a chain of events that extended even beyond Britain and thirteen of her colonies in North America.

After provincials seized authority in the late summer and early fall of 1774, King George III, his ministers, and Parliament could have ceded to the rebels' demands by repealing the Coercive Acts, accepted the loss of a colony, or attempted to crush the rebellion. Choosing the third option and realizing that rebels were amassing a military arsenal, King George banned the importation of arms into New England. It was at this point, in late 1774 and early 1775, that the dispute between Britain and Massachusetts spilled over to the European mainland and across the seas. Holland, France, Spain, and the Austrian Netherlands (now Belgium) manufactured munitions for the world market. Vessels registered to these nations and others, including Denmark and Sweden, carried these to America and elsewhere. According to international code, Britain had the right to prohibit the importation of any given item by foreign ships into its possessions, but the ruling immediately antagonized foreign manufacturers, merchants, and seamen who profited by the weapons trade.[1]

Enforcement of the ban led to resentments and a diplomatic war. British ambassadors told their counterparts in other European nations that the Crown would seize any "foreign Ships which may be found with prohibited Goods, or warlike Stores destined for His Majesty's Colonies in America." Threatened outright, a French official fired off a response: British vessels must not "come near our possessions under any circumstances to visit those of our ships loaded with all that is necessary for the consumption and defense of *our* Colonies." In translation, this meant that French vessels were free to carry weapons to French Martinique in the Caribbean. In similar fashion, Spanish vessels could ship armaments to Spanish Hispaniola, Danish vessels to St. Croix, and Dutch vessels to St. Eustatius. These islands had long been conduits for smugglers dealing with contraband goods, and illicit arms could readily pass from there to the North American continent.[2]

When New England provincials and British officers tussled over armaments in Charlestown, Portsmouth, Newport, or New London, other nations might not have noted or cared, but they would if a British ship tried to strip a French or Dutch ship of its cargo. "If the English policy to keep constantly cruising ships . . . is not offset by identical measures, it gives them at the onset certain advantages over us that might well destroy the fragile principles of justice," M. Garnier, of the French foreign department, advised Count de Vergennes, France's foreign minister. "Offset by identical measures"—this was the language of retaliation, the initial sparring in an escalating trade war that, step by step, would evolve into a real one.[3]

After Britain extended its ban to cover all trade with Europe, colonial rebels worked closely with European merchants to smuggle contraband arms and supplies into America. Early in 1778, these contacts facilitated a formal alliance between France and the United States, and in short order Spain and the Netherlands joined France to create an anti-British alliance. To protect their vessels from predatory British ships, Russia, Denmark-Norway, Sweden, Prussia, and Portugal formed a League of Armed Neutrality. What we know today as the American Revolution became a global war, fought in good measure on the high seas. Britain had to contend not only with thirteen American colonies that had declared their independence, but also with a Franco-Spanish armada in the English Channel; Dutch vessels that protected the Cape of Good Hope on the southern tip of Africa and that cruised the North Sea; a Franco-Spanish siege of Minorca and Gibraltar in the Mediterranean; a colonial rebellion in India aided by a French fleet; and ongoing struggles with French, Spanish, and Dutch navies in the Caribbean.

That war, in a larger sense, was a continuation of the struggle for global dominance that had been going on for centuries, but this particular phase of the war had its origins in the executive order of October 19, 1774, that banned all arms trade with New England—and that, in turn, can be traced to the acquisition of arms by Massachusetts townships, the Massachusetts Provincial Congress, and other New England bodies. The never-ending chain of actions and reaction blurs the boundaries separating local, national, and global. What happens in a particular *here* can reverberate far beyond.

ACKNOWLEDGMENTS

History is a collaborative enterprise, and we've benefited from the interest other historians have shown in our enterprise. As the narrative took shape, we received feedback on the entire manuscript from John Bell, who hosts the Boston 1775 blog and is eminently knowledgeable on all matters concerning Revolutionary Massachusetts. John steered us to sources whenever we were stumped and ably responded to questions we posed over the months.

Others provided valuable insights after reading portions of the manuscript pertaining to their specialties. We owe much to Joel Bohy, Historic Arms & Militia specialist for Skinner Auctioneers and an appraiser for PBS's *Antiques Roadshow*, who has been studying the ins and outs of the Battles of Lexington and Concord for years; Jim Hollister, Education Coordinator and Historic Weapons Supervisor at Minute Man National Historical Park; Alex Cain, author of *We Stood Our Ground: Lexington in the First Year of the American Revolution*; and Richard Trask, Town Archivist for the Danvers Archival Center, Peabody Institute Library. Don Sherblom, of the Vought House Revolutionary Loyalist Homestead, inspired our "Note on Nomenclature," which we hope will alert readers to common linguistic concerns in Revolutionary Era narratives.

We are greatly indebted to scholars of earlier times who edited compilations of primary sources: William Lincoln, who in the 1830s collected and published the journals of the Massachusetts Provincial Congress and the county conventions of the committees of correspondence; and L. Kinvin Wroth, George H. Nash III, Joel Meyerson, Patricia A. Young, and Catherine Schagh, who in their 1975 publication, *Province in Rebellion*, placed in print 1,140 documents from 1774 and 1775.

Marc Favreau of The New Press was an advocate of this project at its inception and immediately supportive of dual authorship. Always able to see the forest for the trees, he provided editorial counsel.

Public historians over the past few years have helped to increase awareness of the Massachusetts revolution of 1774. These include, among many others, Mel Bernstein, Moderator of the Minute Man NHP's American Revolution Round Table; Jayne Gordon and Kathleen Barker, Education and Public Outreach, Massachusetts Historical Society; Pleun Bouricius, Director of Programs, Massachusetts Humanities Council; Mike Fishbein, President of the Massachusetts Society, Sons of the American Revolution; Jim Moran, Director of Outreach, American Antiquarian Society; Bill Wallace, Director of Worcester Historical Museum; Elizabeth Tivnan, Regent of the Colonel Timothy Bigelow Chapter, Daughters of the American Revolution. A dedicated group of citizens from Worcester has organized an annual reenactment of the dramatic court closure of September 6, 1774, a signature moment in that revolution.

Finally, we offer thanks to two great historians who inspired our work and endorsed our findings, Alfred F. Young and Pauline Maier.

NOTES

Introduction: The Missing Sixteen Months

1. David M. Kennedy and Lizabeth Cohen, *The American Pageant*, volume 1, fifteenth edition (Boston: Cengage Learning, 2014), 118; James West Davidson and Michael B. Scott, *America: History of Our Nation* (Upper Saddle River, NJ: Prentice Hall, 2014), 152.
2. William Deverell and Deborah Gray White, *Holt McDougal United States History: Beginnings to 1877* (Orlando, FL: Houghton Mifflin Harcourt, 2012), 112.
3. John Andrews to William Barrell, August 26, 1774, "Letters of John Andrews of Boston, 1772–1776," Massachusetts Historical Society, *Proceedings* 8 (1864–1865), 348.
4. Gage to Dartmouth, September 12, 1774, Clarence E. Carter, ed., *The Correspondence of General Thomas Gage, 1763–1775* (New Haven: Yale University Press, 1931–33), 1:374; Merrill Jensen, *The Founding of a Nation: A History of the American Revolution, 1763–1776* (New York: Oxford University Press, 1968), 53.
5. Jensen, *Founding of a Nation*, 539–40. Ostensibly, gunpowder produced in Pennsylvania was for future trade, not current use—apparently a political ruse to soften Quaker resistance.
6. William J. Van Schreeven, Robert L. Scribner, and Brent Tarter, eds., *Revolutionary Virginia: The Road to Independence. A Documentary Record* (Charlottesville: University Press of Virginia, 1973), 2:366–67; John Drayton, *Memoirs of the American Revolution* (Charleston: A.F. Miller, 1821), 1:222.

1: Boston: Tea

1. *Boston Gazette*, November 29, 1773.

2. Samuel Adams to Arthur Lee, December 31, 1773, in Harry Alonzo Cushing, ed., *The Writings of Samuel Adams* (New York: G.P. Putnam's Sons, 1904), 3:73–77.

3. Alfred F. Young, "Revolution 1773: The 'Body of the People' at Old South Meeting House," Old South Meeting House website, history page: http://www.oldsouth meetinghouse.org/history/boston-tea-party/revolution-1773-body-people -old-south-meeting-house.

4. John Tyler, *Smugglers and Patriots: Boston Merchants and the Advent of the American Revolution* (Boston: Northeastern University Press, 1986), 143.

5. Abigail Adams to Mercy Otis Warren, December 5, 1773, L.H. Butterfield, ed., *Adams Family Correspondence* (Cambridge, MA: Harvard University Press, 1963), 1:88–89.

6. Benjamin Carp, *Defiance of the Patriots: The Boston Tea Party and the Making of America* (New Haven: Yale University Press, 2010), 52–54.

7. Ibid., 55–58.

8. *Boston Gazette*, February 12, 1770.

9. Samuel Adams, writing as "Valerius Poplicola" in the *Boston Gazette*, October 5, 1772, in Cushing, *Writings of Samuel Adams*, 2:336.

10. Carp, *Defiance of the Patriots*, 8–11.

11. Jensen, *Founding of a Nation*, 434–35; Carp, *Defiance of the Patriots*, 55.

12. Jensen, *Founding of a Nation*, 434.

13. Paul Leicester Ford, ed., *The Writings of John Dickinson* (Philadelphia: Historical Society of Pennsylvania, 1895), 1:460.

14. Francis S. Drake, ed., *Tea Leaves: Being a Collection of Letters and Documents Relating to the Subject of Tea to the American Colonies in the Year 1773* (Boston: A.O. Crane, 1884), 282.

15. Carp, *Defiance of the Patriots*, 87. The "proceedings" of the North End Caucus are printed in Elbridge Henry Goss, *Life of Colonel Paul Revere* (Boston: Joseph George Cupples, 1891), 2:635–44. Much of the documentation for the series of events outlined, from November 2 to December 16, 1773, is reproduced in Drake, *Tea Leaves*. Samuel Adams chronicled these events in his December 31 letter to Arthur Lee (Cushing, *Writings of Samuel Adams*, 3:73–77).

16. Carp, *Defiance of the Patriots*, 91–92,

17. The dispute between Dr. Young and Dr. Warren is reported, with citations, in Ray Raphael, *Founders: The People Who Brought You a Nation* (New York: The New Press, 2009), 58–59. For Young's early advocacy of throwing the tea overboard, see Benjamin W. Labaree, *The Boston Tea Party* (New York: Oxford University Press, 1964), 141–42, 295, note 31; L.F.S. Upton, ed., "Proceeding of Ye Body Respecting the Tea," *William and Mary Quarterly*, third series, vol. 22 (1965): 299; Drake, *Tea Leaves*, 44, 172; George Bancroft, *History of the United States of America, from the Discovery of the Continent* (Boston: Little, Brown, 1879;

first published 1834–1874), 4:274. Young was not the only one considering this simple resolution to the crisis, but he seems to have been the first to propose it in a public setting.

18. *Boston Gazette*, December 6, 1773.

19. The handbill is quoted in Thomas Hutchinson, *The History of the Province of Massachusetts Bay, from 1749 to 1774* (London: John Murray, 1828), 434.

20. Diary of John Adams, December 17, 1773, in Charles Francis Adams, ed., *Works of John Adams* (Boston: Little, Brown, 1850–1856), 323–24.

21. Pauline Maier, *The Old Revolutionaries: Political Lives in the Age of Samuel Adams* (New York: Alfred A. Knopf, 1980), 277; Young, "Revolution 1773."

22. Carp, *Defiance of the Patriots*, 119–20.

23. Upton, "Proceeding of Ye Body Respecting the Tea," 297–98; William V. Wells, *The Life and Public Services of Samuel Adams* (Boston: Little, Brown, 1865), 2:iv and 2:122; Esther Forbes, *Paul Revere & the World He Lived In* (New York: Houghton Mifflin, 1999; first published in 1942), 197; Louis Birnbaum, *Red Dawn at Lexington* (Boston: Houghton Mifflin, 1986), 29.

24. Upton, "Proceeding of Ye Body," 297–98; Drake, *Tea Leaves*, 70; *Boston Evening Post*, December 20, 1773, and *Boston Gazette,* December 20, 1773. A similar report appeared in the December 23 issue of the *Massachusetts Gazette and Boston Weekly News-Letter*.

25. Drake, *Tea Leaves*, 71–72.

26. Carp, *Defiance of the Patriots*, 131–37.

27. Hewes: In a groundbreaking study, Alfred F. Young singled out George Robert Twelves Hewes and compared the two memoirs Hewes dictated with contemporaneous evidence, demonstrating how a commoner could play a significant role in popular politics of the 1760s and 1770s. Alfred F. Young, "George Robert Twelves Hewes (1742–1840): A Boston Shoemaker and the Memory of the American Revolution," *William and Mary Quarterly*, third series, 38:4 (October 1981), 561–623. Young expanded on this study and discussed the Boston Tea Party in historical memory in *The Shoemaker and the Tea Party: Memory and the American Revolution* (Boston: Beacon Press, 1999). Oliver quotation: Peter Oliver, *Origin and Progress of the American Rebellion* (Stanford: Stanford University Press, 1961), 65.

28. "The 'White Hills' of New Hampshire," *Yale Literary Magazine* 10:9 (August 1845), 418; Carp, *Defiance of the Patriots*, 135.

29. Young, *Shoemaker and the Tea Party*, 44–45.

30. Ibid., 43–44

31. Montagu to Philip Stephens, secretary of the admiralty, December 17, 1773, and Leslie to Lord Barrington, secretary of war, December 17, 1773, in William Legge Dartmouth, *The Manuscripts of the Earl of Dartmouth* (London: Royal Commission on Historical Manuscripts, 1887), 2:344. Quoted in Carp, *Defiance of the Patriots*, 125.

32. James Hawkes, *A Retrospect of the Boston Tea-Party, with a Memoir by George R.T. Hewes* (New York: S.S. Bliss, 1834), 41; *Boston Evening Post*, January 3, 1774,

quoted in Richard Frothingham, *Life and Times of Joseph Warren* (Boston: Little, Brown, 1865), 282.

33. Adams to James Warren, December 17, 1773, *Warren-Adams Letters* (Boston: Massachusetts Historical Society, 1917), 2:403–4.

34. Hawkes, *Retrospect of the Boston Tea-Party*, 41; Carp, *Defiance of the Patriots*, 139.

35. John Adams, *Diary and Autobiography*, L.H. Butterfield, ed. (Cambridge, MA: Harvard University Press, 1961), 2:86.

2: London: Crackdown

1. *The Parliamentary History of England, from the Earliest Period to the Year 1803* (London: T.C. Hansard, 1804), 17:1159.

2. Ibid.

3. Boston Port Act, March 31, 1774 (Yale Law School, Avalon Project): http://avalon.law.yale.edu/18th_century/boston_port_act.asp; *Parliamentary History of England* 17:1172, cited in Don Cook, *The Long Fuse: How England Lost America* (New York: Atlantic Monthly Press, 1995), 186.

4. *Parliamentary History of England* 17:1165; Andrew O'Shaughnessy, *The Men Who Lost America: British Leadership, the American Revolution, and the Fate of the Empire* (New Haven: Yale University Press, 2013), 53.

5. *Parliamentary History of England* 16:104; William Stanhope Taylor and John Henry Pringle, eds., *Correspondence of William Pitt, Earl of Chatham* (London: A. Spottiswoode, 1840), 4:346.

6. Burke's speech on American taxation, April 19, 1774, in *Celebrated Speeches of Chatham, Burke, and Erskine* (Philadelphia: Biddle, 1852), 55; *Parliamentary History of England* 17:1266, quoted in Cook, *The Long Fuse*, 189.

7. *Parliamentary History of England* 17:1171, quoted in Cook, *The Long Fuse*, 186.

8. Franklin to Thomas Cushing, March 22, 1774, in John Bigelow, ed., *The Works of Benjamin Franklin* (New York: G.P. Putnam's Sons, 1904), 6:335.

9. "Administration of Justice Act, May 20, 1774 (Yale Law School, Avalon Project): http://avalon.law.yale.edu/18th_century/admin_of_justice_act.asp.

10. *Parliamentary History of England* 17:1193.

11. Hutchinson to Richard Jackson, August 30, 1765, in Edmund S. Morgan, ed., *Prologue to Revolution: Sources and Documents on the Stamp Act Crisis, 1764–1766* (Chapel Hill: University of North Carolina Press, 1959), 108–9; Hutchinson, *The History of the Province of Massachusetts Bay*, 353.

12. Massachusetts Government Act, May 20, 1774 (Yale Law School, Avalon Project): http://avalon.law.yale.edu/18th_century/mass_gov_act.asp.

13. Ibid.

14. Carp, *Defiance of the Patriots*, 93; House of Lords, "Report of the Committee to Inquire into the Several Proceedings in the Colony of Massachusetts Bay," referring to a letter from Lieutenant Governor Hutchinson to the Earl of Hillsborough, April 27, 1770, in *American Archives, fourth series, containing a documentary*

history of the English colonies in North America from the king's message to Parliament of March 7, 1774 to the Declaration of Independence by the United States (Washington, DC: M. St. Clair Clarke and Peter Force, 1837–1846), 1:25–26, http://lincoln.lib.niu.edu/cgi-bin/amarch/getdoc.pl?/var/lib/philologic/databases/amarch/.11.

15. Hutchinson, *History of the Province of Massachusetts Bay*, 221; Massachusetts Government Act, Avalon Project.

16. "Protest, May 11, 1774, House of Lords," Clarke and Force, *American Archives*, series four, 1:93: http://lincoln.lib.niu.edu/cgi-bin/amarch/getdoc.pl?/var/lib/philologic/databases/amarch/.60.

17. Jensen, *Founding of a Nation*, 69.

18. Cook, *The Long Fuse*, 190–91.

19. The Administration of Justice Act was to be in force for three years, regardless of whether payment for the tea was proffered. The Massachusetts Government Act had no sunset clause.

20. Francis Walett, "Governor Bernard's Undoing: An Earlier Hutchinson Letters Affair," *New England Quarterly* 38:2 (June 1965): 217–26. Reacting to the letters, the Massachusetts Council complained of Bernard's "earnest Wish and Endeavor to bring about an Alteration in the Civil Government of the Province at the very Time he was professing himself a warm Friend to the charter" (221).

21. Hutchinson, *History of the Province of Massachusetts Bay*, 409.

22. Peter Orlando Hutchinson, *The Diary and Letters of His Excellency Thomas Hutchinson* (Boston: Houghton Mifflin, 1884), 129.

23. Gage to Hillsborough, September 26, 1768, and Gage to Barrington, September 8, 1770, Carter, *Gage Correspondence*, 1:197 and 2:557.

24. King George III to Lord North, February 4, 1774, in W. Bodham Donne, ed., *The Correspondence of King George the Third with Lord North*, 1768–1783 (New York: Da Capo Press, 1971), 1:164.

25. Dartmouth to Gage, April 9, 1774, Carter, *Gage Correspondence*, 2:158–62.

26. John Shy, *Toward Lexington: The Role of the British Army in the Coming of the American Revolution* (Princeton: Princeton University Press, 1965), 408–9.

3: Salem: Provincial Assembly and Town Meetings

1. Gage to Secretary of State Sir Henry Conway, January 16, 1766, Carter, *Gage Correspondence*, 1:81, quoted in Shy, *Toward Lexington*, 215.

2. Gage to Lord Hillsborough, October 31, 1768, and Gage to Lord Barrington, April 13, 1772, Carter, *Gage Correspondence*, 1:205 and 2:603. For the paucity of materials of a personal nature amidst the voluminous papers left by Gage, see John Shy, *A People Numerous and Armed: Reflections on the Military Struggle for American Independence* (New York: Oxford University Press, 1976), 73.

3. Joseph Warren to Josiah Quincy, November 21, 1774, in Frothingham, *Life and Times of Joseph Warren*, 395; Shy, *A People Numerous and Armed*, 96.

4. Gage to Dartmouth, May 19, 1774, Carter, *Gage Correspondence*, 1:355.

5. John Andrews, "Letters of John Andrews of Boston, 1772–1776," in Massachusetts Historical Society, *Proceedings* 8 (1864–1865), 328. Gage to Dartmouth, May 19, 1774, Carter, *Gage Correspondence*, 1:355.

6. The list of nominees, plus those rejected by Gage, appears in *Boston Gazette*, May 30, 1774. The previous year, Governor Hutchinson had rejected only three of the nominees. John Adams was rejected by both Hutchinson and Gage. See *Boston Gazette*, May 31, 1773.

7. "Governour's Speech to Both Houses," May 26, 1774, Clarke and Force, *American Archives*, series four, 1:358: http://lincoln.lib.niu.edu/cgi-bin/amarch/getdoc.pl?/var/lib/philologic/database/amarch/.351.

8. Dartmouth to Gage, April 9, 1774, Carter, *Gage Correspondence*, 2:158–62.

9. *Boston Gazette*, May 30, 1774; Gage to Dartmouth, May 19, 1774, Carter, *Gage Correspondence*, 1:355.

10. *Essex Gazette*, June 14, 1774, reprinted in James Henry Stark, *The Loyalists of Massachusetts and the Other Side of the American Revolution* (Boston: J.H. Stark, 1907), 131.

11. Resolutions of the House of Representatives of Massachusetts, June 8, 1774, Clark and Force, *American Archives*, series four, 1:399. http://lincoln.lib.niu.edu/cgi-bin/amarch/getdoc.pl?/var/lib/philologic/databases/amarch/.428.

12. *Boston Gazette*, June 6, 1774.

13. Speech by Lord Germain, March 28, 1774, *The History, Debates, and Proceedings of Both Houses of Parliament of Great Britain, 1743–1774* (London: J. Debrett, 1792), 7:107. For the etymology of "Intolerable Acts," see J.L. Bell, "Intolerable Acts," *Journal of the American Revolution*, June 13, 2013: http://allthingsliberty.com/2013/06/intolerable-acts/.

14. For town meeting instructions, see Kenneth Colegrove, "New England Town Mandates," Colonial Society of Massachusetts, *Publications* 21 (1919): 411–49, accessible online through Google Books at http://is.gd/ivsat ; J.R. Pole, *Political Representation in England and the Origins of the American Republic* (New York: St. Martin's Press, 1966): 72–75, 80, 94–95, 161–65, 211–14, 229–40, 441, 541–42; Ray Raphael, "Instructions: The People's Voice in Revolutionary America," *Common-Place* 9:1 (October, 2008): http://www.common-place.org/vol-09/no-01/raphael/.

15. Hutchinson, *History of the Province of Massachusetts Bay*, 353.

16. Resolutions of the House of Representatives of Massachusetts, June 17, 1774, Clarke and Force, *American Archives*, series four, 1:421: http://lincoln.lib.niu.edu/cgi-bin/amarch/getdoc.pl?/var/lib/philologic/databases/amarch/.456. The idea for a general congress was not unique to Massachusetts. Simultaneously, other colonies were also calling for delegates to convene and develop a unified response.

17. "The General Assembly Dissolved by General Gage," Clarke and Force, *American Archives*, series four, 1:422–23: http://lincoln.lib.niu.edu/cgi-bin/amarch/getdoc.pl?/var/lib/philologic/databases/amarch/.457.

18. Dirk Hoerder, *Crowd Action in Revolutionary Massachusetts, 1765–1780* (New York: Academic Press, 1977), 285; John Andrews to William Barrell, August 26, 1774, "Letters of John Andrews of Boston, 1772–1776," Massachusetts Historical Society, *Proceedings* 8 (1864–1865), 348. In letters to his brother-in-law William Barrell, who had recently moved from Boston and was hungry for news, Andrews chronicled events in and around Boston from 1772 to 1776. He described his running narration as "only my crude thoughts, as they arise in my mind," and in that lies their value (342). He never shaped his commentary with publication in mind, and it abounds with voluminous detail that only a letter writer would find worthy of note—a guess at the weight of a corpulent justice of the peace or an off-the-cuff description of a street fight. Filled with news, gossip, and insight, his letters enable readers not just to study revolutionary Boston but to experience it. For the background to Andrews's letters, see pp. 316–22.

19. *Massachusetts Gazette*, August 29, 1774, reprinted in L. Kinvin Wroth ed., *Province in Rebellion: A Documentary History of the Founding of the Commonwealth of Massachusetts, 1774–1775* (Cambridge: Harvard University Press, 1975), 550.

20. *Boston Gazette*, August 29, 1774, Supplement; Salem Committee to Boston Committee, Wroth, *Province in Rebellion*, 816–18; Andrews, "Letters," 346–47.

21. *Boston Gazette*, August 29, 1774, Supplement; Salem Committee to Boston Committee, Wroth, *Province in Rebellion*, 816–18.

22. *Boston Gazette*, August 29, 1774, Supplement; Salem Committee to Boston Committee, Wroth, *Province in Rebellion*, 818; Andrews, "Letters," 347.

23. Andrews, "Letters," 347–48.

24. Andrews, "Letters," 347; Wroth, *Province in Rebellion*, 901; *Boston Gazette*, September 12, 1774; *Essex Gazette*, September 13, 1774.

25. Andrews, "Letters," 348.

4: Berkshire County: Committees of Correspondence

1. Joseph E.A. Smith and Thomas Cushing, *History of Berkshire County, Massachusetts, with Biographical Sketches of Its Prominent Men* (New York: J.B. Beers, 1885), 1:10, 38–39.

2. *Boston Evening-Post*, January 5, July 6, and July 13, 1767.

3. Smith and Cushing, *History of Berkshire County*, 1:308 (Curtis), 119 (Ashley).

4. *Massachusetts Spy*, February 18, 1773 (italics added), reproduced on Wikisource at : http://en.wikisource.org/wiki/Sheffield_Declaration. The vast literature of the "Mumbet" case is too voluminous to cite.

5. *Massachusetts Spy*, February 18, 1773.

6. Thomas Young to Hugh Hughes, August 31, 1772, Massachusetts Historical Society, miscellaneous bound documents.

7. *A Report of the Records Commissioners of the City of Boston, Containing the Boston Town Records, 1770–1777* (Boston: Rockwell and Churchill, 1887), 93–108: https://archive.org/stream/reportofrecordco18bost#page/n7/mode/2up.

8. Richard D. Brown, *Revolutionary Politics in Massachusetts: The Boston Committee of Correspondence and the Towns, 1772–1774* (New York: W.W. Norton, 1976), 95, 109; John Daggett, *A Sketch of the History of Attleborough* (Boston: Samuel Usher, 1894), 122.

9. *Boston Weekly News-Letter*, February 10, 1774.

10. Smith and Cushing, *History of Berkshire*, 1:118–23.

11. Boston Covenant: *Colonial Society of Massachusetts Publications* 18:107–9. Berkshire Covenant: William Lincoln, ed., *The Journals of Each Provincial Congress of Massachusetts in 1774 and 1775, and of the Committee of Safety, with an Appendix, Containing the Proceedings of the County Conventions* (Boston: Dutton and Wentworth, 1838), 652–54.

12. Berkshire Committee to Boston Committee, July 25, 1774, Wroth, *Province in Rebellion*, 753.

13. Boston Committee to Berkshire Committee, July 31, 1774, Wroth, *Province in Rebellion*, 767.

14. *A History of the County of Berkshire, Massachusetts* (Pittsfield, MA: Samuel W. Bush, 1829), 1:366–68; also in J.E.A. Smith, *The History of Pittsfield, Massachusetts, from the Year 1734 to 1800* (Boston: Lee and Shepard, 1869), 194–95. The petition was composed by Timothy Childs, a twenty-six-year-old doctor who had attended Harvard without graduating, and John Strong, a schoolteacher and tavern operator who had graduated from Yale. The "state of nature" concept is discussed in chapter 9.

15. Charles J. Taylor, *History of Great Barrington, Massachusetts* (Great Barrington: Clark W. Bryan, 1882), 288.

16. *Boston Evening-Post*, August 29, 1774. This dispatch was printed in several other newspapers throughout New England. Smith and Cushing, *History of Berkshire*, 126–27. Judges of the Court of Common Pleas were joined by justices of the peace and other local officials to form the Court of General Sessions. Timothy Woodbridge, the recently deceased fourth judge of the Court of Common Pleas, had not yet been replaced.

17. Wroth, *Province in Rebellion*, 606–9. By the time the rumors reached Boston, Ingersoll was said to have been covered with grease ("for want of tar") and feathers, "put down an empty well," and kept there overnight. See John Andrews to William Barrell, August 23, 1774, Andrews, "Letters," 346.

18. Wroth, *Province in Rebellion*, 608–9 (document 203).

19. Gage to Dartmouth, August 27, 1774, Carter, *Gage Correspondence*, 1: 366–67.

20. Andrews, "Letters," 643.

5: Hampshire County: "River Gods"

1. Kevin J. MacWade, *Worcester County, 1750–1774: A Study of a Provincial Patronage Elite* (Boston University: Ph.D. thesis, 1973), 56–58; Bettye Hobbs Pruitt, ed., *The Massachusetts Tax Valuation List of 1771* (Boston: G.K. Hall, 1978),

372–73. John Chandler's "annual worth" was twice that of any other citizen in Worcester.

2. Gregory H. Nobles, *Divisions Throughout the Whole: Politics and Society in Hampshire County, Massachusetts, 1740–1775* (Cambridge: Cambridge University Press, 1983), 114–15.

3. Ibid., 20–35; Robert J. Taylor, *Western Massachusetts in the Revolution* (Providence, RI: Brown University Press, 1954), 11–33.

4. Kenneth Lockridge, "Land, Population, and the Evolution of New England Society," *Past and Present* 39 (1968): 62–80; Nobles, *Divisions Throughout the Whole*, 227; Douglas L. Jones, "The Strolling Poor: Transiency in Eighteenth-Century Massachusetts," *Journal of Social History* 8 (1975): 28–54. Bettye Hobbs Pruitt's analysis of the 1771 Massachusetts tax rolls revealed that about half of the farms had fewer than twenty acres of improved land, and almost half of these lacked either tillage, pasture, or hay land. Half of the small farmers possessed no horse, and almost two-thirds possessed no oxen to work the land. One-third had no milk cows or breeding swine. Many farmers, Pruitt and other scholars have concluded, were far from self-sufficient. See also Bettye Hobbs Pruitt, "Self-Sufficiency and the Agricultural Economy of Eighteenth-Century Massachusetts," *William and Mary Quarterly*, third series, 41 [1984]: 339.

5. Edward M. Cook Jr., "Social Behavior and Changing Values in Dedham, Massachusetts, 1700–1775," *William and Mary Quarterly*, third series, 27 (1970): 573; Nobles, *Divisions Throughout the Whole*, 201.

6. Taylor, *Western Massachusetts in the Revolution*, 55. Three years later, Williams and Worthington, like John Ashley from Berkshire County, were among the distinct minority of assembly members who voted to rescind Boston's circular letter opposing British taxation. Once the Stamp Act was repealed in 1766, commoners did not have the political will to turn out representatives with experience and influence. The river gods had weathered that storm, but greater turbulence would follow.

7. *Boston Evening-Post*, January 5, July 6, and July 13, 1767.

8. Wroth, *Province in Rebellion*, 755–57; Mason A. Green, *Springfield, 1636–1886: History of Town and City* (Springfield: C.A. Nichols & Co., 1888), 275–77. Gage to Dartmouth, August 25, 1774, Carter, *Gage Correspondence*, 1: 364. Williams's letter of resignation was dated August 10; he must have penned it immediately after receiving his official notice of appointment, sent out on August 7.

9. Hampshire County Convention to Boston Committee of Correspondence, August 31, 1774, Wroth, *Province in Rebellion*, 883–84.

10. Diary of Reverend Stephen Williams (transcript copy), Richard Salter Storrs Library, Longmeadow, MA, August 26 and 27, 1774, Book 8, 306. Jonathan Judd Jr., a conservative shopkeeper from Southampton, likewise expressed concern in his diary entry for August 29: "The Heat increases and some from the West have Set out, we hear. Confusion is coming on inevitably."

See Jonathan Judd Jr. Diary, v. 2 (1773–1782), Forbes Library, North-ampton, MA.

11. James R. Trumbull, *History of Northampton, Massachusetts, from its Settlement in 1654* (Northampton, MA: Gazette Printing Co., 1902), 346–48. Clarke was Hawley's wife's nephew, raised by the Hawleys and trained by his adoptive father to be a lawyer. We do not know the friend to whom this letter was addressed. For the size of the crowd, see *Boston Gazette*, September 12, 1774; Franklin B. Dexter, ed., *The Literary Diary of Ezra Stiles* (New York: Charles Scribner's Sons, 1901), 1: 479; Jonathan Judd Jr., Diary, v. 2 (1773–1782), Forbes Library, Northampton, entry for August 31, 1774.

12. Trumbull, *History of Northampton*, 346; *Boston Gazette*, September 12, 1774.

13. Trumbull, *History of Northampton*, 347.

14. Ibid.

15. Judd, Diary, August 31, 1774.

16. Trumbull, *History of Northampton*, 347–48.

17. Ibid., 347; Judd, Diary, September 7.

18. Trumbull, *History of Northampton*, 348. In fact, we have no record of any mob actions that night, nothing "transacted rashly." Reverend Stephen Williams did report that on the evening of August 31, his son Samuel and "Seargt G. Colton" were approached and forced "to Sign Something, I know not what." Even so, had there been violence, Reverend Williams would have been the first to report it, and he did not. See Williams, Diary, 8:309.

6: Massachusetts Towns and Countryside: "Mobs"

1. Gage to Dartmouth, July 27, 1774, Carter, *Gage Correspondence*, 1:363.

2. Gage to Dartmouth, August 27, 1774, ibid., 1:365. Lists of those who assem-bled on each date are in *Boston Gazette*, August 15 and 22, 1774. For a list of the thirty-six appointees, see William H. Whitmore, *Massachusetts Civil List for the Colonial and Provincial Periods, 1630–1774* (Albany: J. Munsell, 1870), 64.

3. Abigail Adams to John Adams, September 14, 1774, in L.H. Butterfield, ed., *Adams Family Correspondence* (Cambridge, MA: Harvard University Press, 1963), 1:152.

4. Trumbull, *History of Northampton*, 348.

5. Charles Francis Adams, ed., *Works of John Adams* (Boston: Little, Brown, 1850–1856), 10:194–95; Daniel Leonard to Thomas Gage, August 31, 1774, Wroth, *Province in Rebellion*, document 158, 1:534.

6. Leonard to Gage, August 31, 1774, Wroth, *Province in Rebellion*, 1:534–535. See also John Andrews to William Barrell, August 23, 1774, Andrews, "Letters," 345–46. The men might well have been drinking—they often did, whether or not engaging in political action—and some might have treated others, but the hint that the crowd could be bought with liquor seems unfounded, particularly in light of other crowd actions that followed.

7. An account appearing in the *Boston Evening-Post* on August 29 agrees in all essentials with Leonard's testimony, save only the part about the rum.

8. Andrews to Barrell, August 31, 1774, Andrews, "Letters," 349–50; see also *Boston Evening-Post*, August 29.

9. *Boston Evening-Post*, August 29, 1774.

10. George Watson to Gage, August 30, 1774, Wroth, *Province in Rebellion*, document 157, 533. Watson's public resignation appears in the *Massachusetts Spy*, September 22, 1774.

11. Dispatch from New London, September 2, 1774, in Clarke and Force, *American Archives*, series four, 1:731; Declaration of Abijah Willard, August 25, 1774, in Wroth, *Province in Rebellion*, 527–28; Lorenzo Sabine, *Biographical Sketches of Loyalists of the American Revolution* (Boston: Little, Brown, 1864) 2:429; *Massachusetts Gazette*, September 8, 1774.

12. Clarke and Force, *American Archives*, series four, 1:731–732. According to Governor Gage, "Mr. Willard was grievously maltreated first in Connecticut when he went on Business, and every Township he passed through in his way home in this Province had previous Notice of his Approach, and ready to insult him, Arms were put to his Breast with threats of instant Death, unless he signed a Paper, the Contents of which he did not know nor regard." See Gage to Dartmouth, September 2, 1774, Carter, *Gage Correspondence*, 370.

13. Charles Nutt, *History of Worcester and Its People* (New York: Lewis Historical Publishing Co., 1919), 198–99.

14. Timothy Paine to Thomas Gage, August 28, 1774, Wroth, *Province in Rebellion*, 528. The September 5, 1774, edition of the *Boston Evening-Post* estimated the crowd at three thousand. An account reprinted in Correspondence Proceedings, Boston, August 29, 1774, Clarke and Force, *American Archives*, series four, 1:745, states fifteen hundred. That day, Paine said "more than fifteen hundred," while the following day he revised his estimate to "more than Two Thousand."

15. Paine to Gage, August 28, 1774, Wroth, *Province in Rebellion*, 528–31.

16. Clarke and Force, *American Archives*, series four, 1:745; Albert Alonzo Lovell, *Worcester in the War of the Revolution* (Worcester, MA: Tyler and Seagrave, 1876), 44; *Boston Evening-Post*, September 5, 1774. One version of the story, part of Worcester's enduring folklore, holds that "in the excitement attendant on the scene, Mr. Paine's wig was either knocked off or fell off. Be that as it may, from that day he abjured *wigs*, as much as he had done *whigs*, and never wore one again. The now dishonored wig in question, he gave to one of his negro slaves, named 'Worcester.'" See Caleb A. Wall, *Reminiscences of Worcester from the Earliest Period, Historical and Genealogical* (Worcester: Tyler and Seagrave, 1877), 81–82. Holly Izard of the Worcester Historical Museum, in personal correspondence, explains that Paine "was dressed to his stature, not showing off or being obnoxiously British. A gentleman's attire at the time included a wig, a cravat, ruffled shirt, embellished waistcoat, overcoat, knee breeches, stockings, and buckled shoes."

17. Gage to Dartmouth, September 2, 1774, Carter, *Gage Correspondence*, 1: 370; Paine to Gage, August 28, 1774, Wroth, *Province in Rebellion*, 530.

18. Andrews to Barrell, August 23 and 24, 1774, Andrews, "Letters," 346. Murray accounted for more than 70 percent of the town's money lent out at interest. See Kevin Joseph MacWade, *Worcester County, 1750–1774: A Study of a Provincial Patronage Elite* (Boston University: PhD thesis, 1973), 8.

19. *Boston Evening-Post*, September 5, 1774; Daniel Murray to John Murray, August 28, 1774, cited in MacWade, *Worcester County Elite*, 152; Sabine, *Loyalists of the American Revolution*, 2:115. Sabine first published this account in 1847.

20. *Boston Evening-Post*, September 5, 1774; *Boston Gazette*, September 5, 1774.

21. Sabine, *Loyalists of the American Revolution*, 2:242–43; Butterfield, *Adams Family Correspondence*, 1:183. For Worcester County judgeships, see William H. Whitmore, *Massachusetts Civil List for the Colonial and Provincial Periods, 1630–1774* (Albany: J. Munsell, 1870), 118.

22. Gage to Dartmouth, August 27, 1774, and September 2, 1774, Carter, *Gage Correspondence*, 1:365, 370; MacWade, *Worcester County Elite*, 147; *Boston Evening-Post*, August 29, 1774; Clarke and Force, *American Archives*, series four, 1:732. A few months later, a Loyalist's letter complained that Ruggles "had his arms taken from his dwelling-house in Hardwick, all of which are not yet returned. He had at another time a very valuable English horse, which was kept as a stallion, poisoned, his family disturbed, and himself obliged to take refuge in Boston, after having been insulted in his own house, and twice on his way, by a mob." See Clarke and Force, *American Archives*, series four, 1:1260–61.

23. Henry S. Burrage, "Colonel Nathaniel Sparhawk of Kittery, in *Collections and Proceedings of the Maine Historical Society* (Portland: Maine Historical Society, 1898), second series, IX:256; *Boston Gazette*, December 5, 1774; Sabine, *Loyalists of the American Revolution*, 2:166–76. The November 16 proceedings of the York County Congress, which urged people to "withdraw all Connection, Commerce and Dealings from him," appears in the *Boston Gazette*, December 5, 1774, and Wroth, *Province in Rebellion*, document 402, 1327–30.

24. Joshua Loring to Thomas Gage, August 31, 1774, Wroth, *Province in Rebellion*, document 160, 537–38.

25. Ibid.

26. Clarke and Force, *American Archives*, series four, 1:731; Declaration of David Ingersoll, in Wroth, *Province in Rebellion*, document 203, 606–9.

27. Joshua Loring to Thomas Gage, August 31, 1774, Wroth, *Province in Rebellion*, document 160, 537–38.

28. Andrews to Barrell, September 9, 1774, Andrews, "Letters," 357–58; Abigail Adams to John Adams, September 14, 1774, Butterfield, *Adams Family Correspondence*, 1:152.

29. Gage to Dartmouth, September 2, 1774, Carter, *Gage Correspondence*, 1:370.

7: Charlestown and Cambridge: Powder Alarm

1. Andrews, "Letters," 347; Gage to Dartmouth, August 27, 1774, Carter, *Gage Correspondence*, 1:366.

2. Brattle to Gage, August 27, 1774, Wroth, *Province in Rebellion*, 604.

3. Andrews, "Letters," 350; *Boston Evening-Post*, September 5, 1774; *Boston Gazette*, September 5, 1774; "Powder taken from the Charleston Magazine," Clarke and Force, *American Archives*, series four, 1:762: http://lincoln.lib.niu.edu/cgi-bin /amarch/getdoc.pl?/var/l ib/philologic/databases/amarch/.863.

4. *Boston Evening-Post* and *Boston Gazette*, September 5, 1774; Andrews, "Letters," 351–52; Dirk Hoerder, *Crowd Action in Revolutionary Massachusetts* (New York: Academic Press, 1977), 288.

5. Andrews, "Letters," 351, 353; *Boston Evening-Post* and *Boston Gazette*, September 5, 1774; Hoerder, *Crowd Action in Revolutionary Massachusetts*, 288–89.

6. Franklin B. Dexter, ed., *The Literary Diary of Ezra Stiles* (New York: Charles Scribner's Sons, 1901), 1:479–81.

7. Diary of Reverend Stephen Williams (transcript copy), Richard Salter Storrs Library, Longmeadow, MA, book 8, 311–13.

8. Andrews, "Letters," 352.

9. Joseph Warren to Samuel Adams, September 4, 1774, Samuel Adams Papers, Bancroft Collection, New York Public Library; reprinted in Frothingham, *Life and Times of Joseph Warren*, 356.

10. *Boston Gazette* and *Boston Evening-Post*, September 5, 1774; *Massachusetts Gazette*, September 7, 1774. Gage's statement was intended for a public audience.

11. *Boston Gazette* and *Boston Evening-Post*, September 5, 1774; Wroth, *Province in Rebellion*, 542–43; Andrews, "Letters," 352.

12. Thomas Young to Samuel Adams, September 4, 1774, Samuel Adams Papers, Bancroft Collection, New York Public Library.

13. Warren to Samuel Adams, September 4, 1774, in Frothingham, *Life and Times of Joseph Warren*, 356; *Boston Evening-Post* and *Boston Gazette*, September 5, 1774; Edward Hill to John Adams, September 4, 1774, in Butterfield, *Adams Family Correspondence*, 1:149.

14. Hoerder, *Crowd Action*, 289–90.

15. Ibid., 290.

16. Benjamin Hallowell to Gage, September 8, 1774, Wroth, *Province in Rebellion*, 609–12; *Boston Evening-Post* and *Boston Gazette*, September 5, 1774; Andrews, "Letters," 352.

17. Andrews, "Letters," 352–53; *Boston Evening-Post* and *Boston Gazette*, September 5, 1774.

18. Ibid.; *Massachusetts Gazette*, September 7, 1774, reproduced in Clarke and Force, *American Archives*, series four, 1:764–66: http://lincoln.lib .niu.edu/cgi-bin/amarch/getdoc.pl?/var/l ib/philologic/databases/amarch /.864.

19. Ibid.

20. Stiles, *Diary*, 481.

21. *Boston Evening-Post* and *Boston Gazette*, September 5, 1774; William Tudor, ed., *Deacon Tudor's Diary* (Boston: W. Spooner, 1896), 49.

22. Andrews, "Letters," 355.

23. Gage to Dartmouth, September 2, 1774, Carter, *Gage Correspondence*, 1:370.

24. Ibid.

8: Worcester County: Militia

1. Gage to Dartmouth, August 27, 1774, Carter, *Gage Correspondence*, 1:366–67.

2. Ibid., 1:366.

3. MacWade, *Worcester County Elite*, 29–31, 79; the genealogy of the Chandler clan is traced in Nutt, *History of Worcester*, 74–79.

4. American Political Society, Minutes, American Antiquarian Society. Viewable on the documents page of rayraphael.com.

5. Franklin P. Rice, ed., *Worcester Town Records from 1753 to 1783* (Worcester: Worcester Society of Antiquity, 1882), 230–33; *Boston News-Letter* and *Massachusetts Gazette*, June 30, 1774; *Boston Gazette*, July 4, 1774.

6. American Political Society, Minutes; Albert A. Lovell, *Worcester in the War of the Revolution: Embracing the Acts of the Town from 1765 to 1783* (Worcester: Tyler & Seagrave, 1876), 26; Kenneth J. Moynihan, *A History of Worcester, 1674–1848* (Charleston, SC: History Press, 2007), 67.

7. American Political Society, Minutes.

8. "The Work of a Blacksmith," *Forge: The Bigelow Society Quarterly* 25:3 (July 1996): http://bigelowsociety.com/Blacksmith.html.

9. Rice, *Worcester Town Records*, 87, 131, 162, 180, 203, 215; American Political Society, Minutes. Images of the scratched-out document can be viewed on the document page of rayraphael.com.

10. American Political Society, Minutes; Allan French, *General Gage's Informers* (Ann Arbor: University of Michigan Press, 1932), 15; "General Gage's Instructions, of 22d February/75, to Captain Brown and Ensign D'Berniere," and "Narrative, &c.," Massachusetts Historical Society, *Collections* 4 (1916): 204–18.

11. American Political Society, Minutes; Rice, *Worcester Town Records*, 234, 238–39, *Massachusetts Gazette*, September 15, 1774; *Boston Evening-Post*, September 19, 1774; William Lincoln, *History of Worcester, Massachusetts, from Its Earliest Settlement to September, 1836* (Worcester: Charles Hersey, 1862), 83; Lovell, *Worcester in the War of the Revolution*, 38, 41. The original town records are stored today in the basement of Worcester's City Hall. The inked-out pages are reproduced on the document page of rayraphael.com.

12. William Lincoln, ed., *The Journals of Each Provincial Congress of Massachusetts in 1774 and 1775, and of the Committee of Safety, with an Appendix, Containing the*

Proceedings of the County Conventions (Boston: Dutton and Wentworth, 1838), 631, 629.

13. Lincoln, *Journals of Provincial Congress/County Conventions*, 631–35; Wroth, *Province in Rebellion*, 894–97. In the well-known and influential Suffolk Resolves passed in early September, Bostonians would proclaim that King George III was their "rightful sovereign" and "justly entitled" to their allegiance.

14. Ebenezer Parkman, Diary, September 6 and 7, 1774, American Antiquarian Society. Breck, Ebenezer's son, gave an account of the day to his father, a minister from Westborough, who recorded the day's events in his diary. The diary can be accessed on the documents page of rayraphael.com.

15. Lee Newcomer, *The Embattled Farmers: A Massachusetts Countryside in the American Revolution* (New York: King's Crown Press, 1953), 2–5.

16. "Staves and fife": Parkman, Diary, September 6. Council Proceedings, August 31, 1774, Wroth, *Province in Rebellion*, 525; Gage to Dartmouth, September 2, 1774, Carter, *Gage Correspondence*, 1:370.

17. American Political Society, Minutes; Parkman, Diary September 7, 1774. Parkman reported that "a few companys had arms," and a secondhand account from an anonymous Tory reported that "about one thousand of them had fire-arms." See Boston's *Weekly News-Letter*, February 23, 1775, and New York's *Rivington's Gazette*, March 9, 1775.

18. Lincoln, *Journals of Provincial Congress/County Convention*, 635.

19. Parkman, Diary, September 7; Lincoln, *Journals of Provincial Congress/County Convention*, 635–37.

20. Parkman, Diary, September 7; Lincoln, *Journals of Provincial Congress/County Conventions*, 637. A more detailed narrative of the day's proceedings appears in Ray Raphael, *The First American Revolution: Before Lexington and Concord* (New York: The New Press, 2002), 130–38.

21. Lincoln, *Journals of Provincial Congress/County Conventions*, 637; Andrew M. Davis, *The Confiscation of John Chandler's Estate* (Boston: Houghton Mifflin, 1903), 224.

22. Lincoln, *Journals of Provincial Congress/County Conventions*, 639.

23. Ibid.

24. Ibid. Rice, *Worcester Town Records*, 322, 389, 439. Artemas Ward was also on that ballot, although he too lost.

25. Lincoln, *Journals of Provincial Congress/County Conventions*, 641.

26. Ibid., 642.

27. Fred Anderson, *A People's Army: Massachusetts Soldiers and Society in the Seven Years' War* (Chapel Hill, University of North Carolina Press, 1984), 27.

28. Lincoln, *Journals of Provincial Congress/County Conventions*, 643.

29. Minutemen covenant for Ipswich, January 14, 1775, in Herbert T. Wade and Robert A. Lively, *This Glorious Cause: The Adventures of Two Company Officers in Washington's Army* (Princeton: Princeton University Press, 1958), 9.

30. Lincoln, *Journals of Provincial Congress/County Conventions*, 643–44.
31. Ibid., 643.

9: Philadelphia and Cambridge: Two Congresses

1. Jensen, *Founding of a Nation*, 475.
2. Committee of Philadelphia to Boston Committee, May 21, 1774, Clarke and Force, *American Archives*, series four, 1:341. http://lincoln.lib.niu.edu/cgi-bin/amarch/getdoc.pl?/var/1 ib/philologic/databases/amarch/.322. The intercolonial network of committees of correspondence and colonial assemblies that organized this meeting sent invitations not only to the twelve colonies that attended but also to Quebec, Nova Scotia, St. John's Island, Georgia, East Florida, and West Florida, all of which declined to dispatch deputies. Even so, the vast majority of British citizens on the continent had representatives in the most broadly based convention yet to be assembled in British North America. The Albany Congress of 1754 had attracted delegates from only seven colonies, and the Stamp Act Congress of 1765 only nine.
3. Resolutions of the House of Representatives of Massachusetts, June 17, 1774, Clarke and Force, *American Archives*, series four, 1:421: http://lincoln.lib.niu.edu/cgi-bin/amarch/getdoc.pl?/var/lib/philologic/databases/amarch/.456.
4. John Adams, *Diary and Autobiography*, L.H. Butterfield, ed. (Cambridge: Harvard University Press, 1961), 2:96–97 (June 20 and 25).
5. Ibid., 2:97–98, 103–6 (August 10, 20, and 22).
6. Ibid., 2:114 (August 29); Dave DeWitt, *The Founding Foodies: How Washington, Jefferson, and Franklin Revolutionized American Cuisine* (Naperville, IL: Sourcebooks, 2010), 49; City Tavern website: http://www.citytavern.com/history3.html.
7. Adams, *Diary and Autobiography*, 2:109 (August 23).
8. James Warren to John Adams, July 14, 1774, *Warren-Adams Letters* (Boston: Massachusetts Historical Society, 1917), 1:26; Adams, *Diary and Autobiography*, 2:122 (September 5).
9. "I am not a Virginian, but an American," Patrick Henry, the firebrand from the large colony of Virginia, famously pronounced. Ironically, Henry's comment is often used to demonstrate national unity at this moment in time, but its political effect was self-serving. Following his logic, if state identities were eliminated, voting would have to be proportional, and this would give Virginia, by far the largest colony, an overwhelming influence in Congress. See Adams, *Diary and Autobiography*, 2:125.
10. John Adams to Abigail Adams, September 8, 1774, *Adams Family Correspondence*, 1:150–1. Accessible on the Web at National Archives, Founders Online: http://founders.archives.gov/?q=Volume%3AAdams-04–01&s=1511311112&r=99; Silas Deane to Elizabeth Deane, September 7, 1774, *Letters of Delegates to*

Congress, 1:35, Library of Congress, American Memory: http://memory.loc
.gov/ammem/amlaw/lwdglink.html.

11. Silas Deane to Elizabeth Deane, September 7, 1774, *Letters of Delegates to Congress*, 1:35; John Adams to Abigail Adams, September 8 and 18, 1774, *Adams Family Correspondence*, 1:150–1 and 157–8. *Aut Mors Aut Libertas* appeared as a banner to Gadsden's column in *South Carolina Gazette and Country Journal*, February 11, 1766.

12. William Lincoln, ed., *The Journals of Each Provincial Congress of Massachusetts in 1774 and 1775, and of the Committee of Safety, with an Appendix, Containing the Proceedings of the County Conventions* (Boston: Dutton and Wentworth, 1838), 601–5. The proceedings of other county conventions appear on 609–60.

13. *Journals of the Continental Congress*, September 17, 1774, 1:39, at Library of Congress, American Memory: http://memory.loc.gov/ammem/amlaw/lwjclink.html.

14. Adams, *Diary and Autobiography*, 2:134–35.

15. Silas Deane to Elizabeth Deane, September 7, 1774, *Letters of Delegates to Congress*, 1:35; Joseph Reed to [Charles Pettit?], September 4, 1774, quoted in Jack Rakove, *Beginnings of National Politics: An Interpretive History of the Continental Congress* (New York: Alfred A. Knopf, 1979), 45; *Journals of Continental Congress*, October 8, 1774, 58–59.

16. *Journals of Continental Congress*, October 11, 1774, 61–62.

17. Samuel Adams to James Warren, writing from Philadelphia, fall of 1774, *Warren-Adams Letters*, 26. This letter was clearly written from Philadelphia, as stated in the *Warren-Adams Letters*, but it could not have been written on May 21, as indicated there. Adams was not in Philadelphia at the time, and the context would not fit. It does mesh perfectly with everything else Adams was writing in September and October 1774.

18. Samuel Adams to Joseph Warren, September 25, 1774, Cushing, *Writings of Samuel Adams*, 3:159.

19. John Adams to Joseph Palmer, September 26, 1774, and Adams to William Tudor, October 7, 1774, Robert J. Taylor, ed., *Papers of John Adams* (Cambridge, MA: Harvard University Press, 1977), 2:173, 187–88.

20. Robert McKenzie to Washington, September 13, 1774, and Washington to Robert McKenzie, October 9, 1774, W. W. Abbot and Dorothy Twohig, eds. *The Papers of George Washington* (Colonial Series), (Charlottesville: University Press of Virginia, 1983–) 10:161 and 10:171–72.

21. Worcester Committee to Boston Committee, August 15, 1774, Boston Committee of Correspondence, Correspondence and Proceedings, Bancroft Collection, New York Public Library, microfilm reel 2, letter 498, reproduced in Wroth, *Province in Rebellion*, 808.

22. Ibid. For intelligence on Gage's intentions, see Donald E. Johnson, *Worcester in the War for Independence* (Clark University PhD Thesis, 1953), 63; and John Andrews's letter of August 13: "It's currently reported that a regiment is to go to

Worcester to protect the Court, which is to sit there soon." In Andrews, "Letters," 341.

23. Boston's August 17 response to Worcester's letter is in Wroth, *Province in Rebellion*, 812–13.

24. Wroth, *Province in Rebellion*, 689–92. For county populations in 1776, see Lincoln, *Journals of Provincial Congress/County Conventions*, 755.

25. Court Closures: Of the nine counties in contiguous Massachusetts, only Suffolk and Essex did not close their courts, but that did not mean they were on a different page. Suffolk contributed its influential resolves, and Essex, also because of the proximity of British troops guarding Governor Gage in Salem, adopted a different strategy. The Essex County committees of correspondence devised an ingenious plan to avoid what could have been a cataclysmic confrontation with British Regulars. Rather than close the courts and force officials to walk the gauntlet, Essex County activists allowed the judges to do business, but only by virtue of their original appointments *before* the Massachusetts Government Act. This was an innovative and decidedly nonviolent method of staging a revolution: by a twist of logic. The convention resolved that since "no authority whatever" could legally alter the authority of the judges, they would continue to enforce the old laws "as if the aforementioned act of parliament [the Massachusetts Government Act] had never been made." By local decree, they nullified an act of Parliament and proclaimed "that all civil officers in the province, as well as private persons, who shall dare to conduct in conformity to the aforementioned act . . . are unfit for civil society; their lands ought not to be tilled by labor of any American, nor their families supplied with clothing or food." In conclusion, they declared their willingness to go to war: "If the despotism and violence of our enemies should finally reduce us to the sad necessity, we, undaunted, are ready to appeal to the last resort of states; and will, in support of our rights, encounter even death, 'sensible that he can never die too soon, who lays down his life in support of the laws and liberties of his country.' " While threatening war, they prevented Gage from initiating one by *not* staging a massive public demonstration, as activists had done in the western counties. See Lincoln, *Journals of Provincial Congress/County Conventions*, 616–18.

Instructions: Ray Raphael, "The People's Voice in Revolutionary America," *Common-Place* 9:1 (October 2008); Kenneth Colegrove, "New England Town Mandates," Colonial Society of Massachusetts, *Publications* 21 (1919): 411–49. Accessible online at http://is.gd/ivsat; J.R. Pole, *Political Representation in England and the Origins of the American Republic* (New York: St. Martin's Press 1966): 72–75, 80, 94–95, 161–65, 211–14, 229–40, 441, 541–42.

26. Plymouth Instruction, September 30, 1774, Wroth, *Province in Rebellion*, 1305; Andrews to Barrell, October 6, Andrews, "Letters," 373–74.

27. Rice, *Worcester Town Records*, 244; Wroth, *Province in Rebellion*, 1312. These pages of the *Worcester Town Records* are reproduced on the documents page of rayraphael.com. This wording originated in the American Political Society,

which drafted and approved the instructions the day before the town meeting. See American Political Society, Minutes, October 3, 1774.

28. This was precisely the program John Adams and Samuel Adams warned against. If Timothy Bigelow were able to convince a majority of the upcoming Provincial Congress to "raise" such a government, Massachusetts would likely lose the support of the Continental Congress. But the people of Worcester were expressing only a wish, not a demand. They instructed Bigelow also "to give diligent attention" to the advice of the Continental Congress, and "if your advices from Said Congress should not perfectly coincide with these our instructions respecting the mode of Government for this Province, you are to desist in acting any further on that matter untill you have further instructions." The people of Worcester had expressed their views, but they would not insist on them to the point of disunity. (Wroth, *Province in Rebellion*, 1313.)

29. Thomas Gage, Proclamation Dissolving the General Court, Wroth, *Province in Rebellion*, 554.

30. Lincoln, *Journals of Provincial Congress/County Conventions*, 6.

31. Joseph Warren to Josiah Quincy, Jr., November 21, 1774, reprinted in Frothingham, *Life and Times of Joseph Warren*, 395; Andrews, "Letters," 373. On October 16, after the Provincial Congress had been meeting for five days, John Pitt reported to Samuel Adams, who was still attending the Continental Congress, that the delegates from Boston were "by far the most moderate Men." See John Pitt to Samuel Adams, October 16, 1774, Samuel Adams Papers, Bancroft Collection, New York Public Library.

32. Joseph Warren to Samuel Adams, September 4, 1774, in Frothingham, *Life and Times of Joseph Warren*, 358; Charter of Massachusetts Bay, 1629, (Yale Law School, Avalon Project): http://avalon.law.yale.edu/17th_century/mass03.asp.

33. Gage to Dartmouth, October 17, Carter, *Gage Correspondence*, 1:379; Andrews, "Letters," 380–81; James Lovell to Josiah Quincy Jr., October 28, 1774, Clarke and Force, *American Archives*, series four, 6:948: http://lincoln.lib.niu.edu/cgi-bin/amarch/getdoc.pl?/var/lib/philologic/databases/amarch/.1092.

34. Wroth, *Province in Rebellion*, 81–82. Although the farming regions of Massachusetts were well represented in the Provincial Congress, the most radical of the country revolutionaries were not even there. Wroth observed that most of those elected to the Provincial Congress were well-to-do men not very representative of their constituencies. Twenty-two percent were merchants, lawyers, or doctors—far above the statistical norm for a rural society. According to the 1771 tax assessments, 60 percent ranked among the wealthiest 10 percent of their towns, and virtually all ranked in the top half. About 85 percent had previously held public office; more than 70 percent of the former representatives to the General Court had been elected to serve their communities in this new capacity (see *Province in Rebellion*, 80–81). The local revolutionaries who had closed the courts, for whatever reasons, had turned to many of their old leaders when it came time to put together some semblance of a new government. Perhaps it was their

desire not to be perceived as a "mob"; perhaps they didn't want to rock the boat any more than necessary; perhaps they reasoned that previous experience would serve as an asset in the tasks ahead. In any case, the Massachusetts revolution of 1774 signified more a change in governmental structure than in representational leadership.

35. Galloway's plan, introduced on September 28, is in *Journals of Continental Congress*, 1:43–48. It can be accessed at TeachingAmericanHistory.org: http://teachingamericanhistory.org/library/document/galloways- plan-of-union/.

36. *Journals of Continental Congress*, 1:116–21. The annotated text can also be accessed at: http://en.wikipedia.org/wiki/Petition_to_the_King.

37. *Journals of Continental Congress*, 1:64–80.

38. Ibid., 1:75–80. A complete text of the Continental Association is reprinted in Jack Greene, ed., *Colonies to Nation, 1763–1789: A Documentary History of the American Revolution* (New York: W.W. Norton, 1975), 247–50, and can be accessed at TeachingAmericanHistory.org: http://teachingamericanhistory.org/library/document/galloways-plan-of-union/.

10: New England: Arms Race

1. Andrews, "Letters," 373; "Address of the County of Worcester," October 5, 1774, Wroth, *Province in Rebellion*, 1212–14. This address is sometimes attributed to an earlier date, but Wroth cites evidence contradicting the earlier dating.

2. Andrews, "Letters," 373.

3. Abigail Adams to John Adams, September 22, 1774, *Adams Family Papers: An Electronic Archive*, Massachusetts Historical Society: http://www.masshist.org/digitaladams/.

4. Salisbury Family Papers, American Antiquarian Society, Worcester; Andrews, "Letters," 360; William Tudor to John Adams, September 17, 1774, in Robert J. Taylor, ed., *Papers of John Adams* (Cambridge, MA: Harvard University Press, 1977), 2:166–67.

5. "The General has set about two hundred soldiers to work on fortifications this morning," John Andrews reported. Gage wanted to buttress the wall and its two gates with additional timbers, but there he ran into a snag: "The townspeople are in general very uneasy and dissatisfied with the Governor's fortifying the entrance; so much so, they cant get any one workman to assist 'em. They've got an engineer from New York, who is trying what he can do with a number of carpenters and masons out of the army. They talk of sending to New York for a number of mechanics to affect it: It is my opinion, if they are wise, they wont come." See Andrews, "Letters," 359, 355. Yet try as they might, the people of Boston could not keep Gage from fortifying the entry to their town. The general set his own soldiers to work, not only in "repairing and mantling" the wooden structures, but also "throwing up an entrenchment," as armies did in preparation for battle. See Thomas Newell, "Diary of Mr. Thomas Newell,"

Massachusetts Historical Society, *Publications* 15 (1877), 358 (entry for September 19).

6. Newell, "Diary," 357; Andrews, "Letters," 356, 358.

7. Andrews, "Letters," 354, 356.

8. Ibid., 356–57.

9. Ibid., 359–60.

10. Ibid., 362.

11. Ibid. Both cannon-stealing incidents are reported and analyzed in J.L. Bell, "Behold, the Guns Were Gone: Four Brass Cannon and the Start of the American Revolution," presented at the Boston Area Early American History Summer Sessions, 2001, Massachusetts Historical Society, 12–23.

12. Lincoln, *Journals of Provincial Congress/County Conventions*, 636.

13. By calling for each town to acquire and prepare field pieces, the Worcester Convention was taking the lead. The Suffolk County Convention, in its famous resolves issued a few days later, had advised citizens "to acquaint themselves with the art of war as soon as possible, and do, for that purpose, appear under arms at least once every week," but it said nothing about field pieces, and with good reason: if it had done so, moderate delegates to the Continental Congress, thinking that Massachusetts was too aggressive, would likely have withheld their support. A lust for field pieces would have overstepped the thin line between preparing for the possibility of war, which was acceptable, and egging on, which was not. For those wishing a peaceful reconciliation, puffing up chests to get their way with London was one thing, but acquiring cannons would be too graphic. For most of Massachusetts, though, the line demarking acceptability was drawn differently. Even those patriots who opposed offensive measures could not argue against doing everything possible to prepare for a British military assault—and "everything" included field pieces. Hence the mad scramble to procure as many as possible as quickly as possible.

14. "Six good pieces": Benjamin Kent to John Adams, September 23, 1774, quoted in Bell, "Behold, the Guns Were Gone," 25. Bell conjectures that these may have been the cannons that hardware merchant William Molineux, one of Boston's chief street leaders, purchased from another merchant, Joseph Webb, and tried to deliver to country patriots. "Fifty Cannon": William Tudor to John Adams, September 17, 1774, in Taylor, ed., *Papers of John Adams*, 2:166–67. "About 20 pieces of cannon": Quoted in Bell, "Behold, the Guns Were Gone," 7. This was reported to Brigadier General Earl Percy, recently arrived to assist General Gage.

15. Lincoln, *Journals of Provincial Congress/County Conventions*, 23, 28.

16. Ibid., 29–30.

17. Ibid., 31–33.

18. Ibid., 33, 38–39.

19. Ibid., 35; George Henry Preble, *Genealogical Sketch of the First Three Generations of Prebles in America* (Boston: David Clapp & Son, 1868), 53.

20. Lincoln, *Journals of Provincial Congress/County Conventions*, 33–34, 41.

21. Andrews, "Letters," 381.

22. Gage to Dartmouth, September 12, 1774, Carter, *Gage Correspondence*, 1:374; Gage to Barrington, October 3, November 1, and November 2, Carter, *Gage Correspondence*, 2:656, 2:658, and 2:659.

23. Dartmouth to Gage, October 17, 1774, Carter, *Gage Correspondence*, 2:174.

24. King George III to Lord North, November 18 and 19, 1774, W. Bodham Donne, ed., *The Correspondence of King George the Third with Lord North, 1768–1783* (New York: Da Capo Press, 1971), 1:215–6. These letters are also in Sir John Fortescue, *Correspondence of King George the Third* (London: Frank Cass, 1967), 3:153–54, but both dated November 18. Peter Orlando Hutchinson, ed., *The Diary and Letters of His Excellency Thomas Hutchinson, Esq.* (Boston: Houghton Mifflin, 1884), 1:297.

25. King George III speech to the House of Lords, November 30, 1774, Clarke and Force, *American Archives*, fourth series, 6:1465: http://lincoln.lib.niu.edu /cgi-bin/amarch/getdoc.pl?/var/lib/philologic/databases/amarch/.1769. On November 19, North confessed to Hutchinson, "I will venture to tell you that Parliament was dissolved on this account—that we might, at the beginning of a Parliament, take such measures as we could depend upon a Parliament to prosecute to effect." See Hutchinson, *Diary*, 1:298.

26. Lord Suffolk to King George III, October 17, 1774, and Lord North to King George III, October 18, 1774, in Fortescue, *Correspondence of King George the Third*, 3:147–48; "Order in Council," Wroth, *Province in Rebellion*, 1206–7; Dartmouth to Gage, October 19, 1774, Carter, *Gage Correspondence*, 2:176; Gage to Dartmouth, December 15, 1774, Carter, *Gage Correspondence*, 1:385–86. Enclosed in Dartmouth's letter to Gage, which transmitted the council order, were the letters from the British ambassador to Holland, Sir Joseph Yorke, that told of the Dutch shipment.

27. Gage to commissioner of customs, December 6, 1774, Wroth, *Province in Rebellion*, 1231; Gage to Dartmouth, December 15, 1774, Carter, *Gage Correspondence*, 1:385–86; Charles Dudley, collector, and John Nicoll, Rhode Island comptroller, to the customs commissioners in Boston, enclosure to letter dated December 20, 1774, in Fortescue, *Correspondence of King George the Third*, 3:159; Bell, "Behold, the Guns Were Gone," 33; Boston1775.blogspot.com/, December 14, 2013.

28. Wroth, *Province in Rebellion*, 1206 (footnote 3); *Boston Gazette*, December 12, 1774.

29. John Cochran to Governor Wentworth and Wentworth to Gage, December 14, 1774, http://www.mocavo.com/New-Hampshire-Provincial-and-State-Papers -Volume-7/563856/446; George Meserve, collector, and Robert Traill, comptroller, to customs commissioners, December 16, 1774, enclosure to letter dated December 20, 1774, in Fortescue, *Correspondence of King George the Third*, 3:161.

30. Wentworth to Gage, December 14, 1774: http://hdl.handle.net/2027/uc1.$b 727987 or http://www.mocavo.com/New-Hampshire-Provincial-and-State -Papers-Volume-7/563856/446.

31. John Wentworth to George Erving, January 5, 1775: http://www.library
.unh.edu/special/index.php/exhibits/capture-of-fort-william-and-mary
/wentworth6. "Mr. Benning Wentworth" was not the former governor, who
had died in 1770. Fischer, *Paul Revere's Ride* (New York: Oxford University
Press), 56, referencing the *New York Journal*. Several documents relating to
the Portsmouth event are presented in Charles L. Parsons, "The Capture of
Fort William and Mary, December 14 and 15, 1774," *New Hampshire Historical Society Proceedings* 4 (1899–1905), 18–47: http://babel.hathitrust.org/cgi
/pt?id=uc1.sb727987.

11: Salem, Worcester, or Concord: Where Will the British Strike?

1. Gage to Barrington, October 3, 1774, Carter, *Gage Correspondence*, 2:656. Dartmouth told Gage that a satisfactory resolution depended on the governor's "fortitude and discretion." (Dartmouth to Gage, Carter, *Gage Correspondence*, October
17, 1774, 2:174.)

2. Gage to Dartmouth, September 25, 1774, Carter, *Gage Correspondence*, 1:375.
Gage was referring to a letter he had sent to Thomas Hutchinson on July
12 but is not extant. King George III to Lord North, November 19, 1774,
Donne, *Correspondence of King George the Third with Lord North*, 1:216, and
also in Fortescue, *Correspondence of King George the Third*, 3:154, but dated
November 18. Peter Orlando Hutchinson, ed., *Diary and Letters of His Excellency Thomas Hutchinson*, 1:297. The reaction in London was described by
William Knox: "What turned us all so much against Gage was his telling
Governor Hutchinson that, in his opinion, the only thing to be done was
to suspend the Acts, and, in the mean time, make preparation for enforcing
them." Quoted in John Shy, *Toward Lexington: The Role of the British Army
in the Coming of the American Revolution* (Princeton: Princeton University
Press, 1965), 411.

3. Gage to Dartmouth, September 25, 1774, Carter, *Gage Correspondence*, 1:375.

4. William Emerson, *Diaries and Letters of William Emerson*, 1743–1776, Amelia
Forbes Emerson, ed. (Boston: Thomas Todd, 1972), 59; Lincoln, *Journals of Provincial Congress/County Conventions*, 505.

5. Lincoln, *Journals of Provincial Congress/County Conventions*, 505–11; spy report of
March 3, Wroth, *Province in Rebellion*, 1972.

6. Lincoln, *Journals of Provincial Congress/County Conventions*, 507.

7. Ibid., 509–10.

8. Ibid., 510–11.

9. French, *General Gage's Informers*, 147–201.

10. Wroth, *Province in Rebellion*, 1969.

11. Ibid.

12. Ibid., 1968.

13. Gage to Dartmouth, March 4, 1775, Carter, *Gage Correspondence*, 1:395. Brass cannons, because they were so much lighter than iron ones, were highly prized.

14. Charles M. Endicott, "Leslie's Retreat, or the Resistance to British Arms, at the North Bridge in Salem," *Proceedings of the Essex Institute* (Salem, MA: William Ives and George Pease, 1856), 1:89–135. Endicott's narrative blends contemporaneous accounts with recollections of informants who were children at the time but heard the stories from their parents and neighbors. Fortunately, he attaches both his primary and his secondary sources, articles from the *Essex Gazette* of February 28 and March 7, and oral histories taken in the middle of the nineteenth century. Quotations here are from the narrative of William Gavett, a child at the time, who confesses he saw the Regulars march by but nothing more, and who states that his account is based on "what I was afterwards told, the subject being very often discussed in my hearing for a long time." Some of these oral histories are supported in part by contemporaneous evidence. According to accounts in the *Essex Gazette*, for instance, gondolas were scuttled and breasts were pricked, but whether Whicher bared his breast and dared the troops is not confirmed.

15. *Essex Gazette*, February 28 and March 7, 1775, reproduced in Endicott, "Leslie's Retreat," 124, 126.

16. The "Provincial grand magazine" quotation is from "Extract of a Letter from Boston, to a Gentleman in Philadelphia, April 5, 1775," Clarke and Force, *American Archives*, series four, 2:255. The rest is from Jerome Carter Hosmer, ed., *The Narrative of General Gage's Spies, March, 1775* (Boston: Bostonian Society, 1912), 10–11. Gage's instructions and the spies' report also appear in "General Gage's Instructions, of 22d February, 1775, to Captain Brown and Ensign D'Bernicre," and "Narrative, &c.," Massachusetts Historical Society, *Collections* 4 (1916): 204–18. These documents were originally published by Boston printer J. Gill in 1779 under the title, "General Gage's instructions, of 22d February 1775, to Captain Brown and Ensign d'Bernicre [i.e., De Berniere], (of the army under his command) whom he ordered to take a sketch of the roads, passes, heights, &c. from Boston to Worcester, and to make other observations; with a curious narrative of occurences during their mission, wrote by the ensign; Together with an account of their doings, in consequence of further orders and instructions from General Gage, of the 20th March following, to proceed to Concord, to reconnoitre and find out the state of the provincial magazines; what number of cannon, &c. they have, and in what condition. Also, an account of the transactions of the British troops, from the time they marched out of Boston, on the evening of the 18th, 'till their confused retreat back, on the ever memorable nineteenth of April 1775; and a return of their killed, wounded and missing on that auspicious day, as made to General Gage. (Left in town by a British officer previous to the evacuation of it by the enemy, and now printed for the information and amusement of the curious.)"

17. Hosmer, *Narrative of Spies*, 12–14.

18. Ibid., 12–30. Nineteenth-century writers guessed that the horseman was Timothy Bigelow, but we have no contemporaneous evidence for this.

19. Hosmer, *Narrative of Spies*, 18; Report of March 8, 1775, Wroth, *Province in Rebellion*, 1974; French, *General Gage's Informers*, 15: https://archive.org/stream /narrativegeneraooberngoog#page/n4/mode/2up.

20. French, *General Gage's Informers*, 11–13.

21. Hosmer, *Narrative of Spies*, 31–33.

22. Spy report of March 26, Wroth, *Province in Rebellion*, 1976. "These consist of 8 field pieces, 2 mortars, 70 half Barrels Gun powder, 100 hogsheads Salt, 350 Barrels flour, 200 Quintals of fish, 300 stand of Arms with some Bread Pease, Beans &c," the report specified. See April 14 minutes of the committee of safety, Lincoln, *Journals of Provincial Congress/County Conventions*, 514.

23. Emerson, *Diary*, 69, 66.

24. Ibid., 68.

25. Ibid., 114–16.

26. Lincoln, *Journals of Provincial Congress/County Conventions*, 513, 99.

27. Hawley to Thomas Cushing, February 22, 1775, Lincoln, *Journals of Provincial Congress/County Conventions*, 748–51.

28. Wroth, *Province in Rebellion*, 1555.

29. Andrews, "Letters," 400.

30. Ibid., 401.

12: Massachusetts: Sixteen Days

1. *Boston Gazette*, April 3, 1775; James Warren to Mercy Otis Warren, April 6, 1775, *Warren-Adams Letters* (Boston: Massachusetts Historical Society, 1917), 1:44. The text of the New England Trade and Fisheries Act can be accessed at Clarke and Force, *American Archives*, series four, 1:1691–95, on the Web at: http:// lincoln.lib.niu.edu/cgi-bin/amarch/getdoc.pl?/var/lib/philologic/databases /amarch/.1903.

2. Emerson, *Diary*, 70–71; Fischer, *Paul Revere's Ride*, 309.

3. Lincoln, *Journal of Provincial Congress/County Conventions*, 117; Franklin B. Dexter, ed., *The Literary Diary of Ezra Stiles* (New York: Charles Scribner's Sons, 1901), 1:530. Six days later, the *Salem Gazette* also reported that the patriots' army was to form at Worcester. See Frothingham, *Life and Times of Joseph Warren*, 453.

4. British spy report of April 9, Wroth, *Province in Rebellion*, 1779–80.

5. Ibid.

6. Lincoln, *Journal of Provincial Congress/County Conventions*, 121.

7. Ibid., 120–29.

8. Wroth, *Province in Rebellion*, 1978; French, *General Gage's Informers*, 21–22. French dates this report April 11, but Wroth says April 7, the date of the verso in which it was found.

9. Lincoln, *Journal of Provincial Congress/County Conventions*, 135; Wroth, *Province in Rebellion*, 1983, 1981.

10. Lincoln, *Journal of Provincial Congress/County Conventions*, 137.

11. Ibid., 139–40.

12. Ibid., 141–42.

13. Ibid., 142–43.

14. Ibid., 756.

15. Ibid., 146–47.

16. Emerson, *Diary*, 70; Samuel Swift to John Adams, March 31, 1775, Taylor, *Papers of John Adams*, 2:409–10. See also Joseph Warren to Arthur Lee, April 3, 1775, *American Archives*, fourth series, 2:255. URL: http://lincoln.lib.niu.edu/cgi-bin/amarch/getdoc.pl?/var/lib/philologic/databases/amarch/.2247, and "Extract of a Letter from Boston, to a Gentleman in Philadelphia, April 5, 1775," Clarke and Force, *American Archives*, series four, 2:255: http://lincoln.lib.niu.edu/cgi-bin/amarch/getdoc.pl?/var/lib/philologic/databases/amarch/.2240.

17. Hosmer quoted in Fischer, *Paul Revere's Ride*, 87; James Warren to Mercy Otis Warren, April 6, 1775, *Warren-Adams Letters*, 1:44–45.

18. James Warren to Mercy Otis Warren, April 7, 1775, *Warren–Adams Letters*, 1:45.

19. *Massachusetts Gazette*, April 3–10, 1775; Andrews, "Letters," 402; Lincoln, *Journal of Provincial Congress/County Conventions*, 142–43.

20. Jill Lepore, *Book of Ages: The Life and Opinions of Jane Franklin* (New York: Alfred A. Knopf, 2013), 169–70.

21. For when Gage received the letter and its copy, see Gage to Dartmouth, April 22, 1775, Carter, *Gage Correspondence*, 1:396. A discussion of the circuitous routes taken by the letter and its copy is in John Alden, *General Gage in America* (Baton Rouge; Louisiana State University Press, 1948), 233–44. For icy waters, see *London Gazette*, February 11, 1775, dispatch from Copenhagen on January 24: https://www.thegazette.co.uk/London/issue/11535/page/1.

22. Dartmouth to Gage, January 27, 1775, Carter, *Gage Correspondence*, 1:179–83.

23. Fischer, *Paul Revere's Ride*, 88; Andrews, "Letters," 403–4.

24. Paul Revere to Jeremy Belknap, circa 1798, Massachusetts Historical Society, Collections Online: http://www.masshist.org/database/99.

25. Isaiah Thomas, *History of Printing in America* (New York: B. Franklin, 1967 reprint; first published in 1810), 180–81; Nutt, *History of Worcester*, 245; Ray Raphael, *Founders: The People Who Brought You a Nation* (New York: The New Press, 209), 177–78.

26. Lincoln, *Journal of Provincial Congress/County Conventions*, 515–16.

27. Ibid., 516–17.

28. Ibid., 515–18.

29. Recollection of Richard Devens, undated, in Frothingham, *History of the Siege of Boston*, 57–58; Fischer, *Paul Revere's Ride*, 90–91.

30. Fischer, *Paul Revere's Ride*, 93–94; French, *General Gage's Informers*, 36 (HMS *Boyne*) and 38 (Mackenzie diary).

31. Gage to Lieutenant Colonel Francis Smith, April 18, 1775, in French, *General Gage's Informers*, 31–32.

32. Elbridge Henry Goss, *The Life of Colonel Paul Revere* (Boston: Howard W. Spur, 1909), 221. This version, revised in 1783, is a slight revision of Revere's original 1775 deposition, in which the last sentence ended " . . . by way of Watertown to take them, Mess. Adams and Hancock, or to Concord." See Fischer, *Paul Revere's Ride*, 399.

33. Revere gave three accounts of his ride, the first a deposition to the Provincial Congress within days of the event; the second a slight revision of this deposition in 1783; the third a detailed letter to Jeremy Belknap around 1798. All three appear in Edmund S. Morgan, ed., *Paul Revere's Three Accounts of His Famous Ride* (Boston: Massachusetts Historical Society, 1961).

34. The myriad events of that night are chronicled in Fischer, *Paul Revere's Ride*, 138–64. Although several of the stories are folkloric and lack contemporaneous sources, the overall picture of a countryside come to life is plausible, given the preparations of each community.

35. Abigail Adams to Mercy Otis Warren, December 5, 1773, Butterfield, *Adams Family Correspondence*, 1:88–89.

13: Lexington and Concord: War

1. Gage to Smith, April 18, 1775, French, *General Gage's Informers*, 32.

2. Ibid., 29, 31–2.

3. Frederick Mackenzie, Diary, in John H. Rhodehamel, ed., *The American Revolution: Writings from the War of Independence* (New York: Library of America, 2001), 5; also in French, *General Gage's Informers*, 35–36. Fischer, *Paul Revere's Ride*, 115–17. On pages 313–15, Fischer provides valuable context for estimating the numbers of the British expedition.

4. Fischer, *Paul Revere's Ride*, 114–18, 123.

5. Lister published his account in 1782 and Sutherland on April 27, 1775, in a letter to Gage's secretary, Samuel Kemble. They appear in French, *General Gage's Informers*, 39–40 (Lister) and 42–26 (Southerland).

6. Recollection of Richard Devens, undated, in Frothingham, *History of the Siege of Boston*, 57–58; Fischer, *Paul Revere's Ride*, 90–91.

7. Deposition of Solomon Brown, Jonathan Loring, and Elijah Sanderson, in *Narrative of the Incursions and Ravages of the King's Troops*, a pamphlet of depositions published by the Massachusetts Provincial Congress on May 28, 1775. On May 3 the Provincial Congress sent the depositions to the Continental Congress, which placed them in its official journal. These can be accessed on the Web at Library of Congress, American Memory, A Century of Lawmaking for a New Nation, *Journals of the Continental Congress*, 2:28–44 (Brown, Loring, and Sanderson appear on page 28). Several of these depositions, along with some taken in subsequent weeks, are reprinted in Lemuel Shattuck, *A History of the Town of Concord, Middlesex County, Massachusetts* (Concord, MA: John Stacy, 1835), 341–51. Depositions also appear on the Library of Congress website, Teachers, Classroom

Materials, Presentations and Activities, American Revolution: http://www.loc
.gov/teachers/classroommaterials/presentationsandactivities/presentations
/timeline/amrev/shots/concern.html. Half a century later, Sanderson offered an
expanded rendition of his encounter with British officers, and William Munroe,
also of Lexington, commented on it. See Elias Phinney, *History of the Battle of
Lexington* (Boston: Phelps and Farnham, 1825), 31–33; and Charles Hudson, *History of the Town of Lexington, Middlesex County, Massachusetts* (Boston: Houghton Mifflin, 1913), 538–41.

8. David Hackett Fischer presents a map of the alarm's spread in *Paul Revere's Ride*,
146.

9. Deposition of John Parker, *Journals of the Continental Congress*, 2:31.

10. Fischer, *Paul Revere's Ride*, 124–26. The story of the widow Rand, appearing
in a local history written a century later, is introduced by "tradition informs us
that . . ." See Samuel Adams Drake, *History of Middlesex County, Massachusetts*
(Boston: Estes and Lauriat, 1880), 311–12. Many such stories, perhaps enriched
by repeated telling, continue to enliven our accounts of the advent of the Revolution.

11. Sutherland to Kemble, April 27, 1775, French, *General Gage's Informers*, 44–46.

12. Fischer, *Paul Revere's Ride*, 69; French, *General Gage's Informers*, 50.

13. Wroth, *Province and Rebellion*, 1299–1301.

14. Jonas Clarke, *A Brief Narrative of the Principal Transactions of that Day, Appended
to a Sermon Preached by Him in Lexington, April 19, 1776* (Lexington: Lexington
Historical Society, 1901), 7; Fischer, *Paul Revere's Ride*, 400 (Lexington's militia
roll and numbers present); *Journals of the Continental Congress*, 2:31 (Parker deposition).

15. *Journals of the Continental Congress*, 2:31.

16. For the numbers in the leading contingent, see Fischer, *Paul Revere's Ride*, 189.

17. *Journals of the Continental Congress*, 2:35; Phinney, *Battle of Lexington*, 32.

18. *Journals of the Continental Congress*, 2:31; Fischer, *Paul Revere's Ride*, 189, 400.
Fischer accepts these later quotations at face value, as do many others. If Parker
did say such things, the fact that nobody reported them at the time reveals the
bias of contemporaneous accounts, which were used to collaborate what Fischer
calls the "myth of injured innocence." More plausibly, recovered memories at
a later time were imposed on an event that had assumed iconic status. Viewing
this incident as the opening of a "war" is easier to do with historical hindsight,
once there *was* a war. A local militia captain threatening to shoot his townsmen is
inconsistent with the communitarian underpinnings of New England militias in
1775. Jonas Clarke, when arguing that provincials did not shoot first, noted "the
absurdity of the supposition that 50, 60, or even 70 men, should, in the open field
commence hostilities with 12, or 1500, of the best troops of Britain," which was
"the number we then supposed the brigade to consist of." For this same reason,
provincials would not have treated the commencement of war in such a cavalier
manner. See Clarke, *Brief Narrative*, 7.

19. French, *General Gage's Informers*, 58–59.

20. Smith's account: French, *General Gage's Informers*, 62. Victory volley: Clarke, *Brief Narrative*, 8–9.

21. Mackenzie, *Diary*, 13.

22. Robert A. Gross, *The Minutemen and Their World* (New York: Hill and Wang, 1976), 25–26, 40–41, 63, 69. For a full picture of Barrett, see 76–82.

23. Formation of Concord's minutemen: Town meeting of September 26, Wroth, *Province in Rebellion*, 854. Instructions to Barrett: Lincoln, *Journals of Provincial Congress/County Conventions*, 513. Barrett's accounting: Shattuck, *History of Concord*, 97–98.

24. Lincoln, *Journals of Provincial Congress/County Conventions*, 513, 517.

25. Ezra Ripley, *A History of the Fight at Concord* (Concord: Allen & Atwill, 1827), 13; Shattuck, *History of Concord*, 103–5.

26. Emerson, *Diary*, 71–2; Gross, *The Minutemen and Their World*, 119.

27. Frothingham, *Siege of Boston*, 64; Letter of Amos Barrett, April 19, 1825, edited and released in 1900 by his great-grandson Henry True, in Josephine Latham Swayne, ed., *The Story of Concord Told by Concord Writers* (Boston: E.F. Worcester, 1906), 49.

28. "We must retreat, as their number was more than treble ours," does not appear in Amelia Forbes Emerson's edition of the diary, but it does appear in renditions printed in *The Complete Works of Ralph Waldo Emerson*, Edward Waldo Emerson, ed. (Boston: Houghton Mifflin, 1876), 11:568, and Swayne, *Concord Writers*, 46.

29. Emerson, *Diary*, 71–2, Emerson, *Complete Works*, 11:568, or Swayne, *Concord Writers*, 46.

30. 1832 account: Shattuck, *History of Concord*, 105–6, and Fischer, *Paul Revere's Ride*, 204 and 409, n. 9. Diary: Emerson, *Diary*, 72, Emerson, *Complete Works*, 11:569, or Swayne, *Concord Writers*, 48. Shattuck and Fischer, along with most later writers, treat the later quotation as fact, even though the substance and tone of Emerson's diary appear to preclude his making such a statement. Fischer quotes Emerson's diary without attribution, introduced only by "one man remembered," giving the diary and an account written fifty-seven years later equal weight.

31. Emerson, *Diary*, 72, Emerson, *Complete Works*, 11:568, or Swayne, *Concord Writers*, 47; Ripley, *Fight at Concord*, 19; Shattuck, *History of Concord*, 107–9; Gross, *Minutemen and Their World*, 121. It remains unclear how much Gage knew about the various locations of the stores. Earlier spy reports had cited specific places, but in a document labeled "Intelligence April 18, 1775," an informant notified him that most of the "military Stores," excepting four "Field Pieces" in the "Town House" and some powder and ball under the watch of Barrett, had been moved to other towns. The provisions, the spy said, were still there, although he admitted that he did not know the outcome of the committee of safety and supplies meeting on April 17 and he made no mention of the meeting on April 18. We do not know for sure whether this report was sent to

Gage on the 18th or he received it on that date. Several spy reports are labeled "Intelligence received" and then the date; one was labeled "Intelligence sent" and the date. This one, and several others, simply said "Intelligence." Further, even if Gage received it on the 18th, he might already have given Smith his orders. His instructions to Smith focus largely on the military wares to be found in Concord, suggesting that Gage had not yet received this latest intelligence or for some reason doubted or ignored it. (Wroth, *Province in Rebellion*, 1982; French, *General Gage's Informers*, 25–27.)

32. William Munroe Special Collections, Revolutionary-Era Concord Town Records, Concord Free Public Library. Thanks to Joel Bohy for leading us to this source.

33. Emerson, *Diary*, 72, Emerson, *Complete Works*, 11:568, or Swayne, *Concord Writers*, 47; Ripley, *Fight at Concord*, 20–21; Shattuck, *History of Concord*, 104; Fischer, *Paul Revere's Ride*, 207–8.

34. For the numbers on each side at that moment, see Ripley, *Fight at Concord*, 21; Shattuck, *History of Concord*, 110–11; Fischer, *Paul Revere's Ride*, 209 and 212. For the council on Punkatasset Hill, see Ripley, *Fight at Concord*, 22–14; Shattuck, *History of Concord*, 111; Frothingham, *Siege of Boston*, 68. Gross's and Fischer's accounts are based on these nineteenth-century narratives.

35. French, *General Gage's Informers*, 88–89 (Sutherland) and 79–80 (Lister).

36. Ibid., 89–90.

37. For the depositions of numerous militiamen, see *Journals of the Continental Congress*, 2:36–39. Many of these have identical wording, suggesting the possibility that the deponents were offering an official line rather than giving their personal observations. Lister's account is in French, *General Gage's Informers*, 80. Emerson's quote is from his diary, Emerson, *Complete Works*, 11:569, or Swayne, *Concord Writers*, 47.

38. Shattuck, *History of Concord*, 114.

39. Fischer, *Paul Revere's Ride*, 249.

40. Lord Percy to the Duke of Northumberland, April 20, 1775, in Charles Knowles Bolton, ed., *Letters of Hugh, Earl Percy, from Boston and New York, 1774–1776* (Boston: Charles Goodspeed, 1902), 54.

41. British casualty numbers are from Fischer, *Paul Revere's Ride*, 321. Howard Peckham gives a slightly different figure: 70 killed, 182 wounded, and 22 captured during the retreat, plus 2 killed and 9 to 11 wounded earlier in the day. Peckham lists the provincial's toll for the day at 49 killed, 39 wounded, and 5 missing. See Howard Peckham, *The Toll of Independence: Engagements & Battle Casualties of the American Revolution* (Chicago: University of Chicago Press, 1974), 3.

42. Lord Percy to General Harvey, April 20, 1775, Bolton, *Letters of Percy*, 53.

43. Warren to Arthur Lee, April 27, 1775, Frothingham, *Life and Times of Joseph Warren*, 471.

44. Lincoln, *Journal of Provincial Congress/County Conventions*, 515–6.

45. Ibid., 231.

Postscript: Local Events, National Narratives, and Global Impact

1. Kevin Phillips, *1775: A Good Year for Revolution* (New York: Viking, 2012), 30–32.

2. Lord Rochford, British secretary of state, to Lord Stormont, British ambassador to France, January 27, 1775, in William B. Clark, ed., *Naval Documents of the American Revolution* (Washington, DC: U.S. Government Printing Office, 1966), 1:388. The message Stormont was to pass on to his French counterpart can be accessed at: http://www.ibiblio.org/anrs/docs/E/E3/ndar_v01p03.pdf. Similar warnings were delivered from Lord Suffolk, an assistant secretary of state, to envoys in the Hague, Sweden, and Denmark. (Clark, *Naval Documents*, 1:396–97.) M. Garnier to Count de Vergennes, French Foreign Minister, February 14, 1775, in Clark, *Naval Documents*, 1:400 (emphasis added). For munitions smuggling through the Caribbean, see Phillips, *1775*, 32–33.

3. Garnier to Vergennes, February 20, 1775, in Clark, *Naval Documents*, 1:404.

INDEX

About the Authors

Ray Raphael's seventeen books include *A People's History of the American Revolution*, *The First American Revolution*, *Founding Myths*, *Founders*, and *Constitutional Myths*, all published by The New Press. He is currently a senior research fellow at Humboldt State University and associate editor of *Journal of the American Revolution*. **Marie Raphael**, author of two historical novels, has taught literature and writing at Boston University, College of the Redwoods, and Humboldt State University. They live in Northern California.

Publishing in the Public Interest

Thank you for reading this book published by The New Press. The New Press is a nonprofit, public interest publisher. New Press books and authors play a crucial role in sparking conversations about the key political and social issues of our day.

We hope you enjoyed this book and that you will stay in touch with The New Press. Here are a few ways to stay up to date with our books, events, and the issues we cover:

- Sign up at www.thenewpress.com/subscribe to receive updates on New Press authors and issues and to be notified about local events
- Like us on Facebook: www.facebook.com/newpressbooks
- Follow us on Twitter: www.twitter.com/thenewpress

Please consider buying New Press books for yourself; for friends and family; or to donate to schools, libraries, community centers, prison libraries, and other organizations involved with the issues our authors write about.

The New Press is a 501(c)(3) nonprofit organization. You can also support our work with a tax-deductible gift by visiting www.thenewpress.com/donate.